# PLAYBOY SWINGS!

# PLAYBOY SWINGS!

How Hugh Hefner and Playboy Changed the Face of Music

## BY PATTY FARMER

### CONTRIBUTIONS BY WILL FRIEDWALD

BEAUFORT
BOOKS

PLAYBOY SWINGS

TO AL BELLETTO, DAVID BRENNER, JOAN RIVERS,
JULIE WILSON, STEVE ROSSI,
and all the other talented and dedicated entertainers who
left us much too early.

# Contents

# BY VICTOR LOWNES

When Patty Farmer told me that she was planning a book about the music produced and presented by Playboy, I knew she was onto something, because music has always been as much a part of the Playboy experience as beautiful women. And—though I can't play any musical instrument and I doubt that my singing voice would get me into even the most desperate choir—I like to think that I had something to do with that. Before you dig in and enjoy the many stories Patty has gathered from all those who helped make Playboy the institution it is, I'd like to share my own perspective on how we got started. You might as well hear it from the source!

I had been traveling between Chicago and New York on business in the years after I graduated from the University of Chicago. One night, I saw a mention of a little club called RSVP on East 59th Street, in an article in *Park East* magazine. I stopped in and was enchanted by a singer there, Mabel Mercer, a half-English, half-American chanteuse. I've spoken with Patty at length about my passion for Mabel, and there's more about her in various chapters throughout, but for now, suffice it to say that she was one of a kind.

One night in 1954, I gave a party for the comedian Jonathan

Winters. My good friend, the photographer Mike Shea, brought along a young guy who was putting out a new magazine. I'm sure you can guess that the magazine was called *Playboy* and Mike's friend was Hugh Hefner. To entertain my guests that evening, I played a recording I had made of Mabel. Hefner was so impressed he asked me if I would write an article about the singer for *Playboy*—which I did. It was the only piece I ever wrote for him, but it was the start of my career as *Playboy*'s promotion director.

Playboy became the most successful magazine to be launched post-war in the United States, but I knew there was still more we could do. Four years later, when Hef ran a piece about the delights of a Chicago nightspot called the Gaslight—which used the gimmick of giving each member a key to the place—it came to me. We should open up our own club! I knew it would fit in perfectly with the image we were trying to create.

I could see the club in my mind even as I presented the idea to Hef. He soon saw it too, and the more we discussed the pros and cons, the more attractive the idea became. We were in the middle of these discussions when I pushed yet another idea on Hef—one that he was equally pleased about: a jazz festival.

My interest in jazz had begun long before Playboy. I had had Huddie Ledbetter, better known as Leadbelly, as a houseguest in my Chicago pad for a couple of months; and the legendary guitarist and singer Big Bill Broonzy had entertained at my parties.

But there's quite a difference between loving jazz and producing an event. Organizing the first Playboy Jazz Festival in 1959 proved quite a challenge. You'll read all about our search for a venue and all the resistance we encountered from the Roman Catholic Church of Chicago, and others. Fortunately, Arthur Wirtz, a big Chicago real-estate man, came forward and agreed to let us hold the festival in his Chicago Stadium. I don't think for one minute that Arthur believed we could fill the place—certainly not in the middle of August, when Chicagoans like to spend their leisure time outdoors. But minor miracles do happen. There was hardly a name band or famous singer who didn't perform, as Patty describes in Chapter Three. The show was an enormous, unrepeatable triumph. I became even more certain that we could run a club of our own—and I knew just the man who could help us do that: the restaurateur Arnie Morton.

Starting this entirely new project—yet blending it in with the Playboy image we were building with the magazine—called for enormous concentration on every detail. Most of the planning took place in the Playboy offices, where we all worked long into the night—and that included Hefner. By a stroke of good luck, Arthur Wirtz—now convinced of our power since we'd filled his stadium—offered us his empty premises on Walton Street for a share of the profits. All that was left was to find exactly the right staff, entertainment, equipment, décor, and everything else. The Bunny idea came later... you'll real all about that in Chapter 6 (but I hope you realize that my version is the correct one!).

We opened the first club on Leap Year night, February 29, 1960. Looking back, it's easy to see why the club was so successful. Through the magazine, we had promoted the novel idea of a place of entertainment and pleasure with charming attractive girls in attendance, but free of the lewdness that could easily be found in Chicago nightlife at that time. The first live entertainment we offered was a trio playing background music in the club's Living Room—one of several rooms that had been designed to look as much like a bachelor flat as possible. Originally, we had decided against having performers in the cabaret, but I kept going back to the idea of live music. I think I was still under the influence of Mabel Mercer. I knew what live music could do to people, the kind of atmosphere it could create.

In spite of the fact that we paid those early performers very little, and none of them was famous at the time, I guess I was right. Our members told us that live entertainment was exactly what they wanted. Soon music became central to the plan, and I hired Mabel herself (my immortal aphrodisiac) to head our first major cabaret presentation. As you'll read, we had no great stage or lighting set-up for her and somebody had the bright idea of having the audience lounging around on cushions while Mabel sat in her signature chair. I'm afraid she wasn't too big a hit with our Playboy audience. After that, while Arnie Morton refined and polished the restaurant and bar side of the business, I went off in continuous search of new talent.

We were soon established in a way we had never intended—as a cabaret club presenting the best new acts available. And we remained so.

After more discussions and planning sessions late into the night, Hefner agreed that we should quickly begin opening Playboy Clubs in new cities. We planned franchises in New Orleans and Miami, both of which were later re-purchased by Playboy. Another Playboy Club was planned for Phoenix, Arizona. And ultimately, I flew east to find us a site in the Big Apple—all while continuing to scout talent for Chicago. I needed artists who could hold the attention of a lusty crowd busy with food, drinks, and the obvious attractions of the Bunnies.

Looking back, it's astonishing what turned up. A young singer making a name for herself, Barbra Streisand, was mentioned to me and I went to see her in a club in Greenwich Village. I offered her a contract at $350 a week to perform in Chicago for a three-week run, four shows a night, seven nights a week. She accepted with pleasure—that is, until she was offered the lead in a musical on Broadway. We let her out of her contract but she repaid us by appearing on the cover of the magazine.

When I first booked Dick Gregory, he was working at a car wash. That engagement was the start of his climb to fame and fortune—another story you'll read in this book, straight from Dick himself. I even hired the soul singer and pianist Aretha Franklin for $250 dollars a week. Of course, it was at the very outset of her amazing career.

The U.S. clubs were soon joined by resort hotelsin Jamaica,

Nassau in the Bahamas, and of course the famed Playboy Club and Casino in my hometown of London, which I opened in 1966.

My interest in cabaret has not waned. My wife Marilyn (a former Bunny) and I often attend the annual Cabaret Conventions put on by the Mabel Mercer Foundation in New York, and we were thrilled to welcome the new cabaret venue in London called the Crazy Coqs. In fact, we were there just the other night, guests of this book's charming author.

Lorna Luft was in the audience that night and greeted us warmly, echoing the sentiments of so many entertainers I have talked to over the years: "I loved the Playboy Clubs and their cabaret rooms— I have great memories of working in them."

I could go on and on about Playboy, but perhaps it's time for someone else to speak. Aren't we fortunate that Patty Farmer has tracked down just about everyone who contributed to making Playboy what it is, from Bunnies and bartenders to the top names in music and comedy? And, as you'll soon find, they were all thrilled to reminisce about old times and talk about what Playboy has meant to them and to their careers. At the risk of sounding immodest, I'll add that it has meant a lot to the world, as well.

—VICTOR LOWNES III

# Introduction

# BY GEORGE WEIN

It's a pleasure for me to write this introduction to *Playboy Swings*, a new book that tells the whole story of the involvement of Hugh Hefner (and Playboy Enterprises) with music—and jazz in particular. I've met Patty Farmer many times, and know that she's an inspired author and a meticulous researcher, and, of course, I've known Will Friedwald for years. But more importantly, I've been close to Hugh Hefner for many decades now—we go way back together.

From the beginning of his career, Hugh Hefner has made no secret of the fact that he was a big jazz fan, and has always gone out of the way to support the music he loves—he puts his money (and other resources) where his taste is. But that's not the only reason that I've always felt a kinship with "Hef"—it's also partly because he and I both started around the same time. *Playboy* magazine's first year was 1954, and that was the same summer that we launched the Newport Jazz Festival. Both our organizations have prospered in parallel, with all of our ups and downs, for over sixty years now.

From the beginning, it was clear that the mixture of Playboy and jazz was a very good combination. I had first met Hef in the 1950s, but sadly, I wasn't able to get to Chicago for the first Playboy

Jazz Festival in 1959. But it was a very big deal at the time—it got wonderful reviews and generated a lot of publicity. In March, 1960, Hef was kind enough to invite me on his TV show, *Playboy's Penthouse*. Not only did I bring Anita O'Day with me (she was always a trip—and a native Chicagoan, like Hef) but he even allowed me to play piano and sing the blues on national television. That might have been a first!

The roots of the Playboy Jazz Festival at the Hollywood Bowl go back to the mid-1970s. Around that time, I began hearing occasionally from Dick Rosenzweig, Vice President of Playboy Enterprises. Dick told me that Hefner was interested in doing a new Playboy Jazz Festival, and they wanted my organization, Festival Productions, to be involved. I got that call from Dick several times, but it never led to anything. Finally, it was about 1978, and we were separately making plans for the 25th anniversary of both the Newport Jazz Festival and of *Playboy*. I got a call from Dick, and he said they were ready—they wanted us to do a festival. That's when we came up with the Hollywood Bowl concept, and we've been going strong together ever since.

Darlene Chan was with me from the very first one in June 1979, and she's been a major part of making the Playboy Jazz Festival the remarkable success that it's been. In the beginning, it was the two of us, but she's been responsible for most of the festivals thus far. As far as the talent goes, we know who Hef likes, but he's always given us a free hand and never held us to a specific instruction to book anyone in particular. He liked Mel Tormé and Bill Cosby—and so do I! Mel played the Bowl every June for years and years, and, up to 2013, Bill was the only emcee we ever had. Playboy was very supportive of Bill in the beginning, giving him work in the clubs when he needed it, and he's more than returned the favor by continuing to host the festival every year.

In 1979 we put together a great show, and every year they're still terrific. Historically, Los Angeles has never been a great jazz town like

New Orleans or New York, but we found an audience for the music. Crossover jazz is still big on the West Coast; it doesn't mean much in New York, but everything goes in phases. That also goes for smooth jazz; Darlene always has three to four smooth jazz groups included. Back in '79, it was unbelievable to sell out 17,000 seats two nights in a row—34,000 seats total!—but we did it. And we still do it!

Hef has always been very generous in his dealings with us. Traditionally, I would always come west for the festival and also for the press conference beforehand. In fact, for years I would challenge myself, while driving to the press conference, to come up with some kind of funny story I could tell about Hef. Hef and I love to kid each other! There was one press conference where I looked straight at Hef while I told all the reporters the following story: "In all my years of coming here, I've never been fixed up with any of the Playboy girls. But I was in my hotel the other night and there was a knock on my door. A voice said, 'Its room service.' I hadn't ordered anything but I opened the door and there were two beautiful young ladies—obviously sent by Hef." Then I looked at him and I said, "I'm sorry, friend. It's too late!"

It wasn't true, just a story I made up to amuse Hef. He loved it when I told those kinds of little stories, and we built up a very nice relationship. He'd come down and have lunch with me while we were getting things ready, always in his pajamas. He loves jazz, and he loves sitting in the front box for the entire festival with two blondes next to him. Well, he just got married again, so, the next time I see him he'll probably only have one blonde with him.

I have had nothing but pleasant, wonderful experiences with Playboy and the Hollywood Bowl. My favorite story about the Playboy Festival involves the famous revolving stage, which is basically the same idea that our friend Victor Lownes devised for the 1959 festival.

Around 1982, I put together an all-star group with Dizzy Gillespie, Gerry Mulligan, J.J. Johnson, Dexter Gordon, and Max Roach.

I mean, it was a real all-star group. I told Dizzy, "you run this set," and asked him to make sure each musician was featured separately—but they could only take five minutes to do their individual set.

Well, Gerry killed with a beautiful ballad, and Dizzy had the crowd swinging, and then Dexter did his solo, which of course was amazing—but he did the melody with three or four choruses, and then went into vamps, cadenzas… he just played on and on. Because we were going way over schedule, I frantically motioned to Dizzy, "take him out!" Now, one of the fabulous things about the festival is that revolving stage. When an artist is done, somebody presses a button and it swings around to present the next feature. So Dizzy pressed the button on Dexter! Dexter later said to me, "Hey, George, when you ask someone to play five minutes you really mean it? It's not a suggestion?"

I'll never forget that!

—GEORGE WEIN

Part One

# THE ORIGINAL SWINGER

# 1

# BIRTH OF A LIFESTYLE

t's fall 1953. A twenty-seven-year-old veteran (of both the Second World War and the publishing business) named Hugh Hefner is looking over a pile of pages on a card table in his rather small apartment in Chicago. It's a rough layout for a magazine, just a basic idea, really, that Hefner has come up with. Hefner, who is already known to his friends as "Hef," has a plan to create a men's magazine which he wants to call *Stag Party*.

Sixty years later, that term is archaic. A stag party, in the days before the sexual revolution (which Hefner would help to bring about), was a private party for men only, sometimes under the guise of a bachelor party, in which alcoholic beverages were plentiful and so-called "stag films," soft-core porn reels of burlesque dancers, were screened; or, better yet, live strippers entertained in person. Think of a stag party as "burlesque take-out."

The burlesque houses (which were more than strip clubs because, unlike the emporiums of today, they offered comedy and live music as well as female flesh) were to theater what the men's magazines of the era were to publishing. The "skin rags," as they were pejoratively called in the industry, featured cheesecake shots of young girls in swimsuits or less, often posed fetchingly on bearskin rugs. Generally speaking, these weren't readily available on the more visible newsstands or magazine racks. You had to go out of your way to ask for them, and they were stashed in the back, away from the impressionable eyes of wives and children.

If Hef had kept the title *Stag Party*, it's safe to say that the term would be in the Urban Dictionary today—and the magazine would have surely been somewhat successful. Nobody ever went broke publishing semi-nude pictures of women. But Hef had another idea, one which involved making a conceptual leap. At the last minute, he changed the title of his forthcoming magazine to *Playboy*.

There was no doubt as to what a magazine called *Stag Party* might contain, but what did he mean by *Playboy*? The term had never been associated with anything positive; there were more salubrious synonyms for it in French, including *bon-vivant* and *dilettante*. It referred to a man of means who didn't necessarily have to work for his money, a plutocrat who lived "the good life," and who had expensive hobbies such as travel, high-stakes gambling, and fast cars, horses, and—yes—women. In short, a playboy was a wealthy ne'er-do-well.

Before Hefner, it wasn't anything that anyone aspired to be. John Millington Synge used the term in the title of his classic Irish drama *Playboy of the Western World* (1907), but he meant the term sarcastically; the titular character is a braggart and a poser, claiming to be something he isn't. To call someone a *playboy* was insulting from the Victorian age up through the Great Depression and World War II, when everyone wanted to be a "real man" who valued work over play. Hefner had probably never heard the word "branding" before 1953, but in the sense that it means making something positive out of what has been perceived as negative, that's precisely what he was doing.

Hefner wasn't strictly a writer, or at least he wasn't as a good a writer as those whom he would soon hire. But he was more than an editor in the traditional sense of the term. Today, he might be called a "conceptualist," a man who saw the very big picture. The first piece of text in the first issue of *Playboy* read, "If you're a man between the ages of 18 and 80, *Playboy* is meant for you. If you like your entertainment served up with humor, sophistication, and spice, *Playboy* will become a very special favorite."

After informing the reader that this new publication was not for women (he advised sisters, wives, and mothers-in-law to go back to "your *Ladies Home Companion*"), he described the new effort as a "pleasure primer styled to the masculine taste." He then took a potshot at sports and outdoorsy publications: "Most 'magazines for men' spend all their time out-of-doors... We'll be out there too, occasionally, but we don't mind telling you in advance—we plan on spending most of our time inside." Using the editorial "we," Hef added, "We like our apartment. We enjoy mixing up cocktails and an hors d'oeuvre or two, putting a little mood music on the phonograph and inviting in a female acquaintance for a quiet discussion on Picasso, Nietzsche, jazz, sex." Thus, even before you've reached the first picture of the first girl, Hef has turned the traditional notions of both a playboy and a men's magazine completely around.

The first issue was forty-four pages and hit the stands in November 1953—but there was no date on the cover, just in case Hef needed more than a month to sell all the copies he was planning to print. Hef had cannily written a letter to potential distributors that was so convincing he received advance orders for 70,000 copies—but he was knowledgeable enough about the magazine business to know that shipping 70,000 was hardly the same as selling them. If customers didn't actually buy them from the stands, they'd be shipped right back soon enough.

He needn't have been so cautious. The first issue, with Marilyn Monroe waving proudly on the cover, sold better than anyone could have anticipated: 54,000 copies. The second issue was released before the end of December, and featured the signature *Playboy* rabbit (not to be confused with the latter-day Bunnies—the rabbit was male) in his dressing gown and bow tie, with his paws around two beauty-pageant-like cuties in swimsuits and sashes that read, "Merry Christmas." From that point on, *Playboy* was a monthly venture—and by the third issue, it was so successful that Hefner was able to move the entire enterprise to its own office at 11 E. Superior Street in Chicago.

Hugh Marston Hefner was born in Chicago on April 9, 1926, the elder of two sons. His brother Keith would later work for him and play a key role, especially, in the development of the Playboy Clubs. His parents were Caroline and Glenn Hefner, both schoolteachers. After high school, Hefner served briefly in the army during World War II, where he obtained early publishing experience by working on the military newspaper. After the war, he attended the University of Illinois, graduating with a BA in psychology. While at college, Hef edited a college humor magazine called *Shaft*, in which he initiated a feature he called, "Coed of the Month," showcasing singularly attractive college girls. The first was Carol "Candy" Cannon.

For a few years after college, Hefner was something of a nonstarter; he briefly pursued a graduate degree in sociology at Northwestern University but dropped out. He then got a job as a copywriter at *Esquire* magazine. When the magazine relocated from Chicago to New York, Hef was offered the opportunity to move with them. Feeling that New York City would prove too expensive for his growing family—which now included his wife Millie and infant daughter Christie—he asked for a salary increase of five dollars a week. *Esquire* refused, so, in January 1952, he quit. Many years later, *Esquire* ceremonially presented Hef with a supersized five-dollar bill; they clearly understood what those five dollars had cost them. To this day, the bill is on view in Hef's game room at the Beverly Hills Playboy mansion.

Hef would not be out of work for long. Deciding that the timing was right, he mortgaged his young family's home and borrowed additional money to help finance his dream of owning his own magazine. That capital also included a thousand dollars from his mother, who didn't necessarily believe in the value of semi-nude ladies, but who, as Hef said years later, "believed in her son." By December of the following year, he was previewing what would eventually become the cornerstone of one of the most recognizable international brands in the world—*Playboy* magazine.

The first issue was a remarkable success, thanks to a combination of Hefner's street smarts and an almost unbelievable piece of good luck. The year 1953 was also the breakthrough one for Marilyn Monroe, who had risen from extra to leading lady over the course of roughly five years. But in 1949, well before anyone had heard of her, Norma Jean Baker (as she was then known) had posed for a nude photo that had been used on a calendar. Hefner knew the infamous photo well, and when he determined that it had never been published in a magazine, he secured the rights to it from the photographer and made Marilyn—if not exactly the first Playmate (he hadn't yet devised that term)—then certainly the first and, quite possibly, the all-time most famous *Playboy* model. The issue was an instant success, thanks to Marilyn's looks and Hefner's brains.

Marilyn was labeled "Sweetheart of the Month," but by the second issue, Hef had come up with the term "Playmate." The blonde bombshell would always remain a lucky charm for Hef, even in death. In January 1964, he published a tribute to the iconic actress (who had died at age thirty-six in August 1962) that included photos from her last, unfinished film, *Something's Got to Give*. Many years later, Hef would buy the burial vault beside Marilyn's at the Westwood Memorial Park Cemetery, so he could lie for eternity beside his first cover girl.

The famous double-page Playmate spread didn't appear until the third issue, and the three-page fold-out centerfold made its debut in March 1956, featuring the many assets of actress Marian Stafford. For the first six months, Hefner purchased shots that photographers brought to him, but from the seventh issue on, he commissioned his own photo shoots (the first model for these was Eve Meyer). Over the years, *Playboy*'s famous pictorials included no-holds-barred (and no-gents-bored) appearances by Anita Ekberg, Brigitte Bardot, Sophia Loren, Gina Lollobrigida, Jayne Mansfield, Kim Novak, Raquel Welch, Linda Evans, Stella Stevens, Barbara Bach, Veruschka, Tina Louise, Arlene Dahl, Victoria Principal, and a bevy of other beautiful celebrities who vied for inclusion.

Hugh Hefner taking time to showing off layouts to a few of the ladies. August 16, 1961, Chicago. Image by Bettmann CORBIS

Doubtless, many of the very first *Playboy* readers put down their two quarters primarily for the famous shot of Marilyn in the altogether. But it wasn't the superstars who made *Playboy* such a success; it was the girls next door. Sex and sexy women were not the exclusive province of Hollywood. It was part of Hefner's rationale to show that women who worked in offices, waited tables, pushed pencils, and lived in sorority houses could be as desirable as the latest super-starlet. In Hefner's universe, the average woman was far above average. The flip side of that message was that it didn't take a "different" kind of woman to enjoy sex (or even exhibitionism); there were plenty of nice girls who would take it off for you under the right circumstances.

In previous men's magazines, the girls inevitably looked like strippers and their photos were obviously shot in a photographer's studio. It was part of the genius of Hef and his staff that they considered the context. Rather than seeming to disrobe for pay, these girls were having just as much fun being seen as their male viewers were having in seeing them. And this, apparently was no illusion. Thousands of women, from all professions, submitted their photos for consideration as Playmates. They may have been airbrushed and idealized, exquisitely coiffed and made-up, but in the most important way, they were down to earth and real—not steely-eyed professional beauties. And they appeared in relatable settings such as picnics, swimming pools, and dormitories.One memorable shot—of Lynn Turner, Miss March 1956—showed her ripping a copy of *TV Guide* magazine in two; clearly, watching television was not her preferred pastime.

Hef's special brilliance was in grounding his fantasy in reality, thus increasing both the credibility and the eroticism. The *Playboy* mantra was "nice girls do." When Janet Pilgrim became Miss July—aka, "*Playboy*'s Office Playmate"—it was a perfect blend of fact and fantasy. Miss Pilgrim, whose *nom-de-pictorial* was apparently inspired by the Betty Grable movie *The Shocking Miss Pilgrim* (1947), was actually Charlaine Karalus. And, while she actually did work in the *Playboy* office, she was also dating Hef, and he talked her into posing *sans top* for a centerfold. So her "back-story" was partially true. Most of the narrative written about the models and centerfolds were strictly the invention of Hef and his well-paid writers.

For Hef, the story behind the image was as much of a turn-on as the image itself, and the Christmas centerfolds came with the most important stories. The legendary (and notorious) Bettie Page (Christmas 1954 / January 1955) was shot wearing a Santa hat and nothing else; Miss Pilgrim returned to pose under a Christmas tree for the January 1956 issue.

*Playboy* wasn't through with Charlaine Karalus yet—she was appointed the corporation's first "celebrity ambassador," and was dispatched to appear at Chicago events where she would pose (fully-clothed) for amateur photographers, sign autographs, and, in general, promote good will for the cause of the *Playboy* experience. Soon, the magazine was sending out other Playmates as models for various car shows, boat shows, and the like, at the rate of $50 a day. At one point, Miss Pilgrim was also hired to congratulate anyone (via telephone) who bought a lifetime subscription to the magazine. Such good taste and judgment clearly required a personal response. To this day, being a centerfold means more than a one-time exposure, and the girls' contracts specifically stipulate that they aren't allowed to radically change their appearance or engage in any behavior that might reflect adversely on the company.

Although, in the pages of *Playboy*, sex was no longer sinful or dirty, it was rare to see somebody reading it in broad daylight, and most public libraries didn't carry it. Nevertheless, major authors such as Ray Bradbury and John Steinbeck were hardly ashamed to be published there—quite the opposite. Which brings us to yet another reason for Hefner's remarkable success; the new publication was much more than all bare skin and double *entendres*. Dr. Paul Gebhard of the Kinsey Institute observed, "Hefner's genius was to associate sex with upward mobility."

\* \* \*

Al Podell, who served on the *Playboy* staff in the early days, remembered that Hefner was a workaholic and even something of a nerd regarding his obsessions, which included jazz, movies, and other forms of popular culture. But as the magazine's success grew, Hefner began to fashion himself as the role model for *Playboy's* ideal reader.

The first issue included a story by Bob Norman denouncing ex-wives who received alimony payments as "Gold-Diggers": "When a modern-day marriage ends, it doesn't matter who's to blame. It's always the guy who pays and pays and pays and pays." This provoked a lively discussion in the letters page for months to come. Much of the best early fiction was taken from the public domain, including the classic "Introducing Sherlock Holmes," by Sir Arthur Conan Doyle (with a rather lurid original illustration depicting the legendary detective's drug use) and "A Horseman in the Sky," by the late Ambrose Bierce. And if it wasn't PD, it was often second hand, including Ray Bradbury's *Fahrenheit 451* and Shepherd Mead's *How to Succeed in Business Without Really Trying*, both already published as books but now serialized in the magazine.

Very early in the game, Hef was going for the gold: the best writers, the best illustrators, the best cartoonists, and the prettiest models. His ambitions took a major leap forward in 1956, when he hired Auguste Comte Spectorsky as the magazine's literary editor. He was officially credited as "A. C. Spectorsky," but was known to friends and fellow workers as "Spec," in a rough counterpart to "Hef." Born in Paris in 1910, Spectorsky helped bring, as the rough-hewn Chicagoans would have said, a little class to the joint. He was a genuine, card-carrying member of the New York literati, with impeccable credentials—such as having served on the staff of *The New Yorker*.

*Playboy* had already published Ray Bradbury (in 1956 they commissioned an original story by him titled "The First Night of Lent") and now the literary heavyweights kept coming, among them P.G. Wodehouse, Arthur C. Clarke, and eventually, Kurt Vonnegut, Joseph Heller, Norman Mailer, Margaret Atwood, and many others. Before too long, Spectorsky became Executive Editor and Publisher, the most important man after Hefner in shepherding the content of the magazine. Spec also became a semi-regular on the first Playboy TV series, *Playboy's Penthouse*, assisting Hef with the informal interviews of authors and writers such as Rona Jaffe (the author of *The Best of Everything*, one of the bestselling novels of 1959, and a hit film in 1960) on the first episode.

With and without Spec, Hef would continually push the envelope. One of his most prominent writers early on was Charles Beaumont, who seemed to stand for the same things that Hef did: superior music and sexual freedom. Early on, Beaumont wrote a piece of what was called "jazz fiction," titled "Black Country," as well as an extended profile of Louis Armstrong in 1955. But his most famous—or, at the time, infamous—short story in the magazine was an allegorical piece entitled "The Crooked Man," set in a world where same-sex love was the law of the land and "straight" couples had to hide in the closet.Hef immediately realized he had gone too far; advertisers were up in arms, and so were readers. He promised, apparently with his fingers crossed behind his back, never to do anything like that again. But he could have said anything he wanted at that point, and it wouldn't have mattered. The story had been published, the point had been made, and he knew that there was no getting the genie back in the bottle—or the lovers back in the closet.

In 1962, Spec and Hef stepped in it again, with a short story byCalder Willingham titled "Bus Stop," in which a seventeen-year-old girl is sexually assaulted by a grown man. Again, major advertisers threatened to pull out if they did anything like that again, and Hefner formally apologized, though he continued to campaign for women's rights and gender equality.

Advertising, in general, was tricky. *Playboy* rejected eighty percent of the companies who sought to run ads in the magazine, holding out for more prestigious businesses that promoted the same image they themselves were building. Yet, the mainstream corporations shied away from displaying their services and goods in such a controversial publication. *Playboy* didn't land its first major account until February 1955, and even it was vaguely suggestive: Springmaid sheets.

In a 1962 interview, Victor Lownes, who had been a vice president of the company almost from the beginning, said, "Hef isn't what you'd call a real intellectual; I doubt that he reads ten books a year." Hefner was highly intelligent, but—in spite of what his readers might have assumed—he started out awkward and unpolished. A role model for his readers on multiple levels, he saw himself as an average guy who aspired to the higher things in life. But unlike Spec, the intellectual, and Victor, the connoisseur of the best food and wine, Hef had to fashion himself into the *Playboy* Ideal—and in the process, he brought his legion of eager readers with him. Attracting the highest class of women, he showed them, required cultivating one's taste in literature, music, cuisine, and the rest of the finer things in life.

An even more idealized—if fictitious—role model for *Playboy*'s readers was James Bond, the British super-spy created by Sir Ian Fleming. A number of the classic Bond novels were serialized in *Playboy,* at the rate of roughly one a year: *On Her Majesty's Secret Service* (April, May, and June 1963), *You Only Live Twice* (April, May, and June 1964), *The Man with the Golden Gun* (1965), and *Octopussy* (1966).Sir Ian himself would become an asset to the Playboy empire when he helped scout out a location for the Playboy Club in Jamaica, an area of the world in which he was an expert.

J. Paul Getty, widely-regarded as America's richest man, was a real-life role-model. In 1960, Hef and Spec talked the sixty-eight-year-old multi-millionaire into lending his name to a series of stories about what it was like to possess great wealth. In 1965, Playboy Press gathered this wisdom into a book titled *How to be Rich.*

From the first issue, Hefner vowed to stay away from politics, and as late as 1960, when the nation debated the merits of Kennedy vs. Nixon, *Playboy*'s way of dealing with the election was to endorse

Professor Irwin Corey, "the world's greatest authority"—and frequent Playboy Club headliner—as a representative of the "Playboy Party." And a swell party it was! Finally, in 1974, the magazine entered the political fray in earnest by publishing the reporting of Carl Bernstein and Bob Woodward on the Watergate incident. Their articles became the basis for the bestselling book and film, *All the President's Men.* It took nearly two decades, but ultimately *Playboy* moved from being apolitical to playing a key role in the un-making of a United States President.

That didn't mean they'd lost their sense of fun, of course. The magazine consistently included sports, games, puzzles, quizzes, and of course the cartoons that were overseen personally by Hef. *Playboy*'s cartoons, which frequently depicted voluptuous, beautiful, and willing young ladies alongside rich but clueless old geezers, were always a key part of the equation. The first great cartoonist to be featured in *Playboy* was probably Jack Cole, who had already made a major contribution to popular culture as the creator of Plastic Man, the most "durable" superhero of the WWII era. His girls were even more visually appealing, albeit no less pliable, than his most celebrated creation. Cole was responsible for some of the most appealing visuals in the sixty-years-and-counting of *Playboy,* in his short tenure there. Tragically, Cole committed suicide in 1958, under circumstances that are still highly mysterious.

After Cole, the next great artists to be featured by Hefner were LeRoy Neiman—whose famous "Femlin" was a ubiquitous presence on the "Party Jokes" page—and Shel Silverstein. The incredibly diverse Silverstein first came to the attention of the world by drawing cartoons for *Playboy* in 1956, and later compiled a highly original hand-drawn travel diary for a long-running section titled *Innocent Abroad*. There seemed to be no end to Silverstein's gifts: After proving himself as a cartoonist, he went on to become a children's book author and illustrator (*Where the Sidewalk Ends*), recorded several classic jazz albums as a vocalist, and probably made his biggest impact and profit, as the composer and lyricist of a series of iconic country and western songs including "A Boy Named Sue," for Johnny Cash.

*Playboy's* humor extended beyond cartoons. Bawdy adult humor in a verbal rather than visual format could be found on the Party Jokes page. And there were opportunities for shopping beyond the advertisements: The Men's Shop showcased all the necessary *accoutrements* of the well-appointed man about town. What aspiring ladies' man could afford to be without a portable bar, which handily collapsed so you wouldn't have to deal with it the morning after? Or a Silent Valet that maintained the crease in one's trousers while busy without them, and, unlike Jeeves or Smithers, could keep a secret? In the first few years, Hefner worked out the details so exactly that the model has stayed consistent from that time to this.

\* \* \*

Apart from the never-ending supply of beautiful women who were lining up to shed their clothes for Hefner's cameramen, the other major asset that distinguished the magazine and the corporation was the overall excellence of the senior staff. Hef was so fond of his employees that, as a kind of a bonus to them, when *Playboy* prepared its own ads, he often used his staff rather than professional actors and models. If you look closely at vintage issues, you'll spot Victor Lownes, Anson Mount (whose son of the same name would star in the TV series *Hell on Wheels*), Reid Austin, Cynthia Maddox, and others.

By the end of the decade, the three men who set most of the tone for the future of Playboy Enterprises all had monosyllabic nicknames: "Hef," "Spec," and "Vic." Whereas Spectorsky was Hefner's man in charge of the actual content of the magazine, Victor was the guy who ran everything else, and would be the one to suggest to Hefner that the corporation should open its own club.

In many ways, Victor was the man Hef aspired to be—an authentically sophisticated, sybarite playboy to the core. Despite their social differences, upon meeting they quickly formed a deep and lasting bond over their shared interests—music and women—and before long, they were inseparable colleagues. Victor was the one who read the books and drank the wines and compared the vineyards while Hef instinctively knew a good business idea when it came to him.

Victor Lownes III was born in Buffalo, New York, on April 17, 1928, two years after Hef, and spent most of his childhood in Florida. After attending the Military Institute in Roswell, New Mexico (the last surviving cavalry school in the country), he moved on to the University of Chicago. It was there that he met his first wife, Judith, and had a son and daughter. He supported them with various jobs, including working his way up to manager at his grandfather's company, the Silent Watchman Industrial Time Lock Firm of Illinois. But, feeling suffocated by the responsibilities and restrictions of bourgeois suburban life, Victor eventually left his family to pursue a more liberated lifestyle. Thus, both Hef and Victor found themselves divorced—"free men"—during the glory years of *Playboy*.

In 2012, we visited Victor at his luxurious apartment on Manhattan's Sutton Place, where Marilyn, his legendarily gorgeous wife of thirty years, joined us as well. As Marilyn Cole, Mrs. Lownes was one of the most famous *Playboy* women of all time, first as a Bunny in the London Club, then as the first completely nude centerfold model, then as the 1973 Playmate of the Year, then as an intimate companion to Hefner, and finally as Mrs. Victor Lownes.

The first thing Victor wanted to talk about was the music. "My original connection with Hefner came about because I was a huge fan of Mabel Mercer's," he began. "Even before I ever heard of *Playboy*, I would occasionally come to New York on business, and when I did, I would always go to see Mabel perform."

It was in an article in *Park East* magazine that Victor first saw mention of the RSVP Club—a nightclub owned by Irvin Arthur and featuring the regal torch singer Mabel Mercer. It was perhaps not entirely a coincidence that the story was written by A. C. Spectorsky, several years before he would be hired by Hefner and come to Chicago; also Irvin would become a key talent recruiter for the Playboy Clubs.

"I was about twenty-four years old then, hanging out at Irvin Arthur's RSVP Club and going crazy over Mabel," Victor continued. "I would take girls there, and if they didn't like Mabel, if they didn't understand that Mabel was great, I'd just send them off in a car. If a girl said, 'That Mabel can't sing,' I'd just yell, 'Taxi!'"

Mabel Mercer (1900—1984), perhaps the single most important figure in the development of the art form generally known as cabaret-style singing, was a British woman of African descent who settled in America during World War II. She was renowned for a uniquely throaty storytelling style that placed an emphasis on the lyrics over the music. While widespread mainstream success may have eluded her, she had a fierce cadre of fans and was known as a "singer's singer"—admired by Frank Sinatra, among others. Sinatra unabashedly admitted that his exquisite phrasing was greatly informed by Mabel. Many songwriters considered her the finest interpreter of their works, and it was she who showed several generations of singers working in small, intimate nightclubs how to turn the lyrics of a song into a highly personal narrative.

Victor told us, "Frank Sinatra was such an ardent fan that if he was in the audience for one of her performances and someone at a nearby table was talking, he'd actually get up from his seat, walk over, and ask them to be quiet.

"Once," he continued, "I accompanied Mabel to a gig at the Blue Angel in Chicago and taped her performance. Around that time, I was having parties, a lot of them, because I was a new bachelor. One night, I was giving a party for Jonathan Winters. Mike Shea, the photographer, asked, 'Can I bring a friend of mine? He's just started a new magazine.' Of course, that young man was Hefner. We got to talking, and when I played Hef my tape of Mabel, he said, 'She's fantastic. Write about her for my new magazine.' That was the start of my career with *Playboy*. It all started with a shared passion for music."

The article turned out to be Victor's only one. "The editorial department didn't think much of my writing skills, and I very swiftly became the promotional director," he explained. But it happened that Atlantic Records was getting set to release *Midnight at Mabel Mercer's* at the time and needed some liner notes to accompany the disk. They asked Victor for permission to use his article for the purpose and he granted it immediately.

When first starting out, Hefner himself took care of interviewing and selecting the models, as well as editing the magazine in accordance with the *Playboy* philosophy. Victor quickly became his second in command, overseeing the business side and eventually masterminding the establishment of the clubs. You'll hear lots more about—and from—Victor, and his defining role in the organization, in upcoming chapters.

* * *

If there's one entertainer more connected to the *Playboy* story than any other, it would have to be Tony Bennett: He has had the honor of appearing on virtually every single Playboy entertainment platform, including multiple episodes of both TV series (1959-1961 and 1968-1970); many different Playboy Clubs (and, later resorts); and, more recently, the Playboy Jazz Festival in the Hollywood Bowl.

Tony understands the Playboy ethos because he was there from the very beginning. It didn't take long for him to figure out that Playboy's mission wasn't just about sex, or even just about music; the watchword was "fun," and it was a kind of fun that involved attractive people, good music, snappy conversation, and humor. In other words, Playboy was creating a never-ending party that took place within the pages of the magazine, at its jazz festivals, on television—and especially within the clubs. Bob Dylan famously described the composers of the Brill Building as having songwriting "down to a science." Likewise, Hef had party-making and grownup fun down to a science.

Tony and Hef were born the same year, 1926, and both served their country during the Second World War. They met in Chicago in 1956, at a point when Tony had already made a few hit records and Hefner's magazine was barely two years old. Tony loves to tell the story of how he first broke through in Chicago, thanks to another of that city's favorite sons, the legendary Nat King Cole. In the early 1950s, Tony was enjoying a successful run on the singles charts with "Because of You," "Cold, Cold Heart," "Blue Velvet," "Rags to Riches," and others. This led to a string of successful engagements around his native New York.

"I was very big in New York City," he told us. "Everybody knew me. I played Ben Maksik's Town and Country in Brooklyn and filled the place up for two weeks, four times a year. But nobody knew me outside of the east coast. I was pretty much unknown in Chicago, all over the Midwest, Los Angeles…."

Chicago clubs were among the first advertisers in *Playboy*, and one of these was quite possibly the Windy City's most prestigious "nite spot," the Chez Paree at 610 North Fairbanks Court. The June 1956 issue of *Playboy* (which was on the newsstands in May), carried an ad for the Chez Paree that announced Nat King Cole as its featured attraction for the month of May. But at the last minute, Tony was asked to fill in for Cole. "President Eisenhower invited Nat to come to Washington and sing for him at the White House," Tony explained, referring to the White House Correspondents' Dinner that took place on Thursday, May 24, 1956—right in the middle of Cole's run at the Chez Paree. "So Nat said, 'Tell them to get Tony!' That's how he broke me into Chicago. I took Nat's place that night and went over real big at the Chez Paree, and then they booked me regularly after that."

Tony may have left his heart in San Francisco, but he took to Chicago as if it was his second home. He particularly liked hanging out at the Black Orchid on the Near Northside, which was owned and operated by Paul David "Pauly" Raffles. "That's where I met Hef," he said. "Those were great days, those Chicago days. The Black Orchid had great comics like Larry Storch and Jack E. Leonard. Pauly invented the piano bar in the lounge. He had girls in scanty clothes and a little showroom; it was the hippest place to go. You'd see a great show with a comic and a singer, and then they'd have a great piano player like Ace Harris, then we'd all go over to Pauly's apartment at, like, 2 a.m. and stay until seven in the morning, just having big jam sessions.

"There was another spot we liked, too—the Key Club. It was in the back of the Chez Paree, and Erroll Garner would come over there and play after all the public left; it was just the chorus girls, Lenny Bruce, Hef, and all of us guys. Hugh was in the middle of all this. He was a very introverted, quiet guy. His genius was that he saw all this fun that everybody was having and he figured out a way to 'incorporate' it. That's how those Playboy Clubs came about. Which was ingenious! Being a good businessman, he thought, 'I'll take something where everybody's having fun and make it a product. Make it work.' And it worked, boy! It worked into millions and millions of dollars."

\* \* \*

Albert Podell, an assistant editor at *Playboy* from 1958—1959, got involved in the business after attending graduate school at the University of Chicago. "I was a graduate fellow on the Committee on International Relations," he told me. "I had edited my high school newspaper in Brooklyn, which, at that time, had the highest circulation of any high school newspaper in the country.

"In Chicago, I started dating a well-endowed employee at

*Playboy.* One day in 1958 she said to me, 'Hey, you know, they're looking for somebody to edit, and you like to write. Maybe you should look into working at the magazine.' I was getting a little bored with grad school, so I went down to their office. It turned out that they'd been looking for an editor for the past six months! I was given a test—an article to rewrite. They said I could take up to two weeks to do it. I read it that night and mailed it right back to them saying, 'Look, this is a piece of crap, unsalvageable. If I were one of your editors, I wouldn't waste my time or your money on editing it.'

"Apparently, for six months, some of the best editors in the country had tried to make that story work. *Playboy* was just looking for somebody with the judgment to say it was a lost cause! After that, I was interviewed by Hef and A.C. Spectorsky, the author of a popular work of sociology at the time, *The Exurbanites.* They really hired only the best people to work there. They called me up the day after my interview and said, 'You've got the job.'

"The first thing that took me by surprise when I started working at *Playboy* was the white opaque plastic on all the windows. When I asked Hef about it, he said, 'I don't want you to see outside. I don't want the thoughts of my editors to be sullied by the drabness of the mundane world outside.'

"Hef—and he'd be the first person to say so—was totally inept back then. He did everything wrong. He didn't know how to order food in a restaurant, how to pick wine, how to dress.... You get the idea. He created the magazine as a bible or guide for the person he aspired to be: the young, upwardly mobile male. It told guys like him what movies to see, what books to read, how to dress, how to furnish their apartments, how to cook, mix cocktails—all the stuff that Hef himself didn't know.

"When I started working there, there were five of us who edited the whole magazine. We had a small building at 232 East Ohio, and Hef lived there. His office had a bedroom, and at the end of the day, he would just close his door and go to sleep, or whatever, and he'd come out in the morning with a Pepsi in each hand to start the day.

"My job was to oversee all of the nonfiction except jazz and cooking. Hef hit the nail on the head when he told me, 'You know squat about jazz and cooking. Forget those.' So I wrote columns on what movies to see and what stocks to buy. I wrote fashion articles that they published under the name of Blake Rutherford III. I asked Hef, 'Who's this Blake Rutherford III?' and he said, 'C'mon, who's going to take fashion advice from an *Al Podell*?'

"I wrote the articles on how to furnish your apartment and what gifts to give for Christmas. I covered how to take your date to a restaurant and how to seduce her afterwards—all the nonfiction except jazz and cooking.

"I became somewhat famous in the building, because I was dating a woman who worked at the magazine at the same time that I had an outside girlfriend. The outside one found out about the magazine girl and came in one day with a kitchen knife. She chased her from the first floor up to the sixth floor. The fact that these two beautiful women were fighting over me, and that one of them was willing to use a weapon, was really very great for my macho prestige there."

\* \* \*

In 1959, *Playboy* reached its fifth birthday, and there was a lot to celebrate. The magazine's circulation had gone from 70,000 copies for the first issue now to a cool million, and was still climbing to the point where it would reach an all-time pinnacle of seven million in the early 1970s.

It was a cultural phenomenon. On a 1964 episode of the TV sitcom *Bewitched*, the dialogue went like this:

SHE: (upon seeing her husband reading a magazine titled "Gals.") Don't you think it's a little undignified for a man your age to have a lifetime subscription to a magazine like that?

HE: It has some very interesting articles.

SHE: Sure. And they all fold out.

HE: I meant it has intellectual content.

SHE: You mean, the girls wear glasses?

Forty years later, on a 2004 episode of *The Simpsons*, Bart came across his father's hidden stash of *Playdude* magazines, read them, and then led his fellow ten-year-olds in emulating the *Playdude* lifestyle. He was shown reclining in a dressing gown, "smoking" a bubble pipe, and listening to vintage LPs by Miles Davis and Dave Brubeck.

But, even though many a man has told his wife or mother that he reads it "for the articles," the larger truth was that even the articles were about sex in one way or another. While the girls pictured were the prizes that the young male readers were encouraged to compete for, the articles gave them clues as to how those prizes could be won. It wasn't as simple as picking the right tie, shoes, or beverage, but these were all pieces of the puzzle, to be sure.

If we had to define the allure of *Playboy* in a single phrase, it would be "how to have it all." That's quite a promise, but over all these years, Hef and his staff have made good on it, and changed the culture profoundly in the process.

2

# ALL THAT JAZZ

The first issue of *Playboy* included a two-page spread on pages thirty and thirty-one that was notably devoid of female pulchritude. This particular layout signaled what would become *another* signature topic in the magazine: music. It was an illustrated article about the renowned jazz artists known as the Dorsey Brothers.

The photographs were stock—Hefner didn't yet have the budget to commission new ones—but the article itself, by one Arthur Silver, was as fresh as the face of Hef's first "Sweetheart of the Month," Marilyn Monroe. Silver recapped the early lives of the brothers, starting with their training at the hands of their father, a coal-miner and music teacher. Jimmy gravitated to reeds (mainly clarinet, but also alto saxophone) while Tommy took up brass (mostly trombone, but occasionally cornet).

The boys spent their early years in Scranton, Pennsylvania, arriving in New York at the start of the Roaring Twenties—just in time to rise through the ranks of jazz-age dance and show bands, most famously Paul Whiteman's, before launching their own touring band in 1939. It would become one of the groundbreaking groups of the early swing era. Their infamous split—recounted in detail by Silver—resulted in the formation of two separate bands that lasted nearly twenty years each and produced some of the greatest jazz and big-band music of all time.

Silver discussed the brothers' occasional reunions throughout the 1940s, but the climax of the story was a description of the Dorseys' reunion in 1953, at which point Jimmy gave up leading his own band and merged with his younger brother. Although Silver couldn't know it in 1953, that new partnership would last until Tommy's death in 1956, at the age of fifty-one.

To this day, Hugh Hefner favors jazz over any other kind of music. You could say it was his first love. During his high-school days, "Hep Hef" wrote reviews of big-band records for the school paper, and from the original launch of *Playboy*, Hep Hef made sure there was room in the magazine devoted to music.

It's significant that the Dorsey story appeared in the very first issue. At that moment, the duo had already made music history, but were still considered as relevant as ever. Even the way the story was listed in the Table of Contents was significant: under "Jazz." By contrast, a story on the legendary halfback Harold "Red" Grange was labeled "Sports"—not "Football"; and a story on a restaurant in Havana (which was still open to Americans in 1953 and is again as 2014 draws to a close) wasn't labeled "International Cuisine", but simply "Food & Drink." The message was clear: Lots of different sports would be covered in the sports section, many varieties of chow would be discussed under "Food & Drink," and all manner of fashion would be introduced in "Attire"—but there was only one kind of music that Hef considered worth talking about, and that was jazz. Indeed, in the first year of publication there was at least one jazz story every other month.

On the literary front, the earliest issues featured reprints of public-domain fiction such as Boccaccio's tales from *The Decameron* (although, in 1954, some of the bawdiest ones were too salacious even for *Playboy*). Sir Arthur Conan Doyle's Sherlock Holmes stories were illustrated to emphasize their frequent references to drug use.

Two new books were serialized in *Playboy*'s first year: Ray Bradbury's now-classic *Fahrenheit 451* (a work Hef must have loved for its excoriation of book-burning and censorship) and Shepherd Mead's satirical *How to Succeed in Business Without Really Trying*. When that one was adapted into a Broadway musical in 1961, the script included an in-joke: "Mr. Gatch," a middle-aged executive, makes a pass at the young heroine and gets his face slapped, at which point he exclaims, "I'm gonna have to stop reading *Playboy!*"

The fourth issue, which hit stands in April 1954, included a feature about the *Metronome* magazine All Stars, a very sporting example of a new publication paying homage to an older and more venerated one. It may also have started the wheels turning in Hefner's imagination. A few years later, *Playboy*'s own jazz poll would become more influential than those of either *Metronome* or *Down Beat*.

The most prominent musician to be profiled in the first few years of the magazine's history is still the greatest name in jazz, Louis Armstrong. The September 1954 issue included a two-page spread headlined, "Satchmo Bops the Boppers," which praised Armstrong's very canny take-off of "The Whiffenpoof Song." The musical parody, written, arranged, and conducted for him by Gordon Jenkins, used the famous theme song of the Yale Whiffenpoofs to tweak the young modern jazz musicians of the day, known as "beboppers." Of course, "The Whiffenpoof Song" was itself a take-off on a classic poem by Rudyard Kipling. The two-page spread was copiously illustrated with new pictures of Armstrong and his All-Stars in action, taken at the Blue Note in Chicago the previous month.

In the same issue was an innovative piece called "Black Country," by Charles Beaumont, described as a work of "jazz fiction." The cover was also a milestone of sorts; it was the first and only one that didn't feature a pretty girl or some other sexually suggestive image. Instead, it had a very abstract drawing of a jazz band in action, with just a suggestion of the as-yet-not-fully-developed Playboy rabbit logo playing the clarinet.

Just four months later, Armstrong was back in *Playboy*'s pages in a far more substantial story headlined, "Red Beans and Ricely Yours: The Story of Satchmo." This long, diligently researched biographical portrait was also written by Charles Beaumont.

The June 1954 issue offered Bob Perlongo's "Little Boy Blues," which fell into the "Satire" section (then most often occupied by the efforts of Shepherd Mead), a funny short piece about a jazz trumpeter named Alfonso Embouchure.

The August 1954 edition included a piece called "Red Lights and Hot Music," that brought both components of the magazine's focus together rather literally. It was a history of Storyville, New Orleans's fabled red-light district, where both prostitution and jazz flourished at the turn of the century. Written by James H. Lavely, it covered both the music and life at the brothels where that music was frequently heard, celebrating the hard-working girls who earned an honest living there.

*Playboy* never shied away from controversy, and that was as true of its jazz coverage as anything else. Appearing in the January 1955 issue—the same one in which the notorious Bettie Page showed Santa who was naughty as the Christmas Playmate—was a piece called, "West Coast Jazz Is Nowhere." In it, Bob Perlongo argued that West Coast Jazz, a genre coined by the record labels in an attempt to promote a new trend, was in fact a nonexistent category. Sixty years later, the most valuable service to jazz history that the article provides is a few direct quotes from tenor saxophonist Wardell Gray, one of the major musical heroes of the era, who was rarely interviewed. Perlongo's own polemic, about whether the west coast had produced its own "important new school of music," seems somewhat irrelevant today, but the fact that a mainstream magazine was covering jazz in such detail was groundbreaking in 1955.

Perlongo's stance touched off an outburst of reader mail, much of which was published in the May issue and nearly all of which disagreed vehemently with his opinions. The longest rebuttal came from Harry Babasin, a prominent Los Angeles bassist, bandleader, and the owner of Nocturne Records, a short-lived label he founded to document the so-called West Coast Jazz. On the "pro" side came a response from none other than jazz piano great Dave Brubeck, who said that he'd enjoyed the story very much and added, "I don't agree with all of [Perlongo's] points, but it's one of the best pieces I've read on the music that's being played out here."

Brubeck may not have been auditioning for a spot on the masthead, but he got one. His became one of the first celebrity bylines in the magazine when *Playboy* published "The New Jazz Audience by Dave Brubeck," the following August, subtitled, "After 60 colleges in 60 days, Brubeck talks about his music and the people who listen."

Opening with, "An exciting new kind of jazz is being played in America today.

And it is creating a new kind of jazz audience," Brubeck's main focus was on the ways that contemporary jazzmen could continue to connect directly with their audiences. "A few short years ago," he continued, "people liked to dance to jazz and they liked to stamp and clap their hands to jazz. Today, people like to do all of these, but realize jazz is as deserving of attention as classical music. In fact, jazz is America's classical music." He ended with, "Jazz is alive in America today: alive and growing. I'm happy to be a part of that growth."

While the Brubeck story was directed at the initiated jazz aficionado, *Playboy* also catered to the other end of the spectrum, the "hot record" collector, in a piece in the September 1955 issue titled "Collecting Jazz."

Jazz seemed to permeate every aspect of the magazine. In addition to the jazz fiction, jazz satire, and jazz-as-sex offerings, there were features that foreshadowed the turns *Playboy*'s later music coverage would take. In June 1955, there was an article called "Playboy's All Time All Star Jazz Band," by Jack Tracy, the editor of

*Down Beat* (a venerable publication for jazz heads that, like *Playboy*, was published in Chicago). While not a formal poll, it prefigured the Playboy All Star Jazz Polls, still to come, in many ways. Featured at the top of Tracy's dream lineup were three all-time greats: Louis Armstrong, Benny Goodman, and Charlie Parker. Sadly, Parker died while Tracy was midway through writing the article (on March 12, 1955), but that didn't disqualify him from the All Stars. Tracy commented that he was pleased to put together the All Star Band because, unlike the annual *Down Beat* poll, it could include musicians from the entire half-century history of jazz, including those who had gone on to the great bandstand in the sky. Accordingly, in addition to Parker on sax, he named Charlie Christian and Jimmy Blanton as his all-time favorites on guitar and bass.

The letters pages of the era featured another item that anticipated a future innovation of the Playboy organization. As early as the magazine's second year, readers were writing in to report starting up their own "Playboy Clubs." These weren't nightclubs, of course, they were more like traditional mens' fraternal societies. The May 1955 letters page contained news of such clubs forming in New Jersey, Boston, New Orleans, and a dormitory at the University of Illinois. From the ground up, without any encouragement from Hefner, *Playboy* was already becoming something more than a magazine.

Clearly, something was in the air. In 1956, the all-star combination of alto saxophonist Art Pepper and trumpeter Chet Baker (both then associated with the "West Coast School" that Perlongo insisted didn't exist) recorded an album on Pacific Jazz entitled *Playboys.* A few months later, Frank Wess, then best known as a tenor sax soloist with the Count Basie band, cut a session for Savoy Records that would be released under the title *Jazz for Playboys.* The covers of both albums depicted fetching young models rather than the male musicians who were actually playing the music. And in its use of typography, Pacific Jazz didn't just borrow the *Playboy* name; it went so far as to mimic the magazine's distinctive logo.

By 1957, *Playboy* was one of the primary proponents of jazz in the mainstream media. Until then, nearly all coverage of the form had been relegated to specialty publications such as the aforementioned *Metronome* and *Down Beat*. Newspapers and general-interest magazines almost never reviewed or covered any kind of music beyond classical—particularly European symphonies and opera—but Hef, along with his future partner, George Wein, were working tirelessly to change that. As a direct consequence, Hefner and Wein, each in his own way, helped alter the very image of jazz.

Up through World War II, jazz had been something that couples—mostly young ones—danced to. Thanks to its intelligent and relentless coverage of the genre, *Playboy* helped turn jazz into something that sophisticated young men listened to on their newly purchased hi-fi systems while holding martinis. Needless to say, you can't dance while you're holding a martini, so jazz become something that smart people sat still for, paid attention to, and developed opinions about.

*Playboy* was there to help form those opinions. Features in its pages covered the best hi-fi to buy, the best vodka for mixing martinis, and the best jazz albums to listen to while sipping them. The "new jazz audience" that Brubeck had spoken of was made up of the same people who read *Playboy;* both groups, it seems, were predominantly male. Something about tenor saxophonists with beards and berets spinning endless variations on a few chord changes appealed less to women than men. The ladies, it seems, were less interested in music as an abstract art form than as an accoutrement of the social scene. Ultimately, women would benefit from the sexual revolution that *Playboy* helped ignite (though not all of them would see it that way)—but in the 1950s, they didn't read *Playboy*, and they didn't buy instrumental modern jazz albums.

In February 1957, the relationship between *Playboy* and jazz was, you might say, consummated, with the debut of the annual Playboy Jazz Poll. It began with a picture of the drummer Shelly

Manne and the following lines: "All the cats joined in to make the first annual Playboy Jazz Poll the biggest, most successful popularity poll ever conducted in the field of jazz music." How big? "The last of more than 20,000 ballots and the more than 430,000 individual votes have been counted."

* * *

Throughout 1957, the first year of the poll, singer and songwriter Jon Hendricks was hard at work on the album that became *Sing a Song of Basie*, with the collective that would eventually evolve into Lambert, Hendricks, and Ross—the most acclaimed jazz vocal group of all time. He had already noticed all the jazz coverage in *Playboy*, and remembers, almost sixty years later, how surprising it was to see that kind of attention being paid to music in a popular magazine.

As a man of letters himself, Jon remembered that he was immediately attracted to the quality of the writing. "Hef loved to have good writing, so he had people helping him find good writers. He had some wonderful writing done on music. There weren't too many people writing about jazz at that time. Nobody talked about it. It was like a secret! 'What are you going to do?' 'I'm going upstairs and I'm going to listen to my secret music.' Ha ha!

"It didn't stay that way for very long though, thanks to Hefner. He kept on doing everything possible to help the music and the musicians, you know, the artists involved. He was really with them. I thought that was not only humane of him but human!"

In later years, Jon would appear at any number of Playboy venues: the 1959 Jazz Festival in Chicago, multiple episodes of *Playboy's Penthouse* in 1959 and 1960, the Playboy Club in London in 1968, and several years of the Playboy Jazz Festival in the Hollywood Bowl in the 1980s. "*Playboy* was the first national magazine to have a big readers' jazz poll," Jon continued. "Absolutely! They certainly were. And they thought about it, and they were sincere about it. And all of us were just thankful for it, you know, because you go to any other country and they respected their culture, you know, whatever it is, but the United States didn't start respecting each culture until people like Hugh Hefner and others who had money to spend on it did and built it up. He was a rare example of a man with both money and taste. Most people you meet have one but not the other!"

\* \* \*

There had been jazz polls before, in *Esquire* magazine as well as in the specialty publications, but—as usual—*Playboy* did it bigger and better than the rest; just as its girls were prettier and more plentiful, its jazz survey was more extensive than any that had been published previously.

*Esquire*'s poll had focused on the opinions of critics but *Playboy*'s approach was decidedly populist: readers' votes were counted assiduously and their opinions were what determined the winner. And the artist who won their hearts over all others for no fewer than seven of the first ten years was Stan Kenton.

For much of his three decades on the road, Kenton had a following like no other in jazz. His fans were the most dedicated and the most cultist. In the overall field of American music—jazz, pop, whatever—Kenton's fans were devoted to him in the way that *Star Trek* fans worshipped that show. His acolytes were as numerous as they were nerdy. Although Kenton produced many excellent albums of ballads, his music was never really conducive to dancing or making out. His was a highly testosterone-driven sound in which the limits of the brass players, in particular, were tested regularly. It was very much the jazz equivalent of driving the latest sports car and pushing it as fast as it would go.

If Kenton's appeal was mostly masculine, the single most popular tenor saxophonist of the decade was Stan Getz, one of the music's great romantics—who won every year in his own category.

The poll celebrated its tenth anniversary in 1966. To mark that milestone, the magazine published the entire "Decade of Playboy Jazz Poll Winners," as an adjunct to that year's poll. The term *spreadsheet* would certainly have meant something entirely different to a *Playboy* reader in the 1960s than it does today, but the results of ten years' worth of polls was presented in tabular form.

Major winners of the decade included J. J. Johnson, who was virtually unchallenged as the number-one trombonist of the modern jazz era; and, of course, Dave Brubeck. Besides topping the list of pianists for seven out of those ten years, he led the number-one instrumental combo of the entire decade, The Dave Brubeck Quartet, beating out the two most famous Miles Davis quintets of all time. Davis won the top slot on trumpet for seven out of the ten years, sharing the honor with Louis Armstrong and Chet Baker.

The other most consistent winner in the poll was Frank Sinatra, who sat atop the Male Vocalist category for all ten years and then some. In fact, the only reason Sinatra fell off his perch in the early 1970s was that he decided to retire from show business—temporarily, it turned out. That opened the door for Tom Jones, Joe Cocker, and Ray Charles to take home the prize.

As Hefner told the authors of this book, "Sinatra was the Playboy ideal, a man who represented the best in his chosen profession, who was populist and yet sophisticated, a leader and at the same time—in the parlance of the day—a chaser." As usual, Hef nailed it. Sinatra, whose own role model was his best friend, the composer Jimmy Van Heusen, was the ideal of the swinging bachelor. In fact, his 1955 movie *The Tender Trap* was a virtual guidebook to the Playboy lifestyle (just as Shepherd Mead's *How to Succeed in Business Without Really Trying,* although meant as a satire, worked quite literally as a guide to corporate advancement in the grey-flannel era).

Ella Fitzgerald was by far the most popular female vocalist in the poll, winning almost all sixteen years running, except for a few times when the throne was usurped by Barbra Streisand. Yet Fitzgerald was never a personal role model the way Sinatra was; a man who women wanted and men wanted to *be*. Even more than Hefner himself—as Hef freely admits—Sinatra was the ultimate playboy.

For sixteen years, the annual Playboy Jazz Poll was one of the music world's most anticipated events. In 1958, 25,000 ballots were collected, and it was all upward from there. Each year, the art director made the story seem fresh and visually stunning. The 1957 edition featured lots of color photos, and in 1958, the winners were sketched by artist Howard Mueller. After that, the presentation of the poll alternated between photos and top-notch artwork. The most outstanding photos can be seen in the 1961 edition. Up until then, the photo editors had obtained shots from a wide range of photographers and sources, but in the fifth poll, the images were specially commissioned by a single photographer (uncredited, alas, but undoubtedly based in New York). Shot in his studio, the musicians posed on stools and couches in front of colorful backgrounds. Even Sinatra dropped by for his closeup, as did the infamously anti-social Miles Davis, who is shown reclining on a couch, looking relaxed and happy to be there. The most visually stunning photo is a full-page color shot of the year's favored vocal group, Lambert, Hendricks, and Ross. The runner-up is a thoughtfully conceived pose by the Brubeck quartet, with the Dave holding the keyboard from a deconstructed piano.

In 1962, the winners were rendered in drawings by Mike Ramus that were too affectionate and respectful to be described as caricatures. As Hefner put it in his front-of-the-book comments, they were "lightly lined by caricaturist Mike Ramus, whose portraits provide the proper note of harmony for musicologist Leonard Feather."

For the first six years, Feather wrote the text accompanying the illustrations and the statistics, but in 1963 Nat Hentoff took over. That year, the winners were depicted—again by an uncredited photographer—in stylishly blurry, out of focus photos. In retrospect, they almost seem to constitute a visual analogy for where music itself was headed at the time.

In 1965, the musicians were rendered in lovely paintings by Richard Frooman, and all of the winners (again including Sinatra) seem to have sat for him; there's no evidence that he worked from photographs or other existing images.

That 1965 feature represented the visual high point of the poll. In its last years, the illustrative techniques grew increasingly modish. In 1968, the art director used a collage of photographs that almost could have been assembled by Louis Armstrong, who favored the technique in his own visual art. In 1969, artist Alex Gnidziejko came up with some very Peter Max-ish depictions based on photographs; and in the poll's final three years, 1970, 1971, and 1972, voguish artists of the day offered variations on that theme, manipulating photographs with airbrushes and other tools to make them look like paintings and drawings. But, even as the poll itself became less and less focused, the illustrations remained very satisfying.

\* \* \*

Over the years, two additional components were introduced into the poll, starting with "The Playboy All-Stars' All-Stars" in 1959. Readers continued to vote on the general categories, but while those results were being tabulated, Feather informed us, he and the *Playboy* staff contacted all the winners of the previous year's poll and asked them to pick their own favorite performers in each category. So, in addition to the sterling silver Jazz Medals that were awarded to the twenty-nine men and one girl who'd secured a place in the readers' poll, a special group of sixteen "All-Stars," selected by the musicians themselves, was announced. The audience favorites and those the artists selected overlapped quite a bit, but the differences were significant. Top choices on vocals were Frank Sinatra and Ella Fitzgerald in both polls, but the musicians' top choice for tenor sax was Sonny Rollins (over Stan Getz) and for piano Oscar Peterson (over Dave Brubeck). The most notable difference was in bandleader; the musicians picked Count Basie the first year and then Duke Ellington virtually every year after that. Clearly, they didn't want to work for Stan Kenton!

In 1962, the editors introduced one of the most distinctive features of the annual jazz section, a two-page illustration of the "Playboy All-Star Jazz Band." The winners were depicted in matching tuxedos, as if they were members of the same big band, posed behind bandstands featuring the Playboy rabbit insignia where the bandleader's name usually went. The idea was rather outrageous, when you think about it. If you know anything at all about jazz, it's hard to imagine Miles Davis, Dizzy Gillespie, Louis Armstrong, and Maynard Ferguson sharing the same trumpet section—even if they did share the bill at some festivals. The vocal department included not only Sinatra and Fitzgerald, but the trio of Lambert, Hendricks, and Ross.

Because the notion of "All Stars"—a musical *fantasy team,* in today's parlance—was so fanciful, it made perfect sense to render the players in a cartoon-like style; the honor of doing so went to Mike Ramus. This image became so distinctive that for the next ten polls, the art directors continued to present variations on it. In 1963, there was a much more audacious—though no less endearing—cartoon of the winners by Randall Enos.

And so it went—1964 and 1965 brought bold visual layouts in which photos of the winners' heads were placed above a rendering of their bodies on the bandstand, and for most of the remaining years, cartoon illustrations were the order of the day.

The last aspect of the poll to be introduced was the "Playboy Jazz Hall of Fame." Beginning in 1966, readers were asked to vote on entries for an all-time Hall of Fame, which could include anyone in jazz history, living or dead, singer, instrumentalist, or bandleader.

As it happened, the winners that first year were all among the living. "After the ballots had been counted," reported Nat Hentoff, "Louis Armstrong, Frank Sinatra, and Dave Brubeck led all the rest—and by a handsome margin, we might add." This became perhaps the most visually compelling section of the poll. Each year from 1966 to 1972, readers selected three new additions to the Hall of Fame, who would then be depicted in stunning clay sculptures by Jack Gregory that were photographed by Seymour Mednick. Over the poll's final six years, these distinctive sculptures would take up more and more of the section.

Added to the roster in 1967 were Duke Ellington, Ella Fitzgerald, and Count Basie; in 1968, John Coltrane (who died in July 1967, not long before the 1968 poll), Benny Goodman, and Ray Charles. By 1969, some surprising choices began to creep in. In addition to Miles Davis and the recently deceased Wes Montgomery, was Herb Alpert. And by 1970, the honorees were all rock stars: Bob Dylan, John Lennon, and Paul McCartney. In 1971, the anointed were all members of the live-fast-die-young contingent: Jimi Hendrix, Janis Joplin, and Elvis Presley (whose career was actually hitting a new high point in the early 1970s, before his premature demise in 1977). The last three artists to make it into the figurative Hall were Mick Jagger, Jim Morrison (of the Doors), and George Harrison.

\* \* \*

In 1962, *Playboy* inaugurated yet another feature of its cultural coverage: the now-famous *Playboy* interview. The first one appeared in September of that year and, from then until now, these provocative, in-depth interviews with artists and other movers and shakers have been a shining hallmark of the magazine. "I buy it for the articles" began to sound somewhat plausible.

Over the past fifty years, notable figures from every walk of life have been interviewed at length in *Playboy*, including actors, athletes, artists, authors, atheists, comedians, politicians, and industrialists. The diversity of interview subjects is perhaps best illustrated by the two who appeared successively in the November and December 1963 issues: Jimmy Hoffa and Albert Schweitzer.

At this point it should come as no surprise that the interview series was launched on a high note, literally, with Miles Davis interviewed by Alex Haley. Haley, who would go on to write the bestseller *Roots*, would become the best-known *Playboy* interviewer, his subjects including not only Martin Luther King Jr. and Malcolm X (whose relationship with Haley led to their collaboration on his classic autobiography), but the infamous American Nazi George Lincoln Rockwell. All three of these, it might be noted, were later assassinated.

In the inaugural interview, published in September 1962, Miles Davis was infamously frank and, perhaps because his interviewer was also African American, very forthcoming on the subject of race. "In high school," he commented, "I was best in music class on the trumpet, but the prizes went to the boys with blue eyes. I made up my mind to outdo anybody white on my horn." Though Davis was notably frank with Haley, he was hardly hostile. He discussed his highly untraditional stage presence, explained why he didn't announce song titles or banter with the crowd, and stated what might not have been obvious to his fans at the time—that he felt he was always communicating with his audience even when he wasn't looking at them or, sometimes, even facing them. The article remains perhaps our best view into the heart and soul of the man later dubbed jazz's "Prince of Darkness."

The next major musician interviewed was a man who had been a significant influence on Davis—and everyone else. The February 1963 interview with Frank Sinatra, when he was at the pinnacle of his career, would become one of the magazine's most famous. At the time, Sinatra ruled the Ratpack, was cozy with the presidential administration that he had helped elect, and was flying high with the success of his own record label, Reprise Records. He had just completed a triumphant world tour, the most successful ever by a performer at the time, and was making some of the best movies of his career—including *The Manchurian Candidate* and *Robin and the Seven Hoods*.

Sinatra, whose formal education ended after grade school, had never felt confident about dealing with intellectuals—which probably accounts for his reluctance to be interviewed. When Hefner approached him, someone on Sinatra's team came up with the idea of asking the magazine to submit the questions in writing, and having Mike Shore, a writer on the staff of Reprise Records, write out the answers. To this day, no one is sure to what extent the responses came from Sinatra himself; surely some of them reflect his genuine views, while others come across like pure Shore. One thing is certain; when Sinatra said that the quality he most tried to instill in his own singing was "honesty," it was an accurate reflection of his feelings on the subject.

The interview featured a long philosophical section, in which "Sinatra" turned out to be more unconventionally spiritual than anyone realized. "Remember," he ruminated, "they were men of God who destroyed the educational treasures at Alexandria, who perpetrated the Inquisition in Spain, who burned the witches at Salem. Over 25,000 organized religions flourish on this planet, but the followers of each think all the others are miserably misguided and probably evil as well." The interview's most quoted line is, "I don't believe in a personal God to whom I look for comfort or for a natural on the next roll of the dice. I'm not unmindful of man's seeming need for faith; I'm for anything that gets you through the night, be it prayer, tranquilizers, or a bottle of Jack Daniel's."

That last line was later immortalized by singer-songwriter Kris Kristofferson, who was inspired by the interview to write the song "Help Me Make It Through the Night." Sinatra himself never recorded it but Elvis Presley and many others did, and it went on to become a classic country ballad.

The Beatles graced *Playboy* with a collective interview in February 1965, the same month the jazz poll debuted. "England's mop-topped millionaire minstrels," were charming and entertaining, to be sure, though not notably revealing. All four admitted to being *Playboy* subscribers, and when asked about the upcoming opening of the London Playboy Club, they all expressed certainty that it would be a success because of the preponderance of "dirty old men" there. They described themselves as "dirty *young* men."

A later interview with John Lennon, conducted just a few months before he was murdered in December 1980, and published a month after his death, was much more candid. At forty, Lennon was still defensive about his wife and collaborator Yoko Ono, and still angry with his former partner, Paul McCartney. When asked why he chose to move beyond the Beatles, his response was philosophical: "When Rodgers worked with Hart and then worked with Hammerstein, do you think he should have stayed with one instead of working with the other? Should Dean Martin and Jerry Lewis have stayed together because I used to like them together?"

When McCartney was interviewed three years later, he was more forgiving, comparing his experience of Lennon's death to another collective tragedy: "It was the same as the JFK thing. The same horrific moment, you know. You couldn't take it in. I can't."

Lennon and McCartney were hardly the last musical greats to submit to a *Playboy* interrogation. Over the years, many iconic figures from the music world spoke frankly and revealingly, including Quincy Jones, Paul Simon, Sammy Davis Jr., Bob Dylan (twice), Ray Charles, Joan Baez, Elton John, Cher, Dolly Parton, John Denver, Billy Joel—and even Tiny Tim.

In 1968, the jazz poll was redubbed "Jazz & Pop '68," and the heading followed that format throughout its final five years. The 1972 poll was a curious combination of disparate elements; the annual bandstand cartoon depicted *The Tonight Show*'s Doc Severinsen as the bandleader, Chicago as the year's top instrumental group, and the Moody Blues as top vocal group—but they shared the stage with such perennial winners as Stan Getz and Gerry Mulligan. By that point, it was apparent that the music world had become so diverse that no one poll could do justice to all of it. Perhaps for that reason, it took its final bow in 1972.

The sea of changes and diversity within the worlds of jazz and pop could never have been anticipated when *Playboy* magazine was founded with a strong mandate to cover jazz. In 1955, Charles Beaumont concluded his portrait of Louis Armstrong by quoting Satchmo: "The music of tomorrow, or the modern stuff, or all that new-fangled stuff, just don't move the people." But the last word was Beaumont's: "Maybe Louis is wrong. Maybe today's dazzling showers of dissonance, the New Music, the Cerebral Sound-makers, the 'Head Stuff,' will take a firm place and hang onto it. Or maybe it will all fizzle like a fleet of toy rockets and disappear. Whatever happens, one thing is certain. Jazz has lasted for over fifty years… and it will always be vivid and alive and important, always, just as long as it is played by honest artists who have something to say that can't be said any other way. As long as there are men like Louis Armstrong."

We would add, and as long as there is *Playboy*.

Hugh Hefner and Cynthia Maddox arriving in New York on a flight from Chicago to attend a party given by Ella Fitzgerald at Basin Street East, in honor of the winners of the Playboy All-Star

# 3

# "THE GREATEST THREE DAYS IN THE HISTORY OF JAZZ"

B y 1959, *Playboy* was a solid success. The magazine's readership—primarily young, professional men—had made it one of the most notorious and influential magazines in the world. Naturally, Hef was looking for a spectacular way to commemorate its fifth birthday. Given that jazz had always been an essential component of *Playboy's* hip, upscale allure, he, decided to throw a huge jazz party—a festival.

A large-scale event seemed like the logical next move in Playboy's game plan—at least to Hef. The magazine's annual jazz poll had become an anticipated annual event. And, in conjunction with the first one, in 1957, Playboy had released an accompanying double LP called *The Playboy Jazz All-Stars.* The two disks featured previously released performances by the poll winners in a fresh compilation, and *Billboard*—the record business bible—had given it a rave review. "It's a big co-operative venture, quite unprecedented in the industry," they pointed out, and they made it their top jazz pick of the week of December 9, 1957. "Great cover, extremely heavy promotion, and genuine quality make this an outstanding gift offering at $9 tag," they gushed, and crowned it "album cover of the week" as an extra bonus. The package, produced and annotated by Leonard Feather, was such a success that there were follow-ups in 1958 and 1959.

The next frontier was live music and, as usual, Hef wasn't thinking small. The first Playboy Jazz Festival would have to make history. Mind you, the music festival concept was a relatively new one, pioneered and perfected by Hefner's future partner, George Wein, who began producing the groundbreaking Newport Jazz Festival in 1954. The Monterey Jazz Festival, dreamed up by Jimmy Lyons and Ralph Gleason, was first held in 1958 (and has been going strong ever since).

Hef and Victor planned to announce plans for their festival by throwing a press party for the town's many disc jockeys, and the logical venue for the event was their favorite hangout on Chicago's Near North Side, the Black Orchid. The problem was that the club, which had been acquired by impresario Paul Raffles in 1956, had recently declared bankruptcy and closed. It seems that "Pauly" Raffles had moved to Los Angeles, married the daughter of a footwear magnate, and given up show business for shoe business!

Never daunted by a challenge, Hef and Victor pleaded their case to James Kennedy, the federally appointed receiver for the Black Orchid, and he agreed to let them use the shuttered venue on the afternoon of July 12, 1959, before padlocking the front door for good. "It was some wake for the famed ten-year-old café," reported *The Chicago Tribune*, cheekily describing Kennedy as "Rush Street's hottest new club owner!"

Then a far larger problem reared its ugly head: the venue for the festival itself. *Playboy* had been bringing sex and music together in every aspect of its operation, but now it hoped to combine those two ingredients with a third: sports. The Third Pan-American Games—an Olympics-like athletic competition—was scheduled for the end of August at the city's massive outdoor stadium, Soldier Field. Hef and Victor's plan was to stage the *Playboy* event there, in conjunction with the games. But, under pressure from various special-interest groups, the city, which owned the stadium, denied *Playboy* the use of Soldier Field. Apparently, to some self-appointed guardians of morality, the thought of playmates and jazz musicians mingling with wholesome young American athletes and fans was just… wrong. As jazz scholar Chris Sheridan described it, "Plans to set [the festival] aside the Pan-American Games were squashed following a prurient campaign by religious newspapers which were unhappy with *Playboy* magazine per se and concern by Games officials that jazz audiences might damage the athletics track."

Victor remembers the experience as if it were yesterday. "It was supposed to be in Soldier Field, a park owned by the city of Chicago. But when officials of the Catholic Church found out that the event was sponsored by *Playboy*, they complained and the city backed out of the deal. I went to see the manager of the park and he gave me a flat 'no,' as did the Stockyards Arena. So we had to find a venue quick! We approached Arthur Wirtz, who owned the Chicago Stadium [an indoor arena, home to Chicago's hockey and basketball teams]. He let us have it and it all ended very happily. The three-day festival was a big sell-out."

The *Tribune* previewed the festival in an "On the Town" column by Will Leonard that ran on Sunday July 26. Leonard heralded it as just one event in a new "straw hat jazz festival season," comparable to the straw hat theater season more commonly known as summer stock. He expressed surprise and delight at finding jazz being performed out of its usual habitat: "The jazzmen haven't stopped blowing or stomping in the regular smoke-filled rooms of the night sector, but they never have found so many midsummer gigs on concert stages as they have this month and next."

Victor put together the entire event, which included matinee performances as well as three full evenings, working out the logistics with an assistant. "Hefner and I tossed around a lot of opinions about who should be included," he told us. "When you look at

Hugh Hefner and Ella Fitzgerald. Courtesy PEI

the list of musicians we ended up with, you'll see that we got all the greats. We asked and they all came. Not only did we have Ella Fitzgerald and Louis Armstrong, but they played together! Miles Davis was there... *everyone* was there."

Hef later said that he regretted not inaugurating the festival a few years earlier, so that Charlie Parker, who died in 1955, could have played it. Hef did try to bring in Billie Holiday, but she died just weeks before the first downbeat.

Playboy also extended an offer to Nat King Cole, who, like Hefner, was a native Chicagoan (or practically so—his family moved there from Montgomery when the future King was but a four-year-old prince). Regrettably, the great singer-pianist was in the middle of one of his historic South American tours at the time.

"I got a call from the Playboy office while I was in my hotel room in Lima, Peru," Cole reminisced on the October 24, 1959, episode of *Playboy After Dark*. "They said, 'We want you to do a concert!' I said, 'Are you kidding? Why don't you call [my agent] in Chicago, instead of calling me all the way down here?' 'Well, we just wanted to talk to you,' they said!"

On July 26, the *Tribune* published a caricature of the four head-liners scheduled for the first night, Friday August 7: Count Basie and his Orchestra (with vocalist Joe Williams), singer Dakota Staton, Dizzy Gillespie, and comedian Mort Sahl. The Dave Brubeck Quartet and trombonist Kai Winding also performed on Friday, as did Miles Davis, with a quintet featuring alto-saxophone star Julian "Cannon-ball" Adderley. The one tune from that set that survives in recorded form is the trumpeter's classic, "So What." Davis's usual touring group that year was a sextet featuring both Adderley and John Col-trane, but no one seems to recall why Coltrane wasn't at the festival.

The Basie band performed on Saturday night as well, and the show was broadcast by the Armed Forces Network. The Catholic Church may not have approved of the Playboy Jazz Festival, but America's soldiers and sailors apparently did! Basie's show that night was a celebration of his twenty-fifth year as a bandleader, and again featured Joe Williams as well as the vocal trio of Lambert, Hendricks and Ross, then the hottest group in jazz.

Clarinetist Jimmy Giuffre and his trio, which included guitarist Jim Hall and bassist Wilfred Middlebrooks, also played on Saturday, as did the Oscar Peterson Trio, featuring bassist Ray Brown and drummer Ed Thigpen. On Sunday, Ella Fitzgerald—joined by Louis Armstrong—was the big attraction, closely seconded by tenor sax pioneer Coleman Hawkins. Rounding out the events of the weekend were performances by Cab Calloway, Roaring Twenties trumpet star Red Nichols, Duke Ellington and his Orchestra (in town to play the Blue Note), singer David Allyn, trombone legend Jack Teagarden, and rising tenor star Sonny Rollins.

Someone had the out-of-the-box idea of reuniting one of the most famous collectives in the already-long history of jazz in Chicago: the so-called "Austin High Gang." This loosely affiliated group of musicians, all white and from the same generation, was somehow associated with Austin High School on the West Side, though few of them had actually attended. What really united them was that they'd all learned their chops from the original African-American jazz pioneers who'd migrated from New Orleans at the start of the jazz age. The *Tribune* announced that two of the most famous Austin High grads, trumpeter Jimmy McPartland and saxophonist Bud Freeman, would be joined by clarinetist Pee Wee Russell, pianist Art Hodes, and drummer George Wettling.

You'd think it would have been impossible to choose a favorite act among all that talent, but the one artist everybody raved about seeing was Frank Sinatra. Which is interesting, since Sinatra didn't actually perform there! Hefner had reached out to him, but he was in Hollywood at the time, filming *Can Can.* That's when Hef's kid brother Keith had a brainstorm. Since the Chairman wasn't available, how about getting the next best thing: Duke Hazlett!

The younger Hefner recalled, "Duke was a full-time Sinatra impersonator who was already working busily around Chicago. We heard him sing at a club and loved him—he looked like Sinatra and sounded *exactly* like him. So we invited him to perform at the festival."

Here's how Duke remembers it: "I was working a room in Chicago called Le Bistro, and Hugh Hefner came in to see me because he was a fan of Sinatra and I emulate him. Hef said, 'Hey listen, I have an idea,' and he explained to me that he had been looking forward to having Sinatra at his Playboy Jazz Festival, but that he wouldn't be able to appear. He told me his idea and I said, 'Yeah, that sounds like fun, that's what I do!' It was supposed to be a surprise for everyone, but word leaked out and folks on the street heard that Sinatra might show up."

Keith continued, "Right about the middle of the show, the spotlights start swirling and, without an introduction, this guy

Duke Hazlett, Hugh Hefner and Victor Lownes at the Playboy Jazz Festival 1959. Hazlett
Family Archives

walks towards the stage... followed by his entourage, plus security
and a police escort."

"I slowly made my way," said Duke, "with my trench coat
hooked on my finger over my shoulder and, of course, a hat with
a white band à la Sinatra. Count Basie's band was playing as I hit
the stage, and I started singing 'Come Fly with Me.'"

"The crowd went crazy," said Keith. "Duke walked to the center
of the stage and, ring-a-ding-ding, the band started, and he sang two
or three songs, turned, and left. Everyone in the audience, even in
the first row, was sure they had just seen Frank Sinatra!"

The emcee for this landmark event was social satirist Mort Sahl.
Mort told us, "We were all really close at the time. To illustrate
how long ago it was—Hef used to get dressed everyday! Victor and
Hef used to wear three-piece suits before Hef decided to stay in his
pajamas all day. I was appearing at Mr. Kelly's and we became very

friendly. The guys kind of appropriated me, and we'd have lunch every day and then go to the clubs at night. It was a wonderful time, all the clubs stayed open until five o'clock in the morning. They asked me to be a part of the festival out of whatever celebrity I had at the time and it was wonderful. Duke Hazlett was great and the crowd went crazy cheering. They booed me when I took the mic and let them know it wasn't Sinatra they'd just heard!"

In response to our question about his favorite performance, Mort didn't skip a beat in saying, "Stan Kenton. I still have a picture on my wall of Stan and me backstage with a Bunny named Eleanor, who was helping out."

But apparently Eleanor didn't make the cut; Mort went on to marry another Playboy Bunny: the legendary China Lee.

"Evidently, I did very well," said Duke, "because I received a standing ovation. I know it was for Frank, but I like to think it was partially for the way I portrayed him. The next morning, one of the Chicago papers said that Sinatra had made an appearance at the festival and did a fantastic job. So that was quite an evening for me."

"I went to the festival with my brother," said Keith. "We sat in the first row, just us and a girl Hugh was going with at the time. We sat there for two days and nights and—boy! It was unreal. It may have been the greatest thing that happened to jazz ever! You couldn't replicate it, especially when you factor in all the giants who played and sang."

Hazlett had been part of a similar stunt in February 1958, when he made a surprise cameo appearance on *The Steve Allen Show* as Sinatra; to this day many viewers who see the clip, which features Duke singing part of Steve Allen's own "This Could Be the Start of Something Big," assume they're looking at Sinatra.

Even as the greatest jazz artists in the world (and one pretender) were raising the roof of the Chicago Stadium, Hef was planning his next coup—preparing to extend his entertainment empire by opening the first of what he hoped would be many Playboy Clubs.

Duke Hazlett may not have been the real Frank Sinatra, but to Hef he represented real entertainment, the kind that belonged in his clubs. Hazlett would enjoy a long association with the Playboy Club circuit.

Hugh Hefner and Louis Armstrong. Courtesy PEI.

When Louis Armstrong took the stage at the festival on August 9, the moment was tinged with more drama than usual. As his biographer, Ricky Riccardi told us, "Pops had suffered a heart attack in Spoleto, Italy, in late June and didn't resume playing until mid-July. There was a lot of attention paid at first to whether or not he could still blow the horn—he could! He was in great form throughout, but he paced himself appropriately."

The Swedish collector, Gösta Hägglöf, owned a tape recording of that performance, which he passed along to the Armstrong House (where Ricky is the archivist), but Ricky reports that the tape is not of issuable quality. The concert had been broadcast in Europe by the Voice of America, but the Soviet Union attempted to jam the signal, as they routinely did, so the tape is barely audible. This is regrettable, as Pops's version of "Tiger Rag" is said to have been particularly noteworthy. And even sadder still, no recording exists of Armstrong and Ella Fitzgerald performing together that night—at least not that we know of. It's possible that a superior audio record of Armstrong's set, along with the rest of the festival, survives somewhere in the archives of Playboy Enterprises. It's hard to believe that anybody, even the Russians, would have wanted to sabotage Satchmo—but it does give Playboy an interesting distinction as possibly the only organization to have been condemned by both the Catholic Church and the Communist Party.

The fact that the festival ended up at Chicago Stadium rather than the open-air Soldier Field was unplanned, but it turned out to be fortuitous for several reasons. The obvious one was the weather. It was a typically hot Chicago summer with temperatures of ninety degrees recorded at the Pan-American Games. Over at the air-conditioned Stadium, only the music was red-hot. The venue also gave Playboy the distinction of having produced the first indoor jazz festival in America. And finally, the stage at the Stadium provided Victor Lownes with an opportunity to try out his idea for a "turnabout." This was a bisected, revolving stage on which one band could set up in back while another continued playing out front. When the first band finished, the turnabout would gently revolve to reveal the next one. This insured a smooth transition without a lot of down time between acts and no loss of energy or momentum for the audience.

"It was certainly very effective," Victor told us. "I remember the big problem at the Newport Jazz Festival had been that there was a huge lag between groups while they set up. That revolving stage we came up with speeded things up and kept the energy going."

Sonny Rollins remembers the 1959 Festival very vividly. "That first Playboy Jazz Festival was a momentous occasion for me. I already had a little bit of acclaim by that time, and I don't mind saying, I was honored to play there. It's always stayed in my mind as a mark of my commercial acceptance and another degree of achievement." The young saxophonist had already hit an early peak when his fellow musicians voted him the number-one tenor player in the music, as part of the Playboy Jazz Poll. It's an honor he still cherishes.

The single greatest benefit to have come out of the 1959 Festival may have been the fortuitous meeting of Sonny Rollins and bassist Bob Cranshaw. Sonny recalls, "I remember that at the time of the Playboy Jazz Festival, I was looking for a new bass player. Someone recommended Bob Cranshaw and we clicked." Sonny was twenty-nine and Bobby was twenty-six, a native Chicagoan who had worked around the city with the Modern Jazz Trio, among other groups. At the festival, he played with various groups, including the one led by one of Rollins's own heroes, tenor champion Coleman Hawkins. "Now we've been playing together for over fifty years," says Sonny of Bob. Indeed, the Rollins-Cranshaw collaboration has been one of the most enduring partnerships in all of jazz.

Knowing his reputation for practicing up to twelve hours a day, I asked him if he considered himself a perfectionist. "Yes, that has been Sonny Rollins," he said. "I am a perfectionist and I've had to pay for it in a way, but I want to do my very best. I'm never satisfied with what I do and again, I say, that it's important to me to do the best work I can. Jazz music is such a great American art form and it never gets credit for what it means to the world."

As he has been labeled the "greatest living jazz musician," I asked Sonny how he had achieved that peak—and who his biggest musical influences were. "There are so many in the jazz field," he told me, "but I'd have to say Louis Armstrong and Lester Young, John Coltrane, Coleman Hawkins, Art Tatum, Miles Davis, and Thelonious Monk. I could go on and on but these are the demigods and that's not just my opinion; people all over the planet look up to these people. They've spread the music and kept it alive by their genius.

"I studied yoga in India in 1967, and from my swami I observed that people you learn from are designated 'gurus.' I call Thelonious Monk my musical guru. When I was still in school, he hired me. I learned so much from Monk, playing music at his house. Plus, he sort of took me under his wing and showed me around the city and introduced me to the jazz idioms in many different areas of life.

"The first time I met Thelonious, my little band opened for him at a Harlem nightclub. He liked my playing and eventually, after I graduated from high school, I practiced with him and joined his band. Monk was a great, original artist but also a beautiful individual. He was the most honest person I've ever met in my whole life. He showed me so much and I agreed with everything he said, musically. He'd put forth some musical theory and it would really resonate with me, just ring a bell where I'd say, 'Wow, yeah! That's correct.' So that's why I say Monk was the one who influenced me in many, many ways."

I mentioned that it seemed clear that Sonny not only enjoyed jazz but took it very seriously—even more so than most musicians. "You know," he said, "jazz music is such an important social force. Jazz is meritorious; it's not about your color. Early on, black and white musicians crossed those barriers to play with each other because of the music. The music integrated itself because music crosses color lines. It's something big and worldwide. Jazz isn't promoted in America as much as in some other places—it never has been—but it's been embraced all over the world.

"Benny Goodman, who had a big, famous band, hired black musicians and that broke color lines. Great white musicians played with black musicians in that band and boy—you had something big there! So, I'm proud of the jazz tradition, because it's not only about great music, it's also a great social instrument for making America what some people think it should be."

When we turned back to the subject of the Playboy Festival, Sonny said, "Even though I had a few recordings out, when I performed at the Festival I was just making my way into public recognition. So it was a huge honor to be included on the roster, with all those super musicians. See now, Hugh Hefner was a very forward thinking person. Regardless of what people thought about his sexual politics and all that kind of stuff, he was a forward thinking person who wanted to see a free America, a place not just of integration but of advancement. And he took a step in that direction with his Jazz Festival and I was quite happy to have had the opportunity to appear there."

It was shortly after the Playboy Festival that Sonny shocked the world by talking a leave of absence--something that headlining stars just didn't do in those days. His plan was to take a sabbatical from public performing in order to work on new music and experiment with his technique. When he broke the news to Bob, he added that he hoped the bassist would be available to play again on his return--to which Bob replied in the affirmative.

* * *

The first Playboy Festival was a major game-changer for the bassist Bob Cranshaw, as it gave him the chance to work for the first time with Sonny, who would be his closest musical collaborator, but it also was his first of several treasured opportunities to play with one of Sonny's own major inspirations, the father of the jazz tenor saxophone, Coleman Hawkins. Born in the Chicago suburb of Evanston, Illinois, Bob was a semi-regular player at the Cloister, a favorite hangout of Hef and Vic Lownes in the early days of *Playboy*. He worked most regularly in those early days with pianist Eddie Higgins and drummer Walter Perkins, and it would be the three of them who became Hawkins's rhythm section for that one concert. Sonny, as we'll see, only needed two out of the three of them. "I knew Vic and Hef and all the Playboy guys from the beginning.

Yeah, they would come into the Cloister. I was there with Eddie and Walter--they would come in--because it was a nice club, it was kind of a hang out, and they were putting together the nucleus of the Playboy situation. I could hear them talking sometimes about certain things. We were all young guys. We were having a ball, you know? We've watched each other grow over the years. In fact, when I heard they were starting a club of their own, I wanted to put money in it, but they wouldn't let us!"

Sonny had recently returned from a European tour, where, as he had for most of the previous two years, he had been working with a trio, just himself and a bassist and drummer. He had no regular group of his own in the summer of 1959, so when he was hired to appear at the Playboy, he started with the best drummer that he knew in Chicago, Walter Perkins. "He asked Walter to get the bass player that he enjoyed working with, and so when Walter asked me I said, 'Yeah, I'll do it.' And then I started to think, 'Oh heck, maybe I made a mistake. Am I ready?'" Sonny was probably the number one young saxophone player in jazz, one of the music's true superstars, and this concert was going to be a major event, not just on a Chicago scale, but a big festival in an era when festivals were still a huge deal. "I wasn't sure whether I knew enough or had played enough to really be able to handle the job--and so I was really, really nervous. But I said I would do it, so I was going to stick to it. And, of course, as the time came, I just kept getting more nervous. I listened to some of Sonny's recordings, mostly with [bassist] Wilbur Ware, to check out Sonny's psyche and see where he was coming from. Plus, he was going to use a trio, with just myself and Walter — I would have been more comfortable with a piano or guitar."

"The day of the festival, Sonny told us to be there early--we got there *very* early and we set up our stuff, so I was ready. I think at that time we were fourth on the bill, third or fourth on the bill. And now at that time I had met Sonny, but we had never worked together or even rehearsed. So Walter and I are waiting, we didn't know where Sonny was. The first group went on, I think it was the Four Freshmen, and then the second and third group — we were supposed to be the fourth, and each group was set for forty minutes. The third group was a Dixieland band, and by the time they were on, the organizers were asking us, 'have you seen Sonny?' Now the Dixieland band is playing, twenty-thirty-forty minutes, and still no Sonny." Because Sonny hadn't shown up yet, the previous band was told to keep playing and they did, even though the crowd was getting anxious to see Sonny, who was a featured attraction and hadn't been heard in Chicago for a while. "They played for close to an hour, and the crowd was starting to yell 'boo' because they wanted Sonny. And all of a sudden, Sonny shows, and we go on the stage, and we tore it up. I mean, once we started to play together, it was magic. All I can say is that we've been playing together for fifty-five years now and it's still incredible.

"We had never worked with Sonny — there was no rehearsal, in fact I had barely met him at that time. But Walter and I had played together for a long time, so we knew each other and Walter was one of the drummers--he had an incredible *feel*. Really great, great *feeling* drummer, I mean, he could swing his butt off. And I like to think that I was the same way, I tried to have a good *feel* as a bass player. I like for the music to feel good. So everything that I play and how I play go with that kind of situation. That concert was a big deal. I remember that the people were *very* receptive. I mean they were waiting for Sonny. Then, in the middle of one number, I don't remember which, Sonny abruptly changed keys. And I went right with him. He changed keys, and it was like I knew the arrangement. I mean, he changed keys, and I was right there--and he said at that point, as soon as I did that, he knew that I was his bass player.

"So, you know, we finished the concert, and to me it was great. It was really a great situation for me, but for the festival too—and that was the beginning. I mean, those are the things I really remember about that concert, and I've been with Sonny ever since, you know?"

* * *

In addition to its groundbreaking lineup of artists, the festival represented a social milestone. It was the first such event to be racially integrated both on stage and in the audience. Never one to shy away from controversy, Hefner was as open about his commitment to racial equality as he was about his belief in sexual liberation. The first day's gross proceeds were donated to the National Association for the Advancement of Colored People (NAACP), and the festival also served as a benefit for the Chicago Urban League.

From a business perspective, the festival was a raging success. With approximately 68,000 people in attendance, paying up to $5.50 for the most exclusive tickets, the proceeds were substantial even after the NAACP donation. But more important than that, the event provided an opportunity to advertise the Playboy name nonstop, while associating it with the finest in upscale entertainment. With the festival, Playboy became firmly established as something beyond a magazine—it had become a genuine brand.

To this day, Hefner is fond of quoting the judgment of eminent jazz critic Leonard Feather, who said that the weekend of August 9-11, 1959, amounted to the greatest three days in the history of jazz. It seemed a foregone conclusion that Hef and Victor would attempt to repeat the experience the following summer—but they had other rabbits to pull out of their hats. The Playboy Jazz Festival would resume again, but not until an astonishing twenty years later, and in a completely different part of the world. "Playboy was growing extremely fast back then," Victor reminded us. "And remember: We produced the first festival all by ourselves. We just didn't have the time and energy to do another one for quite a long time."

Benny Goodman, Cynthia Maddox, Hugh Hefner and Duke Ellington. PEI

4

# PLAYBOY ON THE RECORD

ugh Hefner's initial exposure to music (and especially to jazz), like that of most people, was through vinyl recordings, and he's always been a record collector. But records were perhaps the one part of Playboy's involvement with music where the commitment was less than total—and, accordingly, the results were half-hearted. With every other venture—the festivals, the clubs, the TV shows—Hefner and his team created something fresh yet classic, something for the ages; but the records, well, they are another story. The albums and singles the company released over the years were always peripheral to other initiatives, but they still comprise a fascinating aspect of Playboy's history.

As we mentioned back in Chapter 2, the first Playboy records were the direct result of the magazine's annual Jazz Polls. Three sets of albums were released between 1957 and 1959, and, from a historical perspective, they amount to an important lead-in to the big events of 1959-1960. The annual poll marked *Playboy's* transition from simply covering jazz to actively presenting it. The first double LP, released in conjunction with the inaugural poll in 1957, was called *The Playboy Jazz All-Stars* and consisted entirely of cuts licensed from the existing labels of the day. But with its carefully art-directed packaging, Hefner proved himself a pioneer of the nascent concept of "branding."

*Billboard*, the bible of the record business, took note, giving the two-LP package a rave review in the December 9, 1957, issue. It even noted that the "great cover, extremely heavy promotion and genuine quality make this an outstanding gift offering at $9 tag." To underscore their approval, *Billboard* named the release "album cover of the week." The two follow-ups, in 1958 and 1959, were greeted with similar enthusiasm.

The 1959 album was the by far the most ambitious: a three-LP set in which each album came in an individual sleeve within a deluxe outer box. But the most notable aspect of the package, released in the fall of that year, was that it featured five live performances from the first Playboy Jazz Festival, held in August in Chicago. These "unique" tracks included performances by pianist Hank Jones and clarinetist Jimmy Giuffre, as well as piano superstar Oscar Peterson, long a Chicago favorite. There was also a standout version of "Body and Soul," by Coleman Hawkins, whose rhythm section included bassist Bob Cranshaw. Finally, there was a notable performance of "How High the Moon," by Ella Fitzgerald. This is the cut that Hef played for Ella, to her apparent discomfiture, on the first episode of *Playboy's Penthouse*. You can find more about that in Chapter 5.

The 1959 package contained one track that had nothing to do with the Jazz Poll or the Festival: the original version of "Playboy's Theme," composed and performed by Cy Coleman as the signature music for *Playboy's Penthouse*. Coleman, a New York based songwriter, pianist, and singer, was an old friend of Hef and Victor, probably from his appearances around the Chicago clubs, and he had already written the hit song "Witchcraft." At the time he was commissioned to write the Playboy theme—which he would introduce "in person" on the first episode of the series—he was working on his first Broadway musical.

Cy Coleman Record

Coleman recorded the theme in Chicago, with a studio orchestra (of mostly classical string players) conducted by Henry Brandon. In addition to being included on the All-Stars album, the track was released as a 45-RPM single credited as "Cy Coleman with Orchestra under the direction of Henry Brandon." The flip side, "You Fascinate Me So," was already a classic at the time, and Cy gave that one a whirl on the first episode of *Penthouse* as well, along with his longtime lyricist, Carolyn Leigh.

"I liked ['Playboy's Theme'] very much," Hefner recalled in a 2006 interview with Chicago journalist Bill Zehme. "It became hugely popular, and was covered… by a number of other groups, including Henry Mancini."

On May 18, 1964, Coleman re-recorded "Playboy's Theme" for Capitol Records and this time the credit read, simply, "Cy Coleman,

His Piano and Orchestra." The flip was a Coleman instrumental titled "Pussy Cat." We've never heard that one, but judging from the title, Hefner would have approved.

By 1964, Capitol Records alone had laid down at least two other versions of "Playboy's Theme," one by Nelson Riddle (on the album *Love Is a Game of Poker*) and the other by Billy May (on *Bill's Bag*).

\* \* \*

The three Playboy All-Star albums and the Cy Coleman single were the extent of the recordings generated by the Playboy organization for roughly a generation—but over the years, a handful of albums were recorded live at the clubs. Atlantic Records, owned and operated by Ahmet Ertegün (who must certainly have been a friend of Hef and Victor's), recorded three albums at the original Chicago Club, including *Live at the Playboy Club* (1961) by the Broadway revue star Robert Clary—today best remembered as a regular on *Hogan's Heroes*. Also recorded there was *The Catbird Seat*, by the highly original "chamber jazz" team of pianist Dwike Mitchell and Willie Ruff (the latter most famous as a French-horn player, but here on bass) in July 1961.

Ertegün recorded several sets by the wonderful cabaret headliner Mae Barnes, but, alas, that album was never released and the tapes seem to have been lost in a warehouse fire decades later. This is indeed a tragedy, since Barnes, who appeared on several episodes of *Penthouse*, was woefully under-recorded. Several lesser-known pianists recorded at Playboy venues as well, namely Harold Harris (in Chicago, 1962) and Paul Mitchell (Atlanta, 1966). But easily the most prestigious Playboy Club recording was *Alone Together,* by the magnificent duo of guitarist Jim Hall and bassist Ron Carter, captured at the New York Club in 1972.

In the 1970s, Playboy Records made a comeback, but it was

also half-hearted. There was no jazz on this incarnation of the label, and that was part of its downfall; rather, the offerings were all soft-edged pop music. The label's most substantial artist, by far, was the great country balladeer Mickey Gilley; its biggest hit single was "Fallin' in Love," by the so-called "soft-rock trio," Hamilton, Joe Frank & Reynolds.

Barbi Benton, Hugh Hefner's one-time girlfriend and costar of the 1968-1970 series *Playboy After Dark*, recorded singles and albums for Playboy Records, but these failed to make much of an impact. The label scored a coup when it signed the Four King Cousins, who had appeared in some of the clubs, but somehow, even one of the most interesting female vocal quartets in history couldn't make any waves.

No wonder the King Cousins packed them in. Each one is prettier than the next! Courtesy The King Cousins.

The whole operation was uncharacteristically softcore, exhibiting a consistent unwillingness to take chances of any kind—

or even to display anything that smacked of individual, personal taste. And the label faced another problem as well. As Larry Waldbillig, of the blog *History's Dumpster*, noted, "There was also the fact that some independent record stores (namely in the Bible belt) refused to stock Playboy Records—possibly out fear of being accused of smut peddling by clueless church ladies." It seems supremely ironic that a label clearly erring on the side of artistic timidity should be considered too edgy for a big swath of the country—but "branding" has a B side, and the label was found guilty by association.

When it had come to the festivals and clubs—not to mention the magazine—it seemed as if Playboy couldn't make a wrong move. With the label, the opposite was true; nobody did anything *right*. The 1970s was a great era for all kinds of music, including punk, metal, and hard funk. It was also the period when Miles Davis literally electrified the music scene with his fusion of jazz and rock elements. Some of his former sidemen formed their own bands and followed suit: Wayne Shorter and Joe Zawinul in Weather Report and Herbie Hancock and the HeadHunters. All of these acts would appear at the Playboy Jazz Festival in the 1980s, but none of them was even considered for the label. In fact, everything about Playboy Records was completely contrary to the business model that had put Hefner on top in the first place: Never play it safe. So it isn't surprising that it was eventually absorbed into Columbia (later Sony) its former distributor.

\* \* \*

Without a doubt, the label's best work was with the county—and-western artist Mickey Gilley. If Gilley isn't a genuine legend of country music, he's certainly close to it. He was from Ferriday, Louisiana, where he and his two very famous cousins, Jerry Lee Lewis and Jimmy Swaggart, were all born within a year of each other in 1935-1936. In fact, if people have heard of Ferriday at all, it is as the birthplace of two musical giants and one rather infamous televangelist.

Jerry Lee and Mickey grew up immersed in the scriptures—so much so that Jerry Lee's friend Johnny Cash later reported that he always seemed conflicted as to whether he should be preaching the Gospel or playing "the devil's music." Apparently, Mickey wasn't quite as troubled by the conflict.

As kids, Mickey and Jerry Lee were as close as brothers, but their careers were hardly parallel. Virtually a child prodigy, Jerry Lee started racking up hits in his early twenties as part of the burgeoning rock-and-roll revolution. His raucous performances were catnip to a new generation of rebellious teenagers. Mickey, on the other hand, was a late bloomer. After years of diligently working the country circuit and playing in nightclubs (including Playboy), he emerged as a national star and a hit-maker about the time that he turned forty. This was in large part due to Playboy Records, who delivered his music to its natural audience: the grown-up set.

"Playboy was always important to me," Mickey told us when we spoke with him. "I played the Atlanta Club when it first opened, and who could forget working in a room with all those beautiful Bunnies standing around?"

In the 1960s, Mickey had recorded some albums on local southern labels. His most promising release was his take on a song that was already a country classic, "Room Full of Roses," which had become a number-one hit on what was still being called the "hillbilly" chart when George Morgan recorded in 1949. "I released it on a local label called Astro Records and the record shot up to the top of the charts here in Houston," said Mickey. "So I jumped on an airplane to Nashville with some copies of the recording, trying to find a record company to put it out nationally for me. Everybody I took it to said, 'Mr. Gilley, you can leave your recording with us and we will get back to you,'—and of course I never heard from them again.

"Around that time, I happened to call a friend of mine in Nash-ville named Eddie Kilroy, who was in the promotional end of it.

He said, 'I've got a company that'll take that record.' And I said, 'Who?' He said, 'Playboy Records.' I actually screamed at him over the phone, 'Are you kidding me? You're telling me Hugh Hefner is in the record business?' I knew he had a magazine and clubs—but a record business?

"But I went into Eddie's office and he threw a little 45 at me, and it had the little Bunny ears on it. I said, 'Wow! Do you think they'll release my record nationally?' He said, 'We can go to Los Angeles and find out.' So we flew out there and visited with Tom Takioshi, the head of the Playboy Records division at that time, and they took 'Room Full of Roses!' It hit the national charts in '75 and then jumped ten to fifteen slots every week until it went up to Number One."

"I think the reason why 'Roses,' did so well nationally is that it was hit in Houston first. There wasn't a lot of competition out there, so when Playboy released it all over the country, their promotional people would call up radio stations and say, 'You know, this record is big in certain areas of the country…' The stations would put it on and get great comments on it, so it went to number one and was good for me *and* Playboy. Then I followed it with three more number-one songs: 'I Overlooked An Orchid,' 'The Window Up Above,' and 'City Lights.' That's four big hits right in a row on Playboy Records."

Mickey achieved superstar status when his music—and his Pasadena, Texas club, Gilley's—were prominently featured in the hit 1980 film Urban Cowboy. Although primarily a balladeer, Mickey also sang some boot-stomping country numbers like, "Don't the Girls All Get Prettier at Closing Time?"

He remembers being well-treated by everyone at the corporation, from Hefner on down. He became friendly with Barbi Benton, and recorded some duets with her. "Hef and Barbi invited me to the Los Angeles Mansion a few times," he said, "and believe me, I was glad to go. I saw sights out there that a country boy like me would never thought he'd ever see with his own two eyes."

When the Playboy Records assets were absorbed into Epic and Columbia Records, Mickey went along to the new corporation and never looked back, but he is proud to point out that the Playboy experience was a turning point in his life and career.

Hef's interest in the 1970s roster stretched only as far as Miss Benton, and he could hardly have been objective on that front. By the 1960s, Playboy had become the number-one employer of musicians and singers in the world, yet that never translated into a wide-ranging or high-quality recording agenda.

Perhaps Hef had been attempting to follow the lead of festival producer George Wein, who made a fortune presenting live music but left the recording of his concerts to others. Hefner's disengagement from the label had the inevitable consequences.

This underscores an important point about Playboy's involvement with records; the only ones that Hefner was personally invested in were the jazz poll collections of 1957-1959 and especially the 1959 Cy Coleman single, which, as mentioned, he discussed with great enthusiasm on the first episode of *Playboy's Penthouse*. As for the roster of talent, Hef's primary interest was in his then girlfriend, Barbi Benton.—the two had met on the *Playboy After Dark* TV series in 1968, when she was only eighteen. Taken with her attractiveness and perky personality, Hef had encouraged her to change her name for showbiz (she had been born Barbara Lynn Klein) and quickly promoted her to the role of his number-one companion on the show. Soon enough, she was playing the role in real life as well. Barbi was serious about both her acting and singing, and after the *Playboy* show wrapped, she graduated to the hit country-music-oriented variety show *Hee Haw*, on which she was a singing regular for four seasons.

Though a native New Yorker, Barbi quickly found her way over to the Nashville side of the charts, becoming Playboy Records' second-biggest country star( after Mickey Gilley), and its best-known female artist. She released four albums on the label: *Barbi Doll* (1975), *Barbi Benton* (1975), *Something New* (1976), and *Ain't That Just the Way* (1978). The first three hit the Country charts.

Barbi's most successful song overall was "Brass Buckles," which dealt in standard country-and-western lyric tropes, like Charley Pride's "Crystal Chandeliers," and Dave & Sugar's "Golden Tears," with a tale of an innocent young girl corrupted by money and fame. It seemed to be autobiographical: "With a mind young and wild / And a body that the devil styled / She could make a man do anything," went one verse. Another was even more pointed: "On every movie screen / You can see this country queen / She's the centerfold of *Playboy* magazine." That was cutting very close to home indeed, and country audiences responded pushing the song as high as number five on the C&W singles chart.

Barbi's other well-known song was "Ain't That Just the Way." Although it never charted for her, it was covered by several others including Lutricia McNeal, and can still be heard occasionally.

The mid-1970s marked the high point of Barbi's career. She continued to act on many TV shows of the era including, *The Love Boat* and *Fantasy Island*, and remained friendly with Hefner long after they ceased to be an "item." She married (not Hef!) in 1979, raised a family, and continues to perform occasionally.

Over the years, only a few albums were recorded live at the Playboy Jazz Festival—quite possibly because the Hollywood Bowl is more conducive to performance than recording. The most famous "Live at the Bowl" album was a record of the 1982 weekend, a double-LP set released by Elektra Musician. This very-well received anthology featured, among others: Dexter Gordon and Woody Shaw; Pieces of a Dream and Grover Washington Jr.; Weather Report and the Manhattan Transfer; the JazzTet with Art Farmer, Benny Golson, and Nancy Wilson; and a special all-star quartet co-led by Freddie Hubbard and McCoy Tyner, with Ron Carter and Elvin Jones. Probably for some sort of contractual reason, this highly successful package has yet to be released in digital form.

The Playboy Festival continues to be chronically under-represented on recordings, probably simply because this has never been the focus of Wein, Hefner, or current festival producer Darlene Chan. In 2002, they made a small but significant attempt to make up for lost time, partnering with Concord Jazz to release CDs of two exceptional concerts: Tito Puente from 1994 (with an all star aggregation that included Hilton Ruiz, Mongo Santamaria, and Dave Valentin), and Mel Tormé with Ray Anthony's orchestra from 1993. This one was especially personal, since the late singer was a very close friend of Hefner's and the bandleader remains one to this day. These two releases went part of the way toward redressing the shortage of Playboy Jazz Festival recordings. In fact, they are so good that we can only yearn for more.

It might seem as if Playboy is out of the recording business forever. After all, in the second decade of the 21st century, the recording industry continues to tailspin down to almost nothing while live performances become ever more important to the international music economy. Still, there's every reason to hope that more Playboy Festival performances will become available, streamed on the Internet (live or after-the-fact) or released in some digital format. We're also still hoping that the 1959 festival recordings will be released comprehensively. Based on the few snippets we've heard, there's no reason to dispute Leonard Feather's summation of this three-day event as the greatest weekend in history.

5

# IN THE PENTHOUSE
# AFTER DARK

Two of the most identifiable brands from the era before *branding* was itself a household word were *Disney* and *Playboy*. Each of these powerhouses appealed to a specific segment within the modern nuclear family, and each expanded into television during the Eisenhower years.

For the first twenty-five years of its history, Disney was known for its films—animated and then live-action—but in the 1950s, Disney also conquered television with an anthology show first called *Disneyland* and later *The Wonderful World of Disney*. If that weren't enough, it pioneered its own version of live entertainment with the first-ever theme park: Disneyland.

Following a parallel course, *Playboy* was just a magazine for its first five years. Then, over the course of roughly six months, from August 1959 to February 1960, Hefner and company launched three new ventures that firmly established the organization as a major presenter of entertainment: the Playboy Jazz Festival, the first Playboy Club, and the first TV series, *Playboy's Penthouse*. The show would run just a season and a half, its first twenty-six shows airing from October 1959 to April 1960 and another seven from September 1960 to March 1961.

Surprisingly, or perhaps not, Hugh Hefner has never talked much about *Playboy's Penthouse,* or its successor, *Playboy After Dark,* which had a similarly brief run beginning in 1968. Considering that his accomplishments also include a magazine that has published continuously for sixty years, a jazz festival that has run for thirty-five, and a string of clubs that stretches around the globe, perhaps he hasn't felt the need. But he did open up about his forays into television in a 2006 interview with Chicago journalist Bill Zehme that accompanied the first DVD release of shows from the series. (Unless noted, all quotes from Hefner here are from that interview.) Hef started by describing the concept: "*Playboy's Penthouse* was made in Chicago in '59 and '60. And out in Los Angeles, *Playboy After Dark*—which is essentially the same show—was done in '68 and '69, and unlike most shows, the notion and the concept behind the show was that rather than simply putting the talent on the stage, and having you watch it from the audience, we turned it into a party instead."

But, why expand into television at all? Hef explained the business reason behind the move—and it is frankly surprising from today's vantage point. "The notion behind the show was—the magazine was hugely successful. We were printing over a million copies a month by 1960, and selling almost all of them, but we were having problems getting advertising, and I was looking for a promotional vehicle that would make the magazine more mainstream—and that was the notion behind *Playboy's Penthouse.*"

What makes this hard to believe is that, if you look at any issue of the magazine from 1959 on, there seems to be nearly as much advertising as editorial content. The record industry, for one, was especially grateful for the coverage its releases were getting in *Playboy*—more than in any other general interest magazine—and the labels ponied up accordingly. But Hef wasn't just interested in the number of ad pages; he was looking for a more upscale variety of advertiser. Instead of selling $4.49 record albums, he wanted to sell $3,000 Chevy Convertibles. And, as he tells it, "It worked! It was within the space of a very short period of time. The combination of the television show and the arrival of the Playboy Clubs gave a *legitimacy* to the magazine that had not been there before, and it became hugely successful. In the 1960s, the circulation climbed from a million copies a month to, by the early 1970s, seven million copies a month. Unthinkable."

In conceiving the television show, Hef made another move that was unprecedented at the time. He made himself the public face of the company. "I'd started the magazine on no money in 1953," he explained, "and within the space of half a dozen years, my whole life had changed; I was by then the Editor/Publisher of the most successful men's magazine in the world, and it was in 1959, quite literally, that I came out from behind the desk and started living the life. I reinvented myself—and became, in effect, 'Mr. Playboy.'"

Though 1959 was the year that Hefner purchased the residence that became known as the original Playboy Mansion, *Playboy's Penthouse* was actually videotaped on a soundstage at WBKB, the ABC affiliate in Chicago. (Surviving footage of the real Playboy Mansion makes it clear that it looked nothing like the setting of TV show. For one thing, it was much darker, and would never have been conducive for filming. Besides, Hef did live there. He surely wouldn't have wanted a film crew traipsing around his house.)

The "penthouse" depicted in the series was very luxurious, but designed to seem within reach of a young, unattached male executive—something your typical playboy could afford to live in comfortably until that inevitable day when he was caught in the tender trap, dragged down the aisle, and carted out to the suburbs to raise a family. Only millionaire stockbrokers (and magazine publishers) could own mansions. So, although the penthouse wasn't really where Hef lived, it made for more copasetic television.

Hefner explained, "It was during a time in which, after World War II, there were a lot of pressures from the government and from society at large to get everybody back into the house, get women out of the workforce, where they had been during WWII. Get everybody married, everybody moved into the suburbs, get the right job and raise the 2.1 children.... but I saw other possibilities in terms of life. And I think that is what *Playboy* was all about. *Playboy,* from the very beginning, was the first magazine for single guys, a lifestyle magazine that defined what it meant to be a guy... and the television show was the living embodiment of that."

The bachelor penthouse idea was part of the brand that Hefner was trying to build. And, as the country grew more affluent throughout the prosperous 1960s and '70s, it was gradually accepted that a mansion could be part of that brand as well. Hefner was lifting the country up by its bra straps. At the end of the first show (October 24, 1959), Hef bid his viewers to "come back next week to 'Penthouse Party,'" indicating that the working title didn't even have the Playboy name in it. The implication is clear: it was the penthouse setting that was all-important—possibly even more so than the Playboy name itself.

The realistic-but-not-real setting was only one of several ways in which art and life mingled. The show always opened with a shot of a Mercedes Benz 300SL careening down Chicago's Lake Shore Drive; it was never actually mentioned on the show, but it was Hef's own car and he was actually driving it. Likewise, there was the matter of Hef's pipe. "The myth is that I took up the pipe as something to do with my hands, during the television show," says Hef. "The reality is, you know, it was a good prop, but I'd started smoking the pipe sometime in the months immediately prior to that and I think I did it simply as a prop. I think it was part of the same thing with the smoking jacket and the Mercedes Benz, and the pipe. I think it was just part of the affectation of becoming who I wanted to be. I mean, in a very real way, it's like Archie Leach becoming Cary Grant. I think, you know, you create the persona that you want to have. And what, of course, is unique about my life is that [I did it in] such a public way, used the magazine as a vehicle for that purpose, and in the process, pointed a direction for other guys and women in terms of how you could live your life."

Even as Hugh Marston Hefner (on one 1969 show, comic Dick Shawn addresses him as "F. Hugh Hefner," a reference to the great comic, writer, and character actor F. Hugh Herbert) was recreating himself as "Hef," he was perfecting the Playboy brand; both elements were essential to *Playboy's Penthouse*. The show made heavy use of the subjective camera, which, while not used much in movies, had been popularized on television in the series *You Are There*. In that show, which ran from 1953 to 1957, historical events were recreated as if they were part of an evening news broadcast, and the camera moved in such a way as to suggest that the viewer was actually part of the action. The actors spoke directly to it, as if it were an actual character. You could say that the technique, as used liberally at the penthouse, foreshadowed today's reality shows.

From the beginning of the first episode of *Penthouse*, viewers were plunged into the middle of the action via subjective camera. We moved from the car on Lake Shore Drive into an elevator and watched the floors light up one by one: 21-22-23-24-25-26-27-28-29… until finally we reached our destination—unmarked. The elevator doors opened and we saw a gentleman in a tuxedo with his back to us, clearly concentrating on the pianist playing the opening theme. Beautiful women in elegant gowns and high heels casually walked about. The first face we recognized was the comedian Lenny Bruce. As the camera moved closer to the man in the tux—who was, of course, Hefner himself—he noticed us and introduced us to the pianist, none other than Cy Coleman, and his own special guest, the legendary jazz trumpeter Charlie Shavers.

Every show opened with a variation on that idea: when the elevator door opened, the party was in full swing with Hefner holding court. Soon enough, he welcomed his "visitors" and introduced the "other guests" who would be dropping by over the next sixty minutes.

With *Playboy's Penthouse*, Hefner and his team had once again figured out a way to add to the evolving Playboy mystique. Far from being just another talk or variety show, it was something completely new and yet comfortable at the same time. "I'm a kid who was raised in a very typical Midwestern Methodist home with a lot of repression," Hef explained, "and I escaped very early on into romantic dreams that were fueled by the movies and the music of my childhood. I was born in 1926, and I grew up during the Depression with the images from the past, from the Roaring Twenties. I came to think of Scott Fitzgerald and *The Great Gatsby*, the Jazz Age, as the party that I thought I had missed. So I think I created a world through the magazine and then the life that gave back the party that I missed. And then parties themselves became thematic for my life and a symbolic response to Puritan repression. So you will see throughout my life, both in the television shows that we do and also life at the mansion, parties are a symbolic way of celebrating life. We're saying, 'We're only here for a little while. Let's make the most of it. And let's do it with some style.'"

The first performance on the inaugural show was of the opening main-title music, "Playboy's Theme," by Cy Coleman—a bluesy jazz riff set against an opulent string orchestra background. It was also the first piece of music actually commissioned by Playboy. Says Hef, "I was looking for a special theme that would combine jazz with a string ensemble, so it would have a beat against a romantic theme. We arranged for a full orchestra, forty pieces—part of the Chicago Symphony Orchestra. Cy, who'd written a number of very popular songs and was a friend, agreed to create what would be called 'Playboy's Theme.' There was a very popular song that André Previn had done called 'Like Young,' and I said, 'This is what I'm looking for.' Later, I got a telegram from André Previn who said that he loved 'Playboy's Theme,' but thought that Cy should have called it 'Like Like Young.'" Perhaps to make amends, on that first show Ella Fitzgerald sang Previn's "Like Young" as one of her three featured numbers.

Cy was also the first guest that Hefner spoke with, and thus the first test of the "party" conceit. Their conversation was neither a formal interview nor completely scripted patter, as on a typical variety show. Rather, the conversation flowed naturally out of the music Cy was playing and his genuine relationship with Hefner. Hef and Cy discussed the recording session; Cy professed amazement that Hef had hired, in effect, a symphony orchestra to back up his little piano trio; and Hef replied that he was so jazzed about the recording that he planned to release it as a commercial single. That, indeed, happened: "Playboy's Theme" was released as a 45-RPM single on the Playboy label. The B side was "You Fascinate Me So," already a classic song by Cy and his longtime lyricist, Carolyn Leigh. He would sing it later on in the first episode.

Cy performed four songs total, all with lyrics by Carolyn Leigh. His rendition of "You Fascinate Me So," became widely popular with so called "cabaret" singers, like Bobby Short and Blossom Dearie. Mabel Mercer would sing it on the Playboy show a month later. Cy sings it later in the show, to a stunning brunette seated next to him on the piano bench, sipping a martini. Her presence made the song all the more fascinating. "Witchcraft" was next. Only two years old, it was already Cy's most successful song, thanks to the 1957 Capitol single by Frank Sinatra. In the TV performance, Cy sang a special verse that he'd written well after the 1957 Sinatra version. Ella Fitzgerald had included the song—with the extra verse—in her 1958 live recording from Mr. Kelly's in Chicago.

Finally, Cy sang a song he'd written with Sinatra in mind, or so he told Hef before he sang it. And thanks to Frank's hit recording, "The Best Is Yet to Come," would ultimately become an even bigger trademark for the songwriter than "Witchcraft." About thirty years later, Cy would reveal that "The Best Is Yet to Come," was, in a sense, a spinoff of "Playboy's Theme." The theme had become so popular that he and Leigh had decided to add lyrics, but when that proved troublesome, they came up with a new melody to support

Carolyn's words instead. The rest, as they say, is history.

One other aspect of Cy's appearance on the first episode is notable—he talked about working on his first Broadway musical, a show that he told Hef would be called *Skyscraper*. As it happened, there were considerable complications in constructing this particular skyscraper. Instead, Coleman's first Broadway show would be *Wildcat*, which starred Lucille Ball and opened in December 1960. *Skyscraper* would make it to Broadway in 1965, but with a score by Sammy Cahn and James Van Heusen rather than Leigh and Coleman.

Cahn and Van Heusen would themselves be on *Playboy's Penthouse* in a show taped on November 24, 1959. It happened that the team was up for an Academy Award at the time, so Hef asked them why they were in Chicago instead of Los Angeles, participating in the Oscar festivities. Sammy drolly responded that during Oscar season, it's always wise to be as far away from Hollywood as possible. Just as wisely, the network held back the episode, airing it in March 1960, shortly before the Oscar telecast on April 4.

In those days, before the era of the "singer-songwriter," composers were rarely heard performing their own songs—though they were occasionally asked to do so at parties, just for fun. And that was exactly the atmosphere that Hef was trying to capture in both of his television shows. The idea was to make viewers feel as if they'd been invited to the private party of a very rich, well-connected, and classy friend—who happened also to be close to the hippest singers, comics, musicians, and songwriters around. And that's the difference between *Playboy* and other shows of its day. Whereas Steve Allen and Ed Sullivan referred to the stars that appeared each week as "guests," on *Playboy* they seemed more like friends.

Songwriters such as Cy Coleman, Sammy Cahn, and Jimmy Van Heusen, who weren't likely to be seen on traditional talk and variety shows, fared best of all on *Playboy's Penthouse*, though the singers did well, too. No one seemed more comfortable than Tony Bennett who, then as now, regarded Hef as one of his best friends. He clearly loved being in the company of Count Basie and Lambert, Hendricks, and Ross. Ella Fitzgerald, who wasn't comfortable being interviewed or speaking in public, never seemed at ease in the penthouse, and looked particularly uncomfortable on one occasion when Hef tried something that he would never do again. While everyone sat around and listened, Hef played an audio excerpt of Ella singing "How High the Moon," the previous August at the Playboy Jazz Festival. As everyone paused their conversations to listen, Ella stood awkwardly with her musicians, waiting to perform and looking as if she'd much rather be singing than listening. Still, the three live numbers that followed—"But Not For Me," "Like Young," and "Get Out of Town"—were among the best of all her many TV appearances of the era. It must have thrilled André Previn to hear his song sandwiched between standards by George Gershwin and Cole Porter.

While the singers generally fared well, the comics were less consistently satisfying. The format was clearly odd for them; they couldn't just take the stage and perform their acts the way they did in clubs or on *Sullivan* or *The Tonight Show*. Their routines had to be somehow worked into a supposedly spontaneous conversation, with Hefner as a willing straight man. They were generally willing to go along with the conceit—and Hef held up his end of the bargain pretty well—but some of the more "Type A" personalities, such as Phyllis Diller and Marty Ingels, exhibited no compunction about taking over the spotlight and making themselves the center of attention for a few minutes.

The first comedian to be featured on *Penthouse* was also the most notorious: Lenny Bruce. "He did the show as a personal favor," recalled Hefner. "We ran a story on Lenny in the later 1950s, and it was the first national exposure that he got. A friend [Shelly Kasten] who ran a Chicago club called the Cloister was looking for new acts, and I'd heard a great deal about Lenny. So I went out to San Francisco with them to look at Lenny's show, and his mother,

Sally Marr, was at the door, taking admissions, and it blew me away. When he came to Chicago to work the Cloister we recorded the entire show for a week and then, from that, published a piece on him that turned out to be the first national exposure that he got, and we became close friends."

Even among comics, who are an admittedly alpha bunch, Lenny was a true provocateur, determined to push the envelope as far as it could be pushed. "We did what we could for him," continued Hef, "because in the 1960s, reflective of how the social, sexual values were changing, there was also a great deal of controversy in terms of censorship et cetera, and *Playboy* was a part of that good fight—and there were casualties to it, and one of the major, early casualties was Lenny himself."

On that premiere episode, Lenny talked for roughly ten minutes in a way that would be hard to categorize as stand-up routine, conversation, or even comedy. He started with a discussion of so-called "sick humor," a label that *Time* magazine had recently saddled him with, and with which he disagreed. Hef disagrees with the categorization, pointing that two of the other comics who got the label, Mort Sahl and Shelley Berman, were anything but "sick." Their comedy was as wholesome as it gets. However, when Lenny mentions that Time included Jonathan Winters on the "sick" list, he concedes that they may have a point. As an example of what might be considered "sick" humor, Bruce related an anecdote from his own life. He told Hef that when his aunt, a very conservative Orthodox Jewish lady, saw that Lenny happened to have a tattoo on his arm, she flew off the handle. According to strict Hebrew law, anyone with a tattoo on his body can't be buried in a Jewish cemetery. Lenny told his aunt not to worry, he said, because he'd left instructions for the undertaker to cut off his arm and bury it someplace else.

That story, Lenny told Hef, was as close to "sick humor" as he got. It was also as close to a joke as anything he uttered in his entire ten-minute segment. His closer was a surprisingly measured exploration of contemporary morality involving Jesus, the Catholic Church, the Communist Party, integration, civil rights, religious freedom, atheism, the United States educational system, Asiatic flu, the American Medical Association, and kids stuck in wells.

The final musical guest on the first episode was Nat King Cole, who walked in just as Cy was finishing "You Fascinate Me So." This was to be Nat's only appearance on the series, and on one level it was a disappointment. The most popular singer in the world at the time—with more hits on the chart than even Sinatra—didn't sing a note or even play the piano! Even so, his conversation was fascinating and the closest thing we have to an authentic on-camera interview. He talked about his career, his future plans, his upcoming albums, and the fact that he was very excited about a project that would eventually be titled *Wild Is Love*, a song-cycle in which he would introduce each track with a brief spoken recitation. Everyone, including Hef and Cy, was enthusiastic about a piece of special material that he'd been performing at the Chez Paree titled "Mr. Cole Won't Rock and Roll," in which he parodied his own hits and signature songs. He insisted that he had no plans to record the piece, preferring to catch audiences by surprise with it in his live shows. He was true to his word. "Mr. Cole Won't Rock and Roll" wasn't heard on record until many years after his death in 1965, and then only as a live performance, never a studio recording.

It may seem absurd today that Nat never sat down at the piano but, as Hef pointed out, "What made [his appearance] particularly unique and controversial was… distinctions of race were simply not there. And in portions of the country, most especially in the South, that was not acceptable and still very controversial. Nat Cole… had his own show for a time in the middle 1950s and it did not last because he couldn't get advertisers, and that was because, as he famously said, 'Madison Avenue was afraid of the dark….' We broke that color line, and I'm proud that we did."

Even Cole's innocuous first line as he sat down on the couch must have been perceived as radical at the time. He turned to Rona Jaffe, author of the best-selling novel *The Best of Everything*, and said that he'd just bought her book and was looking forward to reading it. While this wouldn't raise an eyebrow today, a black man talking casually to a white woman about literature during a party was inconceivable to many in 1959.

* * *

When the original Playboy Club opened in February 1960, the first comic to make a big splash at the new venue was Professor Irwin Corey. The second was Dick Gregory. Most of Dick's memories of those early days in Chicago are in the next chapter, but a few are relevant here.

"I have to tell you something to help you understand the entertainment culture back then," said Dick when we spoke with him about Playboy. "I loved watching Jack Paar and dreamed of being on his show one day. Right after I was profiled in *Time* magazine, I was talking with Billy Eckstine, probably the biggest Negro singer then. He told me that a Negro couldn't sit on Jack Paar's couch. He said, 'All you can do is come, do your act, and leave.'"

In other words, black men could be entertainers but they couldn't be human beings. They were, in Ralph Ellison's almost brutally appropriate phrase, invisible men. Lenny Bruce quoted the same expression somewhere in the middle of his monologue on the first show. The implication was clear: As Eckstine put it, "Pick your cotton, boy."

"I was crushed," Dick continued, "so mad and sad at the same time. Well, Jack Paar reads the *Time* magazine article and calls me. My wife answers the phone, and she's screaming and hollering, 'It's the Jack Paar show!' I hadn't told her what I found out from Billy, but I take the phone, and some guy says, 'Is Dick Gregory there? This is Mr. Silvers, Jack Paar's producer. My God, did you see the article in *Time* magazine? Mr. Paar read it and thinks it's great, and he wants to know if you want to be on the show tonight.' I say, 'No sir, I don't want to work the show,' and I hang up.

"I start crying, and then the phone rings again. This time, I hear, 'It's Jack Paar. Hey, Dick, I know things are probably happening so fast, you think this isn't me.' I say, 'No, I believe it's you.' 'Well, how come you don't want to come on my show?'

"I tell him, 'Because Negroes never get to sit on your couch.'

"He says, 'Well, come on in, I'll let you sit down.'

"That was the first time a Negro sat down on Jack Paar's couch. What I didn't know was that if you sat on the couch, you became part of Jack Paar's family. When I took that seat, my salary went from eighteen-hundred dollars a year to 3.5 million in a year and a half! And all because Hugh Hefner didn't care if you were black or white or purple, only if you were funny or could sing."

Perhaps that story explains why Nat King Cole didn't sing on the first *Playboy* show; it was more important to him to sit and chat with the other guests. One can only imagine what went through the mind of a veteran musician like Louis Armstrong, who had been the victim of institutionalized, legally sanctioned bigotry for fifty-eight years at that point, when he watched it.

Just as *Playboy's Penthouse* was a new kind of television program, the Playboy Clubs, the first of which opened in Chicago in February 1960, represented an entirely new way of presenting entertainment. When Hefner's old friend, Tony Bennett, walked into the penthouse on February 13 1960—less than two weeks before the opening of the original club—that newness was apparent for all to see; it was like the sunshine creeping into every crevice and corner.

That particular show documented the singer at an early pinnacle. When Tony played the big concert houses such as Carnegie Hall—where he debuted in 1962 on the heels of his biggest hit, "I Left My Heart in San Francisco"—he was accompanied by a full orchestra. The same was true of his appearances at the Vegas amphitheaters.

Tony Bennett and Hugh Hefner on Playboy After Dark. Rex USA

But when he dropped by the Playboy penthouse, everything was pared down to the bare necessities. The 1960 show documents Tony working the way he would at the clubs just a short time later, with his frequent accompanist, the brilliant Ralph Sharon, and a trio featuring bassist Hal Gaylor and Tony's longtime drummer and sidekick Billy Exiner.

Tony and Hef started out making small talk and were soon joined by Phyllis Diller, who had just done a comedy routine, and whose trademark cackle could be heard throughout Tony's appearance.

Looking immaculate in his tux, Tony swung out with a bright, bouncy, opener, "Just in Time." He had already helped make this 1956 song from *Bells Are Ringing* into a standard with his successful Columbia single. Seated next to Ralph on the piano bench, he took out a pack of cigarettes and lit one, then hit a more serious note with Gershwin's "Love Walked In." Tony gazed upwards as if in prayer as he sang it, with a joyful expression on his face, as Sharon supplied block chords reminiscent of George Shearing.

After that, Tony briefly introduced the Ralph Sharon Trio, then lunged into "You Can't Love 'Em All," a new Sammy Cahn/Jimmy Van Heusen song written for the Marilyn Monroe movie *Let's Make Love*. He was especially playful with it, toying with the melody and ad-libbing like crazy in a way that wouldn't have worked in a more formal setting. On the line, "There are mountains that you can move," he ran up a staircase then danced his way down, exclaiming, "I feel like Fred Astaire!" On the second chorus, he did something he may never have done elsewhere on film—seemingly out of sheer capriciousness, he hit some deliberately flat notes on the key word, "You *can't* love 'em all, no you *can't* love 'em all!"

Everyone's spirits were unbelievably high as the camera panned around to some of the other guests, among them Count Basie, Jon Hendricks, Dave Lambert, and Annie Ross. But it was Diller who requested the next number from Tony, her favorite song from *The Sound of Music*, which had opened on Broadway just a few months earlier. Tony sang *Climb Ev'ry Mountain* without an overabundance of either piety or levity, keeping it reverent but never saccharine. It may be the most appealing version of the Rodgers and Hammerstein hymn ever recorded.

Holding Diller's hand—or, more precisely, her black opera glove—Tony then swung into an exciting homage to what was already one of his favorite cities, the 1922 jazz classic "Chicago." He was even looser and more jubilant at that point, almost bouncing around the room, throwing in a reference to someone named "Eddie Hubbard" rather than "Billy Sunday" as the guy who was unable to shut down the windy city. As he headed toward a climax, with Diller to his right, Basie to his left, and Hefner behind him, he executed a few time steps as if he had so much energy that singing just wasn't enough; he had to be dancing at the same time.

Looking at the footage now, it's clear what an amazing and unique moment this was—almost as if Hef and Tony were christening the new decade, the new presidential administration, and the new era of entertainment that was about to come, all in a single moment.

For the two years it ran, *Playboy's Penthouse* was a jolly jumble of entertainment without regard for boundaries of any kind. Singers interacted with comedians, jazz musicians chatted with authors, anybody could relate to anybody, and everyone—no matter their particular gift or race—was an honored guest at the party.

* * *

Some of the finest moments in the series were in the presentation of a certain strata of nightclub entertainers, many of whom would later be categorized under the general heading of what has come to be known, in the United States at least, as "cabaret." *Playboy's Penthouse* presented three of the most iconic cabaret stars of them all, Mabel Mercer, Bobby Short, and Mae Barnes, none of whom were likely to be seen on mainstream TV because of their race.

Both Barnes and Short appeared on the episode of February 6, 1960, right around the time of the opening of the original Chicago Playboy Club; and if that wasn't enough, the other musical guest was none other than the legendary Dizzy Gillespie. The show began with what was presented as off-the-cuff comedy by stand-up man Milt Kamen, who essentially performed his stand-up routine, restructured slightly to make it seem more like spontaneous banter with Hef.

Mae Barnes then took the spotlight. A remarkable artist with a fascinating career, Barnes was born in New York in 1907 and became a dancer in all-black Broadway shows such as *Shuffle Along* and the unfortunately titled *Lucky Sambo*. After an auto accident in her early 30s (and an unfelicitous upswing in dress size), she stopped dancing, but by then she had graduated to singing in nightclubs in London and America. After the war, she worked on Broadway and in Hollywood and cut two albums, *Fun with Mae Barnes*, produced by Ahmet and Nesuhi Ertegün for Atlantic in 1953; and *Mae Barnes*, produced by John Hammond for Vanguard Records in 1958. If

Barnes's name is less well known than that of Short or Mercer, it's because she was almost exclusively a nightclub artist.

The February 1960 *Penthouse* appearance provides us with by far the best film of her at work. She sang four numbers total, two standards and two specialties, transforming the standards thoroughly into highly personalized material. She leapt onto "Deed I Do" like a tiger attacking an antelope and, though she had a full rhythm section (her own, not the show's house trio), she punctuated every line with handclaps that resonated with greater volume and more rhythmic accuracy than anything her drummer was playing. At the same time, the way she moved her body around in perfect time suggested a whole new kind of choreography; in effect, Barnes was singing, dancing, and playing the drums all at the same time.

After that short number, her pianist began playing a minor key vamp, but she was not about to let the mood deter her high-flying spirits; she exclaimed to the party-goers, "Oh mercy! I feel so thin tonight!" In fact, throughout the segment (as she apparently did during her actual nightclub act), she was very quick to make "fat jokes," effectively pre-empting criticism of others.

Her next number was "All Men are Evil," which she had performed in the movie *Odds Against Tomorrow*—sort of. In the film, Harry Belafonte as a disorderly drunk joins her from the sidelines, and pretty much ruins the number—her one big onscreen moment—for the sake of the plot. No matter. History corrected itself by giving Barnes the opportunity to sing the song brilliantly on *Playboy's Penthouse*. Co-credited to Belafonte himself, the song is part blues, part Calypso, part folk song, part parable, and a very telling recrimination of male-female relations. Rather than claps this time, Barnes embellished it with dog-like yelps.

Then the unidentified pianist played the famous cradle-rocking vamp for George Gershwin's "Summertime," which includes two choruses, the first slow and the second fast. In the slower opening chorus, Barnes refused to take anything seriously, and there were gags aplenty. Each time she sang, "One of these mornings, you gonna rise up singing," she interpolated a different song. The first time, it was "Wish You Were Here," and the second, it was "Hound Dog." Even during the ending, where she pretended to get serious long enough to toss in an operatic cadenza, contained a few gags.

Following that tour de force, Barnes delivered her most audacious fat joke yet, a protracted sequence where she tried to sit on the piano and failed numerous times, complaining that "this is the slipperiest piano ever!" Hef, sitting on the piano bench, was laughing so hard that he literally had to wipe tears from his eyes. Next came her great party number, "What Will the Neighbors Say?" a fast and exciting slice of rhythm and raillery filled with references to the music of Harlem in the 1930s. Barnes danced furiously, pounded the piano, and belted the number out with joy and jive, as if she could light up all of Chicago with her electricity.

Throughout the show, the most prominent party guests were Dizzy Gillespie and Milt Kamen, who did considerably more patter with Hef than Mae Barnes or Bobby Short. After Milt's comedy routine, Dizzy played and sang his classic bebop novelty love song, "Oo-Shoo-Be-Do-Be." He then sat down next to Hef, who handed him a copy of his new album, *The Ebullient Mr. Gillespie* (on Verve Records). Their conversation turned to the then-current "payola" scandal in the news and how it could be a good thing for jazz, since no jazz musician actually had enough money to participate in the pay-for-play racket. Dizzy then encouraged the party-goers to clap him into the start of what he called "The Shim-Sham-Shimmee on the St. Louis Blues," which he played with the show's house trio led by pianist Marty Rubenstein. Dizzy didn't sing, but after playing a chorus or two of the blues, he placed his famous upturned trumpet on the piano and went into a spontaneous-looking dance routine—the "Shim-Sham-Shimmee" of which he'd spoken. While Diz played his final chorus, Milt Kamen indulged in a very wild, eccentric dance, his rubber legs wiggling and his feet kicking the air. It was a very dynamic ten minutes of Dizzy at his absolute best, proving that he was as vital a combination of musician and entertainer for his era as his mighty predecessor, Louis Armstrong, had been for his own.

Next came Bobby Short. After a conversation with Hef about his nearby hometown of Danville, Illinois, he began the verse to "I Like the Likes of You," and then strolled over to the piano, taking Marty Rubenstein's place at the keyboard in time for the chorus. All five of Bobby's numbers were from his first two albums, *Songs by Bobby Short* and *Bobby Short*, both recorded in 1955. "At the Moving Picture Ball" is a jaunty ragtime-styled number from 1919, which Bobby played in a deliberately rigid, mechanical fashion, as if to sound more like a player piano. His next three numbers were all archetypal Bobby Short songs of the kind that he would become famous for during his thirty-five-year residency at the Cafe Carlyle, starting in 1968. There was a slice of Tin Pan Alley exotica ("An Island in the West Indies"), a Broadway waltz ("The Most Beautiful Girl in the World"), and a Bessie Smith blues ("Gimme a Pigfoot").

Short's major musical inspiration was unquestionably Ethel Waters, but on camera he reminds us more of Al Jolson in the way he continually engaged the crowd and made the most amazing faces. At the end of five flawless numbers, he leapt up from the piano bench into the air, looking exactly like the brash young man that he was.

The November 29, 1959 episode was ninety minutes long, including commercials. The first musical act was Chicago's own Joe Williams, this time backed up by Count Basie's rhythm section featuring guitarist Freddie Green, bassist Eddie Jones, and drummer Sonny Payne—but with another longtime Chicagoan, Earl "Fatha" Hines on piano. It was a case of an Earl sitting in for a Count! The literary guest was Al Morgan, the novelist best known for *The Great Man*, which became a successful film starring José Ferrer. Morgan and Victor extolled Mabel Mercer's greatness and then she appeared, performing five full numbers. The footage is by far the best surviving visual document of Mercer at the height of her height. She performed "Looking at You," (Cole Porter), "Remind Me," (Dorothy Fields and Jerome Kern), "You Fascinate Me So," (Cy Coleman and Carolyn Leigh, which Cy himself had introduced on the premiere episode of *Penthouse* just a month earlier) and "It Was Worth It," by her longtime accompanist Bart Howard.

It's simply amazing to watch Mabel in action. While Mae Barnes and Dizzy Gillespie directed their performances to the party guests, and Bobby Short looked directly at the camera, Mabel displayed the regal bearing she was known for, encompassing the whole wide world in her gaze— the crowd, the camera, the TV audience, everyone.

Throughout, her legendary skills were apparent in abundance. The gem of the set may be "It Was Worth It," a song that impressed

Mabel Mercer. Photofest

Sinatra so much that he later commissioned Bart Howard to write a similar number, expressed from a male point of view, for him. Mabel was known for her waltzes, and to this day, there's no one better at expressing direct emotions in three-quarter time. There was a Yoda-like quality to Mabel, sitting on her throne and dispensing advice to the much younger people around her (she was a few months away from sixty), but with amazing vitality. Watching the tape today, she can still make you feel like she knows all that there is to know about love and life, and that if you listen to her carefully, you will, too.

Bobby Short returned to the program on February 27, 1960, in an episode rich in supper-club headliners. Clearly, Bobby had recently seen the hit Broadway musical *Gypsy*, and performed no fewer than three numbers from that exceptionally rich Jules Styne/Cy Coleman score: "Let Me Entertain You," "Small World," and "Everything's Coming Up Roses."

Barbara Carroll, another pianist/singer, came on next, performing Bart Howard's "Let Me Love You"—a number that is still in her repertoire today, fifty-five years later, at the age of ninety. She followed it with a remarkable piano solo on Ellington and Strayhorn's "Satin Doll." For a long time, that number was almost a cliché among cocktail pianists, a kind of faux-hipster anthem, yet Barbara imbued it with remarkable freshness and originality, employing a lucid, crystalline touch that made the well-worn melody sparkle.

Still, the biggest attraction of the episode was the remarkable Julie Wilson who, like Barbara, is still with us at age ninety. At thirty-five, she was already an amazing entertainer—a singer, comedian, and sexy cut-up in a tight, shiny gown. (How tight? The smile on the face of the gentleman seated directly behind her indicates just how thoroughly he was enjoying the view.) Like many guests on the show, Julie turned Hef into her straight man and he gamely fed her the necessary set-up lines. She smiled, rolled her eyes, and mugged like crazy—and yet the effect of her performance remained remarkably subtle.

Julie's first number, Rodgers and Hart's "I Could Write a Book," was exceptionally jazzy and she belted it with tremendous swing, modulating upward for the second chorus, rocking in rhythm and catching the beat with her hips. By contrast, she stood nearly motionless for "A Man Could Be a Wonderful Thing" a comic turn from her classic live album, *At the St. Regis,* which she dedicated "to all the ladies in the room—as well as the women." Adopting the persona of a sexy sage, her lack of physical movement perfectly paralleled the lack of lyrical movement in a song that derives it's humor from rigid patterns of repetition. In the hands of anyone else, it might have been just be a dopey novelty number, but the ever-droll and sultry Julie made it into a grand statement about the co-existence of the sexes. Julie wouldn't have been so sexy if she wasn't simultaneously so funny, and vice-versa. The gentleman that was seated directly behind her couldn't agree more.

Sammy Davis Jr. was another very special visitor to *Playboy's Penthouse.* By the time he appeared, he had officially left the Will Mastin Trio, the family act in which he'd gotten his start, and had played a prominent role in one of the year's biggest movies, *Porgy and Bess.* He'd also enjoyed his share of television time throughout 1959-1960—several weeks before the debut of the *Playboy* series, he'd been a guest on a show with a similar format, *The Big Party,* co-hosted by the unlikely duo of Rock Hudson and Tallulah Bankhead. But Sammy's *Penthouse* appearance would be his most memorable of the season—and perhaps the single most explosive star turn in the brief history of the show.

As Hef remembered it, the first show of Season Two was actually filmed at the end of Season One, around May of 1960. "We'd stopped doing the first season, and Sammy came into town, and he wanted to do the show," Hef said. "And I obliged him. We literally put the set back together… in a matter of a few days… at CBS, so that one and the next five shows that we did at the end of that season were shot at CBS."

Sammy simply materialized in the middle of the show—just walked in as if completely by surprise in the middle of a number by the Kirby Stone Four, a vocal and comedy group. What were the odds? Sammy just happened to appear in the penthouse as the group was doing an impression of *him*! After a bit of mock outrage, he joined the Stone Four for a few bars, followed by a long and brilliant sequence with his own rhythm section—who just happened to have walked in right behind him. "Be prepared to do anything," he told his accompanist, George Rhodes. "We might attack Castro!" Few viewers watching in 1960 were aware that Davis himself was actually half Cuban.

Sammy made it clear from the start that he was putting aside the formality he'd bring to Carnegie Hall or even the Copa. He was visiting a friend's house and he intended to have fun. Loosening his tie, he sang with a cocktail in one hand and a cigarette in the other. Before, and even during, each number, he bantered with Hef and Victor, who was reclining on a sofa with an attractive companion. At one point—in a moment of genuine spontaneity—Sammy ran up the stairs at the back of the set toward a faux window and was actually off mic for a few minutes—oops!

He did a full twenty-minute segment that included "Lazy River" (with the Kirby Stone Four), "The Gal That Got Away," "The Lady Is a Tramp," "Something's Gotta Give," and "My Funny Valentine." The last number was particularly amazing. Sammy had been jumping all over the place as if he'd just had a double B1 vitamin shot, but as he started to sing the Richard Rodgers ballad, he instantly became someone new, 100 years old and the saddest man in the world. Watching it today, if you were to freeze a frame from "Something's Gotta Give," and compare it to one from "My Funny Valentine," you'd swear you were looking at two different people.

After bringing the room to a standstill, Sammy brought the energy right back up again by kibitzing with Vic and Hef about the lamentable fact that he'd never won the Playboy Jazz Poll. "Your buddy always wins it," replied Hef, referring to Sinatra. Finally, Sammy performed an amazingly high-energy rendition of "Chicago," then hammed up his exit by walking off as Cary Grant, Jimmy Cagney, and Marlon Brando (while Kirby Stone did Boris Karloff).

Before Sam reached the elevator, Hefner intervened and presented him with a puppy named "Playboy" (something that never happened at the Copa), saying, "In a year, he's going to be bigger than you are." With that, Sammy stepped into the elevator, still singing "Chicago."

It was a night to remember and, as usual, the audience was every bit as loose as the performers. "The show was done in such a relaxed and unprofessional way," Hefner remembered. "We served real liquor in the drinks. You can see in some of the shows—because segments were not shot in chronological order, we shot the shows throughout a day and evening and timed them for when the acts were available... so you see some instances... where people were drinking real drinks throughout the entire day and evening and seemingly sobering up."

\* \* \*

There was a price to be paid for the program's bold stance. Stations below the Mason-Dixon Line simply refused to air it, which severely cut into its bottom line and hastened its demise. Hef elaborated, "Well, it was [successful] in the major markets across the country but not in the South. And we knew that we were not going to be able to sell the magazine—sell the show—in the South because of a decision that I made related to the party concept. There were no racial distinctions in the show."

Controversy aside, the program was innovative and appreciated by almost everyone except those who couldn't get past the race issue. Today, it remains a valuable record, not just of cultural attitudes at a crucial moment of change, but of the great performers themselves. The footage of Sammy Davis, Tony Bennett, Mabel Mercer, and many others remains more memorable—and far hipper—than anything presented by Ed Sullivan or any other variety show of its day. Ironically, Hefner's own progressive politics, as much as anything else, were responsible for the eviction notice on the door of the penthouse. If only there had been something akin to HBO in 1961. But also contributing to the show's demise were the increasing demands on Hefner's time. By 1961, the Chicago Club was successful enough that there was talk about expansion into a network, a circuit, an *empire* of entertainment. Television was no longer on the front burner.

\* \* \*

Almost a decade later, Playboy was back on the airwaves with a new show set in a new city. By 1968, the clubs were booming all over the world. The London outpost was particularly successful, along with the clubs in Los Angeles and San Francisco. "The Playboy Clubs were hugely popular in the 1960s," corroborates Hefner. "We'd opened a club in Los Angeles, and I had an apartment—a penthouse apartment, appropriately enough—in the Playboy building on Sunset Boulevard. The club was downstairs and my apartment was on the top, and in that time frame then, in 1968 and '69, we did a new, full-color version of *Playboy's Penthouse* and called it *Playboy After Dark*.

"We were able to do [great] things on the show because we didn't have any networks to deal with, so I was running the show pretty much to suit myself. We didn't have to talk to the suits! And again, both *Playboy's Penthouse* and *Playboy After Dark* are a real reflection of—it's a step back into another time. It has a wonderful retro—sophisticated retro—appeal and of course for me, it was very, very, very personal because it's filled with wonderful memories." This may sound a bit confusing but actually it isn't. While it was on a network, Playboy produced it and picked all the talent—so it was *on* a network but not *produced* by one and the network didn't interfere with what they were doing.

The look of *Playboy After Dark* was quite different from the earlier show. While the 1959—1961 *Playboy's Penthouse* had been populated by grownups in gowns and suits, the 1968—1970 *Playboy After Dark* depicted everyone in a kaleidoscope of colorful 1960s hippie garb that included love beads, flowery jackets, fringe, long hair, and bell bottoms. Tuxedos had looked fine in black and white, but the new show made full use of color. There were so many beards and Day-Glo outfits on the set that any one of the gents could have been mistaken for Sgt. Pepper's rabbi. Hefner himself, on the other hand, hadn't yet affected the Shangri-la style pajamas he would wear from the 1970s onward; as host, he alone wore a tux.

Hugh Hefner, Mabel Mercer, Victor Lownes on Playboy's Penthouse. Photofest

One major innovation was that Hef had a sidekick this time out. "When we were doing *Playboy After Dark* I met—on the show—a young lady called Barbi Benton," Hef recalled. "She was a student at UCLA, pre-med, and a model, and worked as an extra on the show, and I saw her on, I think, the second day of shooting and was smitten and pursued her and that turned into a relationship that lasted for eight and a half years.

"It was Barbi who was really responsible for the Los Angeles mansion. She was looking for a place—I had this apartment on Sunset Boulevard but for home entertaining you really needed something larger—and she was looking for a place where we could play tennis. She found this wonderful, wonderful piece of property and I acquired that in 1971, and it was part of the change in life—I think increasingly in that time frame I was literally splitting my time—and that began really with *Playboy After Dark*.

"I went back and forth between the two cities between '68 and really '75, and by 1975 I had fallen in love with the lifestyle out here, so I simply stopped going back. There was a period referred to as "Captain's Paradise" when I was seeing two primary ladies, Barbi out here and Karen Christy in Chicago. If one remembers the wonderful British comedy called "Captain's Paradise" with Alec Guinness we know that that kind of lifestyle has its own downside, and you pay a price for it, and I did."

There's no question that Barbi added a lot to the show. In addition to her looks and visual charm, she occasionally unleashed a Gracie Allen-like one liner, courtesy of the writers, which she handled with great aplomb and excellent timing.

While *Playboy's Penthouse* had highlighted jazz-oriented singers, established comics, and folk artists, *Playboy After Dark* reflected an increasingly polarized society. To be sure, many guests—including Tony Bennett and Sammy Davis Jr. (as escorted by Pat Lacey, a principal career Bunny)—were selected to appeal to *Playboy's* long-time fans, and they did their jobs as brilliantly as ever. But joining them and other stalwarts such as Vic Damone, Billy Eckstine, and Johnny Mathis, were Sonny and Cher, Linda Ronstadt, Joe Cocker, and Grand Funk Railroad.

By the time *Playboy After Dark* made its debut, mingling the races presented no problem—but the generations?—well, that was another matter. In an attempt to please the widest possible audience, Las Vegas and Haight-Ashbury were thrust together with predictably awkward results. A typical episode might feature Sid Caesar and the Grateful Dead, or Jackie Gayle, Don Adams, and Deep Purple—or how about the one where Larry Storch met Canned Heat?

Despite the "relaxed" dress code, the new show was formal in another sense—rock bands couldn't be expected to play standing around a piano or sitting in front of a fireplace, as Pete Seeger had, so the staging became more elaborate. The Ike & Tina Turner Revue, for example, performed with its full band, plus the dancing Ikettes, on a stage with a full setup. The new "penthouse" felt more like a conventional nightclub, and the artists were shown holding microphones—something that had never happened on the earlier show.

Hugh Hefner, Mabel Mercer, Victor Lownes on Playboy's Penthouse. Photofest

In spite of the stagier setup, *Playboy After Dark* did feature the occasional "spontaneous" drop-in. On a December 1968 episode, the cigar-smoking tambourine player in Sammy Davis's band turned out to be Bill Cosby. Later that same evening, Jerry Lewis and Peter Lawford burst in unannounced in the middle of Davis's number. That visit was a bit unfortunate actually, as they interrupted Sammy's beautiful rendition of "The More I See You," his most intimate number.

Just a handful of major artists, including Sammy Davis Jr. and Vic Damone, appeared on both shows. The most significant one was Tony Bennett, who was an even bigger star in 1968 than he had been eight years earlier. Tony made two appearances on *Playboy After Dark*. The second one, filmed in '69 and aired in '70, is the more remarkable to watch today. While many of the *After Dark* shows featured a seemingly random juxtaposition of guests (Tony's '68 appearance, for example, included George Plimpton and the rock band Steppenwolf), this episode was built around Tony.

The show began with an LP on a vintage 1969 turntable playing Tony's first hit, "Because of You," recorded in 1951. Current-day Tony soon chimed in, walking down the stairs with a stunning brunette model about a foot taller than anyone else in the room. He then belted out an electrifying rendition of Duke Ellington's "It Don't Mean a Thing (If It Ain't Got That Swing)," that pivoted around a drum solo by Tony's old friend Louis Bellson. John Bunch, Tony's accompanist for most of the late 1960s and 1970s, was on piano.

Tony was soon joined by Mitch Miller, the classical oboe virtuoso turned pop record producer who had signed Tony to Columbia Records in 1950. Together, they ran through a lovely rendition of Tony's 1951 hit, "Blue Velvet," complete with prominent oboe obligato. Tony then entertained questions from the crowd, citing Joe Williams, Ella Fitzgerald, Jack Jones, and Peggy Lee as his favorite singers. A bit later, he and Hef introduced entertainer George Kirby, who did his specialty, "Walking Happy," and a set of impressions, including one of Tony. Next, Canadian saxophonist Moe Koffman played a funky soul-jazz number on two tenor saxophones at once. After a few duets with Joe Williams, Tony and the company ran through a few more hits, including "Rags to Riches" (Tony), "I Won't Cry Anymore" (Joe), "The Shadow of Your

Smile" (George), and Tony's own mash-up of his two all-time biggest singles, "I Left My Heart in San Francisco," and "I Wanna Be Around," with Koffman on flute. The show wound down as it had begun, with "Because of You" sung by everyone, including Mitch Miller and Hef.

Of all the episodes of the 1968-1970 series, that show, which ended with Hef toasting Tony as an artist "who leaves his heart in every song he sings," is by far the most exciting.

On the whole, *After Dark* was less memorable than its predecessor, but hardly an afterthought. It, too, was a highly successful hybrid of talk and variety, combining the best features of both formats. And, just as *Penthouse* had been, *After Dark* was a hit in every city that aired it—though the Playboy name was still so controversial that only twenty-three markets took the plunge. It lasted slightly longer than the earlier series—fifty-two episodes versus forty-four—but, ultimately the audience just wasn't large enough to sustain it.

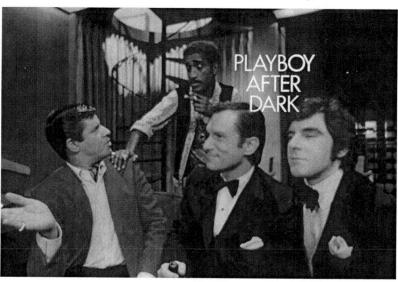

Jerry Lewis, Sammy Davis, Hef, and Anthony Newley on Playboy After Dark 1969. Photofest

Both shows have been re-aired only sporadically since 1971. In 1992, the color shows ran on the Playboy cable channel, providing a rare respite from the cheesecake. In 2006, the first of two packages of shows from both eras was released on DVD, and excerpts from those continue to remain popular on YouTube. Curiously, the DVD sets included only a total of four shows from 1959-1960 series and six from the later show. One might expect it to be the other way around.

Admittedly, humility has never been one of Hef's strong points. But it's hard to disagree with his 1969 statement that his show was "better than the Johnny Carson show or the Joey Bishop Show" and that he was then doing "a better job hosting than Ed Sullivan does."

\* \* \*

So, who was on the invite list at the *Penthouse*? Here's a very selective list of some of the swells who took the elevator to the top floor over thirty-two episodes. For a complete listing, check out the Reference Guide at the back of the book.

THE JAZZ SINGERS: Nat King Cole, Ella Fitzgerald, Ray Charles, Sarah Vaughan, June Christy, Dakota Staton, Beverly Kenney, Beverly Kelly, Della Reese, Carmen McRae, Joe Williams, Anita O'Day, Bill Henderson, Billy Eckstine

THE JAZZ MUSICIANS: Cal Tjader, Bob Scobey & Clancy Hayes, Dizzy Gillespie, Jonah Jones, Woody Herman, Gene Krupa, Buddy Rich

THE PIANISTS: Count Basie, Earl "Fatha" Hines, Ahmad Jamal, Stan Kenton, Eddie Higgins, Dave Brubeck, Dorothy Donegan

THE VOCAL GROUPS: The Four Freshmen, The Kirby Stone Four, The Vagabonds, Lambert, Hendricks & Ross

THE PIANIST-SINGERS: Buddy Greco, Bobby Short, Frances Faye, Nina Simone (in what must have been her first TV appearance)

THE CROONERS: Tony Bennett, Dick Haymes, Vic Damone, David Allen, Frank D'Rone

THE FEMALE POP SINGERS: Barbara McNair, Teddi King, Lurlean Hunter

THE MUSICAL THEATER STARS: Larry Kert, Robert Clary, the entire cast of *The Billy Barnes Revue*

THE COMEDIANS: Joe E. Lewis, George Carlin & Jack Burns, Marty Ingels, Bob Newhart, Larry Storch, Don Adams, Professor Irwin Corey, Phyllis Diller, George Kirby

THE FOLK AND BLUES SINGERS: Pete Seeger, the Gateway Singers, Josh White, Barbara Dane

THE SONGWRITERS: Cy Coleman, Sammy Cahn & Jimmy Van Heusen, Fran Landesman & Tommy Wolfe

THE CABARET STARS: Mabel Mercer, Mae Barnes, Julie Wilson, Sylvia Syms, Barbara Carroll

THE UNCATEGORIZABLES: Dancer Geoffrey Holder, harmonica virtuoso Larry Adler, and the irrepressible team of Mimi Hines and Phil Ford (not to mention Chatter the Chimp)!

\* \* \*

Alta Loma Entertainment, an arm of Playboy Enterprises, has successfully produced TV shows such as *The Girls Next Door, Party at the Palms, Bunny Mother*, and more. In 2011, their eagerly awaited primetime period-piece TV series *The Playboy Club* was cancelled after only three episodes, after pressure from feminist and conservative groups on both sponsors and viewers. It seems nothing has changed in sixty years! In hindsight, perhaps the show would have fared better on a noncommercial channel such as HBO—though the style and content were decidedly conventional.

Starring Eddie Cibrian as Nick Dalton, Laura Benanti as Bunny Mother Carol-Lynn, and Amber Heard as Bunny Maureen, the plot involved the accidental murder of a gangster by a Bunny, and the efforts of both the police and the bad guys to discover who did it. But no show would be worthy of the Playboy imprimatur without a great soundtrack.

The pilot episode included Karen LeBlanc as Tina Turner, singing "Shake a Tail Feather" and "Tina's Wish," complete with Ike and the Ikettes. Pop-singer Colbie Caillat made a fine Lesley Gore, belting out "It's My Party," in Episode Three. And, although we never had the opportunity to see it, Javier Colon was due to depict soul singer Ray Charles singing "Let the Good Times Roll," and Raphael Saadiq was to take a turn as Sam Cooke. Future installments that were never filmed were to have included portrayals of Frank Sinatra, Sammy Davis Jr., Roy Orbison, James Brown, and Dusty Springfield.

When it comes to television, Playboy just can't seem to get a break from the "keepers of decency." Seven episodes of *The Playboy Club,* complete with lovingly recreated musical numbers, were filmed—but sadly only three aired.

Part Two:

# SWINGING AT THE CLUBS

# 6

# SETTING CHICAGO ON FIRE

Victor Lownes remembers when the idea of opening a club was born. He should—he was there. "Here's what happened," he says. "*Playboy* ran an article about Burton Brown's Gaslight Club in Chicago, which had opened in 1953 and was inspired by nostalgia for the 1920s. The waitresses were pretty girls in skimpy outfits, and you had to buy a membership to join. Right after the piece came out, we received over a thousand letters inquiring how to get in touch with them to join. I thought, 'Hmm…' and took the stack of letters to Hef. 'Look at this!' I said. 'Maybe we should open up our own club.'"

In fact, as early as 1955, readers had been writing in to the *Playboy* letters page, inquiring if there were some kind of a club that they could join. Some fans had even started local clubs of their own, as mentioned earlier.

At first, Victor and Hef were really only thinking about a single club, which, naturally, would be in Chicago. But these guys weren't just businessmen, they were visionaries. They'd already propelled the organization into live entertainment and television and had their share of success in both areas. Why not nightclubs?

Why not a whole chain of them?

In 1960, the idea of opening brand-name clubs in different cities was groundbreaking—nobody had ever done it. In the 1930s, there had been a Cotton Club in New York as well as "Frank Sebastian's Cotton Club" in Los Angeles—Louis Armstrong had played at both—but that was purely a coincidence; the two establishments weren't connected. Likewise, two of the most famous jazz clubs in the world were the Blue Note in Chicago, where Duke Ellington played the same weekend he played the 1959 Playboy Festival, and the Blue Note in Paris. But, again, they were owned by different people.

It made sense that Victor would have thought of the club idea—the world of restaurants and nightclubs was his world. Hefner knew about jazz, but Victor was more likely to have a feel for the best location—and he knew where the best chefs and bartenders could be found. Most important, Victor had a visceral sense of what a high-quality club should feel like, while Hef knew what it should sound like.

Still, a move from the magazine business into nightclubs required a big leap of faith. "Right away, Hef agreed that it was a good idea," says Victor. "I admitted that I didn't know anything about the business, but I said, 'I have a friend who runs restaurants. He's got a little place called Walton's Walk on the North Side. Let's go over and talk to him about coming in and managing the restaurant side of the place.'"

The friend turned out to be Arnold "Arnie" Morton, a savvy young restaurateur who later launched the eponymous and wildly successful Morton's Steakhouse chain. Morton would met his wife Zorine at a Playboy event in 1960; they remained married from 1961 until her death in 2005.

"We had this meeting," said Victor, "Hef, Arnie, and I, and before you knew it, we were partners. We divided the new venture four ways: Hef personally had one share, the Playboy corporation had one, and Arnie and I each had one. We each put in ten thousand dollars—it was very inexpensive. We took over the Colony Club site, which was owned by Arthur Wirtz.

"We'd just worked with Arthur on the jazz festival," Victor continued, "and he liked us. The building had been turned over four times before we took it; people were having a tough time making it work. So Arthur let us have it for no rent—just a percentage of the gross. Of course, this ended up being an amazing deal for him! He became a very good friend of ours."

Comic headliner Shecky Greene remembers Wirtz well: "Arthur was an older guy, a gruff, burly man who weighed about 300 pounds. He walked into the Chicago Club one night and the Door Bunny said, 'Sir, may I see your key? Are you a member?' He just mumbled, 'I don't need a key,' and kept walking. So the girl went to the manager and said, 'I asked that guy over there for his key and he just mumbled something. Would you go over and talk to him?' The manager said, 'We don't need to talk to him. He owns the building, so don't bother him again!'"

During the 1950s, Chicago was a mecca for both jazz and nightclubs. Hef and Victor frequented most of them, but there were a select few they thought of as home. The Black Orchid was one of them—and it was probably at least partly because the Black Orchid went out of business in July of 1959 that Hef and Victor decided to open their own club. In fact, the two were such fixtures on the nightlife scene that every club owner and musician in town was friendly with them. Entertainers ranging from Mel Tormé and Sammy Davis Jr. to Ramsey Lewis and Johnny Mathis felt free to stop by the magazine's offices for lunch if they had a free hour. This sense of collegiality would serve Hef and Victor well when they opened their first club.

It was decided that the Playboy Club would be "members only"—but by no means exclusive. Anybody, regardless of race or gender, who applied and paid the twenty-five-dollar fee would be presented with the coveted Playboy Club key—an actual metal key with the bunny-head logo engraved on one side and a numbers-and-letters code etched on the other. Hef's senior archivist, Steve Martinez, decoded it for us: The numbers identified the member and the letters signified the club through which he purchased the membership. The keys had to be presented to gain entry and, needless to say, became status symbols and prized possessions.

The most remarkable aspect of the clubs was the ubiquitous presence of the Bunnies. They seemed to symbolize everything that was new and radical about the enterprise. Other establishments, including the Gaslight Club Victor mentioned, had girls in skimpy outfits—but the Bunny uniform was somehow wholesome and sexy at the same time, like a Disney character or cartoon animal with an "R" rating. The Bunnies established Playboy as a brand. Men lined up around the block to get a look at the girls and just as many girls waited for hours for a crack at getting a job wearing the satin bodysuit, bow tie, and bunny tail.

Two early veterans of the Playboy organization tell stories about the origins of the Bunny uniform, Al Podell and Vic Lownes. Both versions are completely plausible and both revolve around personal conquests—but they don't completely jibe.

The gospel according to Al goes this way. In 1959, he was dating a girl whom Hef had also taken a personal interest in. "Cynthia Maddox was her name," he told me. "She was only about eighteen and worked at the magazine in some lowly position. She was drop-dead gorgeous, sweet and innocent, and had an amazing body. Hef and I kind of started competing for her, which I didn't think was really fair, because he could have almost any woman in the world, and I didn't understand why he needed Cynthia.

"This was in 1959, when Hef was planning the opening of the first Playboy Club but I hadn't yet heard anything about it. One morning, Cynthia walked out of his office wearing this little cotton-tailed thing! I asked her about it and that's how I found out about the club. As part of Hef's courtship, he'd designed the

Bunny costume around Cynthia.

"Many days, at five o'clock, she'd go into his office for a fitting. I don't know what went on in there, but I'd be waiting to take her out and I'd have to wait a pretty long time! One thing led to another and she became Hef's live-in girlfriend for about three years. She was also on the cover of five different issues of *Playboy*—a record—but she never agreed to be a Playmate."

Al laughed. "You couldn't compete with Hefner. He was a lovable guy—charming, wealthy, and he ran the magazine! Who could compete with that?"

Victor's version of the Bunny origin story goes like this. "I was dating a girl from Latvia named Ilse Taurins, and she's the one who suggested that the girls dress as Bunnies. Her mother was a seamstress and made a Bunny costume that we showed to Hef. He'd originally thought the girls in the club should wear shorty nightgowns, but they would have been difficult to serve food and drinks in.

Hef wasn't on board with the Bunny idea at first. He said he's always thought of rabbits as male. When we showed him what Ilse's mother came up with, he liked it but made changes: He wanted the hips cut higher and he suggested adding lace. The collar, cuffs, and black bow tie were his idea, too."

Other designers that have been credited with the legendary design include the well-known African-American designer Zelda Wynn Valdes and Parisian born Chicago dress designer Renée Blot, who supervised production of the outfits by Chicago corset-maker, Kabo. Whoever had a hand in it, the Bunny costume has become so iconic that it is registered with the U.S. Patent Office and can be viewed at the Smithsonian Institution in Washington, D.C.

By the end of the decade, radical feminists would be burning their bras and denouncing the Bunny uniform as a symbol of chauvinist oppression, but in 1960, being a Bunny seemed to many the most liberating job that a young girl could get.

* * *

Every girl who worked in the club wore the Bunny outfit, but there were a number of different jobs to fill, and they came with specific titles. There were Door Bunnies, Camera Bunnies, Cigarette Bunnies, Bumper-pool Bunnies, Cocktail Bunnies, Floor Bunnies, and even a Bunny Mother, who oversaw the work schedules and monitored the girls' comportment and behavior. Each Bunny was required to present herself to the Bunny Mother for inspection every night before going out on the floor. To pass inspection, stockings had to be run-free with back seams straight; regulation underwear had to be in place; and shoes of the prescribed height, style, and color had to be perfectly polished. Even the girls' makeup was scrutinized, and lessons in application were offered when required. A Bunny might be sent back to the dressing room to reapply her face if she'd dared use the wrong shade of eye shadow.

As we mentioned, Keith Hefner—Hef's younger brother—was in charge of all Bunny training, and it was quite rigorous. Bunnies were required to memorize the official forty-four-page "Playboy Club Bunny Manual," whichcovered every move they might have to make and every situation they were likely to encounter. The most important bit of choreography was called the "Bunny Dip," a method for serving and clearing tables that guarded against breasts liberating themselves from low-cut costumes. It involved a slight lean backward while bending the left knee with the right one tucked just behind it. Feel free to try this at home—it isn't easy!

Bunnies were instructed on how to stand (legs together, hips tucked under, and back arched), how to rest, and how to sit. There was even a section in the manual on smoking: The proper method was to take a puff, then set the cigarette in an ashtray. Bunnies were never to take more than one puff at a time, nor were they to stand or sit holding a cigarette. All Bunnies were required to know how to garnish at least twenty different cocktails and identify 140 brands of liquor.

In spite of what might have been going on in the imaginations of the patrons, Playboy Bunnies were strictly forbidden from getting personal with club members. They couldn't date customers, give out their phone numbers, or even share their last names—and they were never to gossip or divulge information about their fellow Bunnies. In fact, they were trained to monitor and limit the amount of time they spent speaking with any one customer.

These restrictions and regulations may have seemed a tad severe, but Hefner and his partners knew that the eyes of the world were upon them. There were plenty of officials who wanted nothing less than to shut down the clubs for good. Any whiff of impropriety could wreak havoc on the licenses they depended upon to stay in business. As Victor recalled, "In keeping with our self-regulating policies, Playboy hired its own private detectives to come into the club and try to seduce and proposition the Bunnies. They went as far as offering them money for sex and then reported back to us. We wanted to spot a problem and correct it if we had to, before anyone else did."

In spite of the draconian rules they would have to adhere to, in every city in which a club opened, beautiful women clambered to audition for a spot in the "hutch." The work seemed glamorous to many, and it certainly paid better than your average waitressing job—better than most office jobs, for that matter. You wouldn't blame a girl for leveraging her assets—would you?

Playboy was a pioneer in another respect, too. From the ratification of the Eighteenth Amendment sanctioning prohibition in 1919—and continuing long after its repeal in 1933—the business of selling alcohol and presenting live entertainment was generally the province of organized crime. New York's Cotton Club, perhaps the single most famous presenter of African-American talent in the 1920s and 1930s, was strictly a mob operation, and so were the original Birdland and Copacabana. The crime families and syndicates were everywhere, especially in the casinos and showrooms of Las

Vegas. The only venues not under the thumb of these organizations were the nightclubs and ballrooms situated in reputable, high-class, and highly expensive hotels —such as the Persian Room at the Plaza and the Wedgewood Room at the Waldorf, both in New York, as well as the Panther Room of the Hotel Sherman in Chicago.

The mob's stranglehold was strongest of all in Chicago—where boss Sam Giancana was reputed to have helped fix the presidential election of 1960. Playboy took great pains to steer clear of any such affiliations. "We just did," says Victor. "That was our policy. Once, we did have some visitors from a certain 'family,' who put forth the idea to Hefner of partnering with us in the clubs. Hef just calmly explained to them that, with the eyes of the Church, conservative groups, and the local and federal governments focused on both Playboy and organized crime with similar intensity, it was not in anyone's best interest to go into business together. Not that we ever would have, but Hef made such a logical argument, they had to agree and go away."

As an added deterrent, Victor had a huge message board installed where members' names were displayed as they presented their keys to the Door Bunny, indicating for all to see that they were in the club. Victor surmised that gangsters would shy away from such attention.In practice, this plan didn't work out quite as he intended. Shadier guests simply used false names, while legitimate members, who, for a variety of reasons, preferred anonymity, were not happy with the publicity.

\* \* \*

In downtown Chicago on a typically frigid February 29ᵗʰ in 1960, amid standing-room-only crowds, the doors to the first Playboy Club opened on 116 East Walton Street; by the end of the first month, close to 17,000 patrons had enjoyed its warm hospitality. Each of its four floors was uniquely designed to showcase a specific genre of entertainment, but overall, there was a uniform feeling in the décor and appointments—definitely masculine—as though one were wandering through the various rooms of a luxurious bachelor pad. At the same time, it was all thoroughly modern, with a spark of excitement. The Playroom, the Penthouse, the Library, and the Living Room were each decked out in posh teak and leather furnishings, and each was more inviting than the last.

Caption TK

It wasn't so much like the actual Chicago Playboy mansion, which Hefner had moved into only a few months before, but it was more like the fantasy ideal of the Playboy penthouse that viewers saw on the *Playboy's Penthouse* TV series, which was still on the air for another year at that point, into the spring of 1961.

The décor was at once classic and completely modern, with an extra tinge of excitement, classy and yet thrilling. The club was a mini-Disneyland for growing men—like Fantasyland, Adventureland, and Tomorrowland; the club had The Playroom, the Penthouse, the Library, and the Living Room. Up to that point, decorating for the male environment was pretty much like a hunting lodge, with photos of outdoor sportsmen with rifles and antlers—everywhere antlers—and the occasional mounted moose head. The ideal Playboy, however, hunted for an entirely different sort of prey, and to that end, the furnishings in all the individual rooms made heavy use of leather and teak.

Yet more than one kind of male appetite was catered to. The food was also decidedly masculine—no afternoon tea with watercress and finger sandwiches: steaks, chops, baked potatoes, and the more manly sort of salad. Arnie Morton engineered the menu so that everything, or practically everything, wouldn't set anybody back anything more than a buck and a half, and a cocktail (whisky soda, please) or a pack of camels (or other smokes) were also $1.50. The uniform prices made it easier both on the customers and on the cotton-tailed wait staff.

And just like Disneyland, the Playboy Club was a success beyond all expectations. Vic and Hef drew on everything that they knew and loved about the other clubs and restaurants that they frequented. The Bunnies were worth coming to see at least once, and the idea of making it a private club with keys, etc., so you weren't just a "customer" but a "member," would lay the groundwork for coming repeatedly. But what would really draw patrons to come back again and again, multiple times a week, was the entertainment. The comics and musicians could enable them to compete with Mr. Kelly's and the London House (now that the Black Orchid was gone and the Chez Paree was about to close), but the Bunnies, the clubby atmosphere, and the reasonable prices gave the Playboy a distinct edge.

In the beginning, they started with a trio, led by pianist Sam DeStefano, who would go on to a long career as musical director and conductor at Playboy venues all over the map. Gradually, the entertainment got increasingly ambitious, and Playboy, which had opened at the very start of the new decade, blossomed along with the swinging sixties. When John F. Kennedy took office a year later, the tone for his presidency had already been set in Chicago, the city that had literally swung the election for him in November.

Over the long haul, the Playboy Clubs would probably be

best remembered for the rising talent that first emerged there, but Victor's first thought was his beloved Mabel Mercer; he'd already made certain she appeared on *Playboy's Penthouse* (first in November 1959, then again in March 1960) and then he hired her to launch The Library room as a cabaret space. Victor told us, "I was pleased, but then it was decided that we should change the décor of [the] room. All the furniture was taken out, and the customers had to sit on big, fluffy cushions on the floor all around the room. It was a dumb idea, but Mabel sang to the assemblage that way. We kept it like that for a while."

While Mabel represented the state of the art of the music most frequently called "cabaret," she was, at age sixty, a past master. Yet Playboy also had its eye on the future; one of the earliest artists that Victor hired for the Chicago Club was Aretha Franklin. In the summer of 1960, she recorded her first album (actually, to be technically correct, it was her second—her very first album was a collection of Gospel songs recorded when she was fourteen) for producer John Hammond of Columbia Records; in this transitional period, she was a jazz artist and as much a pianist as a singer. "We were her first big engagement," says Victor. "Later on, she concentrated on singing, but in 1960, she both played and sang. Keith [Hefner] was the room director and eventually in charge of Bunny training, and he suggested we fire her because he didn't think she was any good. I liked both her playing and singing and said, 'No, we're keeping her.'" To be fair to Keith, this young woman's destiny wasn't clearly written on the wall in 1960, she only turned eighteen in March of that year, and it would have been impossible to predict so early that she would later fuse jazz and Gospel music, and create soul music in the process. Victor feels like he got the last laugh in this instance, "Of course, she became a big star, and we couldn't even think of rehiring her. Occasionally, I remind Keith of his suggestion!"

We talked about Keith's responsibilities regarding the Bunnies, but he initially put his show-biz career on hold to return to

Chicago and shoulder the responsibility of room director. He was Hef's younger brother by two years, and graduated from Northwestern University before moving to New York to be an actor. He's best known as the host of two children's television shows, *Time for Fun: The Johnny Jellybean Show* and *Tip Top Merry-Go-Round,* as well as for appearing in an episode of the popular television series *Get Smart.* Like Hef, Keith always loved the big bands and jazz. He frequented jazz clubs while attending college, and continued to do so once he'd settled into his apartment in New York's Greenwich Village—especially Café Bohemia and the Bon Soir, where Barbra Streisand got her start.

As the empire briskly expanded throughout the sixties, he assumed the duties of director of training and service, implementing policy and procedures for club personnel (including teaching that infamous "Bunny Dip"). When I spoke with him, he seconded Victor's admiration of Mabel Mercer, saying, "I love cabaret and was a huge Mercer fan, listening to her often in New York—independent of Playboy—before the Chicago club even opened."

Keith went on, "The second act ever booked into the Chicago Club was the wonderful cabaret singer and pianist Bobby Short (who had also done the TV show twice in February 1960) and the third and fourth were the comics Jack Burns and George Carlin."

As Keith suggests, it wasn't only singers and musicians who played a role in the success of the Playboy Clubs; star comedians were an important part of the story from the very beginning. The very first comedian to work for Hef is still out there telling jokes today—which is quite something, considering that he passed the century mark in 2014—the legendary funnyman "Professor" Irwin Corey.

Professor Corey was never what you would call a safe choice—he was always trying to challenge the status quo. He's been modestly described as having a left-wing point of view, but his particular brand of humor is perhaps better characterized as anarchic; he's always taken on the status quo—including whatever politicians happened to be in power—and made mincemeat of them.

"Hugh Hefner used to hang out and play gin at the Cloister Inn," the good Professor told us in 2013, when he invited us to his home. This was just around the time of his 99th birthday. "Hef was so bad at the game that he never got to put his initials down, which was something you did when you had a good score. He must have lost thousands of dollars through the years, but we became acquainted and he liked my brand of comedy."

Irwin didn't only challenge the reigning political party; he liked to bite the hand of whoever was feeding him—or at least do what he could to upset the relationship between management and labor. He took pride in breaking the rules. Keith Hefner acknowledged that Irwin was quite a handful. "Corey was always going into the Bunny room, which was not allowed. He chased them everywhere and did all kinds of ridiculous things. He had to be 'spanked' often and didn't get away with as much as he likes folks to think."

In his own book, *Playboy Extraordinary*, Victor wrote about Corey and others whom he believed to be genuine "funnymen": "These men all created one or more comic characters and then established the characters in the public mind to the point that it is impossible for them to be unfunny. Corey's insane professor is as much a part of the funnyman school of humor as Chaplin's magnificent little tramp. Corey's outlandish pedant, who rants and raves and confuses all, derives his comedy value from the same source as the caricature of 'teacher' that the class prize delinquent scribbled on the blackboard a few minutes before the bell rang."

The first star comedian to be associated with Playboy, Irwin was soon working the entire circuit. This led to his first comedy album and, ultimately, a mocking run at the presidency. He credits Hef and Victor for the whole trajectory: "Not only did they like my comedy routine, but they decided I had a lot to say and ran me for president on the Playboy ticket, with Vic as my campaign manager."

This was during the 1960 election that pitted Senator John F.

Kennedy against Richard M. Nixon. As a "third party" candidate, Irwin presented his platform on an LP called, *Win with Irwin*. For a reissue of the album years later, Victor told the story in the liner notes: "'When Corey was appearing at our Playboy Club in Chicago, it dawned on us that it might be a wild idea to run him for president. What we were doing, in effect, was channeling the famed Corey bombast from its main purpose, of being 'The World's Foremost Authority,' onto a very logical sidetrack, by suggesting that Corey would make an excellent 'World's Foremost Executive.' We carried the campaign to its logical extreme, including campaign buttons ['Irwin will run for any party, and he'll bring his own bottle'] and posters ['Corey is the only candidate named Irwin'], and we even hired a sound truck to prowl the North Side of Chicago blaring martial music and booming out the good message to the voting public ['Relief is just a ballot away—elect Corey—then go on relief'].

"But our candidate let us down," Victor concluded, paraphrasing a famous quote from the nineteenth-century statesman Henry Clay. "He simply wouldn't stick with the issues and insisted instead on delighting his audience with the famed Corey zaniness—and only occasionally did he touch on the Corey-Plan-for-Saving-the-Nation. I can't help thinking that we lost a great chief executive when Corey insisted that he'd rather be funny than president."

\* \* \*

Though he didn't realize it at the time, Irwin paved the way for a life-changing engagement for fellow comedian Dick Gregory. "Dick Gregory got the job because I wouldn't work on Sunday," he told us.

We asked if he was a religious man.

"No," he shot back, "but even God got a day off. Dick sent a pot of flowers to me at every job I had for the longest time, thanking me for not working on Sundays. We became friends and did a lot of shows together through the years."

Hef had made his outspoken views on racial equality clear at the Jazz Festival in 1959, and the decisions he made about the magazine and clubs were consistent with these beliefs. Outspoken black comedian Dick Gregory credits him with helping to break down the gates that separated blacks and whites on stage and in audiences. We've already discussed Hef's groundbreaking stance in the south, but in the early '60s, segregation was commonplace above the Mason-Dixon Line as well. Even in Chicago the races didn't mingle much in entertainment venues. Yet it was very early in that club's history that Hef made the shockingly progressive decision to hire the first black Bunny.

"It's undeniable," says Dick, "that Hugh Hefner—aside from what everyone knows or think they know about the girls and all that stuff—believes in humanity. He waged a lifelong battle for racial equality."

In 1938, an amazingly far-sighted entrepreneur named Barney Josephson opened Café Society in New York's West Village, the first truly integrated nightclub. But Josephson was too far ahead of his time and was pilloried during the Red Scare a decade later. When Hef and Victor opened the first Playboy Club as an integrated operation, the move was permanent; there was no going back.

Victor adds, "With the hiring of Dick Gregory, Playboy was the first organization to introduce black cabaret

Dick Gregory. Photofest

performers into essentially white clubs. We didn't discriminate in our clientele either, but there weren't many blacks applying for membership in those early years."

"The way hiring Dick came about is one for the books," Victor told us. He was working in a garage where I parked my car and had it washed. After work one day, I looked at my car and said, 'If you call this car washed, you must be some kind of comedian.' He said, 'I am.' 'Well,' I replied, 'if you're a comedian, come and audition for me at the Playboy Club. If I like your act, I'll book you.'"

Dick picks up the story from there. "About a month later, Irwin Corey, the "Professor," refused to work seven days a week, and my agent called and said, 'You've got a job at the Playboy Club next Sunday for fifty dollars.' Shit, wow! I didn't know there was that much money in the world! I had been making ten dollars a night at the Negro nightclub—the Robert Shaw Club.

"I didn't know much about downtown, but I paid my quarter and got on the bus with my little suit in a plastic bag. Because I wasn't sure where I was going, I got off at the wrong stop and I didn't have a nickel to get back on. I was counting on the money I made that night to get me home! I didn't even know that clubs like that pay your agent. I thought I'd get fifty dollars cash! So I asked somebody, 'Do you know where the Playboy Club is?' The guy said, 'No, but it's that way.' It's snowing, and I'm running—because there's this myth that Negroes can't be on time—and I'm slipping and falling, holding my suit up in the bag, and I round a corner, and about eight blocks away, I see this huge Playboy sign. Thank God!

"I get to the door, and there's a black doorman, and I ask, 'Where's the Caramel Room?' Maybe it was called something else, but he knew what I wanted. 'Second floor to the right,' he said. Aretha was on the first floor. No one had heard of her, and no one knew me—but that's the kind of club it was. So many big people got started there.

"So I get where I need to be, put on my suit jacket in a second, and what I don't know is that Playboy has accidentally booked me to perform for a group of southern white men in the frozen-food business. Playboy was all for integration, but they didn't want to stir up trouble, so someone was waiting to tell me I didn't have to work the show, but they'd still pay me the fifty dollars. But I never talked to the guy, because I was running late! If I had, I would have been happy to get that fifty dollars without working—but my life would have been a lot different. At eight o'clock sharp, I jumped out on stage. And they laughed. One of them actually said, 'You know we're from Alabama?' I said, 'Ain't nothing wrong with that. I spent thirty years in Alabama one night.'

"Two hours later, Victor Lownes went over to the mansion and woke up Hefner. I went on stage at eight. At a quarter to eleven, Hefner came into the room, and at one thirty, I finished the show. They had never seen anything like it in their lives. I'd only been hired for the one show, but they kept me two weeks. And this is where you really see the importance of Hefner.

"To understand how dramatically things have changed, you have to understand how they were for Negroes at that time in history. After the Playboy Club engagement, I worked at Mr. Kelly's in Chicago, and *The New York Times* sent a reporter to interview me. It happened to be a white woman, and after the show, I'm sitting at a table doing the interview, and a white man walks by and says, 'Nigger, what you doing with that white woman?' This is Chicago; the South was much worse.

"To protect myself, I hired a white PR man, so that, in the future, if a white woman wanted an autograph or whatever, I could give it to him and he'd pass it on. He was always with me. That way, it would be assumed that whoever approached me was talking to him and we wouldn't have any trouble.

"While I was performing at the Playboy Club, my PR guy went over to *Time* magazine to ask them to come and cover this young black comic—because there were no Negro comics that anyone was talking about. They didn't say if they'd come, or when. Now here's how the universe—or God—works. The man who covers the space program for *Time* came to town from Cape Canaveral. He and his wife had heard about the Playboy Club and wanted to go—not to work, just to see a show—but when they tried to make reservations, they were told the show was sold out.

"Then someone in the *Time* office remembered the invitation and handed it to them. So the space guy came to see me and when he walked out of there, he was so wiped out that he wrote a big review that really changed my life—and changed the world." By 1963, Dick was one of the highest paid entertainers in the world!

Dick summed up the Playboy experience in his own special way. "The clubs were worldwide, and there was never a scandal. Never shootings; I never heard entertainers say they didn't get paid—they ran a clean ship. And you didn't have to sit at a bar with call girls! You weren't taken seriously if you didn't have a Playboy key. People looked for excuses to flash their key—they'd pretend they were digging something out of their pocket, and then they'd pull out the Playboy key—'Oh, oh… oops…It was *the* status symbol."

It wasn't until February 2, 2015 that the entertainment community honored Dick with a Star on the fabled Walk of Fame.—located on the corner of Selma Avenue. He still credits Hef for his show business success. "There have always been great black comics, but white folks weren't exposed to them until Hugh Hefner put us on stage."

\* \* \*

Way before (and even after) the actress and singer Freda Payne had her mega-hit 'Band of Gold,' she worked the Playboy circuit. Freda told us, "I was happy to be working the clubs and I played at a lot of them—I can't say all of them—but many, many, many of them. At the time, it was considered a good, upscale, kind of hip gig. My first club date was in Chicago, right in the hub of the city. I have to laugh, thinking back to singing there in the mid-60s, because, while I can't remember anything out of the ordinary about my performance, I do remember that Mr. Hefner was still in residence in Chicago and one night, after my show, I was invited to a party at the Playboy Mansion—which was very close to the club. I had never met him before but it sounded like fun.

"I went to the party and was amazed at the swimming pool. To me, it looked like it was sort of in a cave with rocks around; it was really very nice. The girls were all putting on bikinis and I can't remember if I brought one with me or if they were provided, but I put one on and was standing around talking with my agent and a bunch of other people in a circle, when all of a sudden this guy walks over and puts his arm around my waist. Now remember, this is the sixties and we didn't have all the social media that we do today, with everyone's face totally all over, and—as I said—I hadn't met Hefner. I didn't know what he looked like. So I turn around and look at him and say, 'I'm sorry, but get your hands off my waist.' And of course it was Hef! After that, he left the party—right after I said that. I saw him go into the garage and get into his sports car and drive off. That's when my agent told me, 'That was Hugh Hefner!'" Freda paused for a minute and added, "He didn't looked offended—more like, 'Oh, well.'"

It wasn't too long after that, in 1968, that Freda was at her apartment on Central Park West, in New York, and her neighbor, Tamiko Jones, calledto say that a friend from Detroit was in town and wanted to say hi. That friendwas Brian Holland of Holland, Dozier, and Holland. Freda told us, "I went to school with Brian, and he and Lamont Dozier and his brother Edward Holland had become famous because of their hit records with the Supremes, the Four Tops, and many other big, big Motown singers. Well, they had just formed a new record company called Invictus and persuaded me to sign with them. It was really perfect timing, because I didn't have a manager or record contract—I had just ended my association with both a short time prior. I had been on Broadway as an understudy for Leslie Uggams in *Hallelujah, Baby* and I was ready for a change and wanted a hit."

Shortly after signing with Invictus, Freda was offered the opportunity to record "Band of Gold," co-written by Brian and Eddie Holland and Lamont Dozier with Ronald Dunbar. It became her first gold record and sold two million copies. Another gold would follow, but Freda continued to appear at the Playboy Clubs. She said her favorite was the Lake Geneva Club, "because both my mother and Bobby Lucas, my road manager, were able to come enjoy the resort with me. They're both gone now, but we had an exciting time there."

* * *

Since Freda brought up the Playboy Mansion, this is as good a spot as any to explain exactly what the infamous pleasure palace was like.

The jazz festival, the TV series, the clubs... they were all key components in the creation of the Playboy image. And, on another level, so was the first Playboy Mansion, acquired in 1959. Although never seen in either incarnation of Hefner's TV series, it was heavily represented in the 1962 documentary about Playboy and Hefner, *The Most.*

The original Mansion was a striking turn-of-the-century estate located just three streets away from Lake Michigan, at 1340 North State Parkway. When Playboy purchased the seventy-two-room French-brick megalith in 1959, it already included clandestine passageways and sweeping spiral staircases. A face-lift was required to make it suitable for the founder of a company built on pleasure— and when it was complete, the mansion included a game room, a bowling alley, a state-of-the art entertainment center, and a modern twenty-four-hour kitchen.

In the early '70s, Hefner divided his time between his Chicago digs and a new, larger property he called Playboy Mansion West, in Holmby Hills, California. In 1974, the California place became his permanent address and he donated the Chicago property to the Art Institute of Chicago, where they named one of the wings "Hef's Hall" in his honor.

At that point, $15 million was invested in renovating and furnishing the Tudor-style mansion in California—situated on 5.3 acres—all in keeping with the spirited playboy's lifestyle. A Roman bath that could comfortably accommodate eight people was added, along with an indoor pool featuring a subterranean bar, or "Woo Grotto." There are even drying vents in the ceiling of the shower so that, after washing up, you don't have to deal with anything so provincial as a towel—you just flip the switch and soft, hot air envelopes you until you're dry.

A zoo and aviary, including many rare and endangered species of primate and exotic bird, proved a popular destination for visitors from the start. Flamingos, cranes, and a variety of peafowl still freely roam the exquisitely sloping, manicured lawns. The largest privately owned redwood grove in southern California—with over sixty of the majestic trees soaring to seventy feet tall—is located on the grounds, and all of the flora and fauna are maintained in a natural, pesticide-free environment. Hef still calls it home and continues to entertain and welcome guests around the calendar.

Victor Lownes remembered its heyday fondly. "The barroom was amazing. It was in the basement next to the swimming pool and you had to slide down a waterslide to get to it. There was a huge, aquarium-type picture window into the pool so you could see the swimmers swimming about. Hef encouraged nude swimming."

The Canadian-born singer and actress Mimi Hines—who, in 1964, replaced Barbra Streisand in the Broadway show *Funny Girl* and performed the lead role for eighteen months—remembered what she called a "firemen's pole." She told us proudly, "Phil Ford and I had just made an appearance on Hef's TV show, *Playboy After Dark,* and we went to the mansion to hang out. We used to spend a lot of time there, but I'm the only person who ever slid down the pole and then shimmied back *up* it!"

Considering the Mansion's many hedonistic amenities, you can probably understand the purpose of the plaque at the front entrance reading, *"Si Non Oscillas Noli Tintinare."* If you don't swing, don't ring.

The Mansion also included Bunny dormitories on four floors, for special guests and girls visiting from other cities. One of them was Lana Cantrell, who, thanks in large part to her work on the Playboy circuit, would become a major singing star of the late 1960s and early 1970s.

"The Mansion had dormitories upstairs where some of the Bunnies stayed," Lana recalled, "plus four or five apartments. They gave me one of those. It was really neat, because at the end of the living room, which seemed the size of a football field, was a wall with a secret button to press to open the bedroom door. Then you'd press another one and it would close. I lived there for about two years and it was paradise. Sometimes, I'd sit around with Hef, who was usually in his pajamas, and talk. He was a very nice guy and very sweet to me."

\* \* \*

Maurice Hines was in a reflective mood when we caught up with him. He was working on his latest Broadway project, *Tappin' Through Life*, a one-man show which is the culmination of his career thus far, an autobiographical statement roughly in the same vein as Lena Horne's iconic *The Lady and Her Music*. In preparation for that show, he'd been thinking about the various phases of his career: the very early years when he and his brother, the late Gregory Hines, worked together in a dance act called The Hines Kids, then the period when their father joined them and made the duo into a trio billed as Hines, Hines, and Dad—that was the period when they worked for Playboy—and later, when they were simply The Hines Brothers.

Long after their dancing days, when Gregory had a film career as an actor, Maurice's heart remained in the theater as a director and choreographer. But he views the Playboy experience as absolutely essential to the artistic and career evolution of himself and his brother. "I talk about Playboy in the show," he told us, enthusiastically.

At the time that Maurice graduated high school (circa 1961), he and his brother had already been working around the country and the world as The Hines Kids, which he describes as, "strictly a dance act—we didn't sing in the act at that time." Their father, Maurice Senior, a professional drummer, "was mainly playing for all the rock and roll shows." It was their mother, Alma Hines, who wanted the family to travel together by working their father into the act, with the two boys, then seventeen and fifteen, singing as well as dancing. "It was Mom's idea—'The boys sing too. Let's put some singing in the act.' My mother wasn't a driven woman—she wasn't like a stage mother, but she just would say things." One of their earliest appearances as a trio was in the lounge at the Thunderbird in Las Vegas.

Although they were from New York, and spent most of their childhood at the Apollo Theater, they broke into the Playboy circuit at the original Chicago Club about 1961. "We were doing an hour at the Thunderbird, but at the Playboy Clubs, you didn't do an hour, you did thirty minutes. There generally were two acts on each show, an opening act and a closing one. We started as an opening act at the Playboy Clubs, and then became the closing act. They usually had a singer, and then a comedian. The singer did thirty minutes, and the comedian did forty. So we opened and we did our thirty minutes, and then no comedian could follow us because Gregory was funny, too! And then we would tap. Sometimes we worked with a girl singer—usually it was Gloria Loring, a wonderful singer. They had a lot of wonderful girl singers. And then a male comedian. Then we come along, and then we—to be quite frank—we kicked ass!

"We did five shows a night; it was amazing, because we did three in the Penthouse and two in the Playroom, which was smaller. But we only had a trio anyway—a larger band couldn't have fit on the stage. It was small! The smallest stage was in Chicago. It was because it was the first one, so they didn't know they were going to have dancers on the stage. The stages were like postage stamps. Nobody could believe that we could do so much on them. Johnny Carson told us, 'I couldn't believe you guys were tapping on that tiny stage—with a piano, bass, and drums, no less!'

"In fact, that was one of the two most significant things that happened to us as a result of playing the Playboy Club—that's where Johnny Carson saw us, and also where Stanley Kay, who became our manager and our dear friend for life, also saw us. The funny thing was that we had already auditioned for *The Tonight Show*—no less than seven times. But Johnny came and saw us in Chicago and he said, 'Okay. I want you guys on my show.' We thought he'd change his mind once he found out that we failed his audition, but it didn't seem to matter to him. He was true to his word." Of course, both being teenagers, they were constantly improving as a team, so whenever Carson saw them, it makes sense that they would be better than any previous audition.

"We ultimately did the Carson show thirty-seven times while the show was in New York. He absolutely made us! He's a fabulous man. We owe our career to him. Because right about after the sixth time, then we got the Plaza Hotel in New York. We got offers from Puerto Rico, we got to play Miami. Johnny was powerful. Unbelievably powerful! Johnny was famous for helping comedians, but a lot of singers and musicians benefitted from being on *The Tonight Show*: Bette Midler, Diahann Carroll, Mel Tormé, Buddy Rich, Steve & Eydie, Tony Bennett."

After Chicago, the trio moved around to the other early clubs on the circuit. "We couldn't believe the crowds in Chicago. New York was insane, too. New Orleans was just okay—the third show usually was really sparse. But they had a rule that you had to do the show if it was four people, but if it was two then they could cancel the show. But if four people were in the house, we'd do the show. In New Orleans, the late show sometimes was four people, so we'd go on.

"And we were working—we were achieving something, we felt. We were having a good time! It was hard work, five shows a night. When Gregory was doing his television series, the other actors would start to complain about TV being such a grind. But Gregory would say, 'Are you kidding? This is easy! My brother and I did five shows a night with no day off.' You didn't have a day off in Chicago. That was hard. Chicago was hard. Chicago was fun, but five shows a night all week straight was rough!

"The crowds made it worthwhile—they were packed. Of course, they had the Playboy Bunnies, who were sweet—most of them were sweet girls. A lot of them were single mothers. Wonderful girls. People would walk in there thinking they were... well, let's just say that they had a preconceived idea! Now the girls in Chicago, they were some tough girls. If the customers got out of line, the Chicago girls would let 'em know. Some of the others would have to go to the maître d' or the Bunny mother—but those girls, I'll never forget those girls from Chicago. *They didn't take no mess from nobody.* And yet, they were ladies. In Miami, the girls were sweeter—some of them seemed to be a little full of themselves in Miami.

"But other than that, I can't say a bad word about the Bunnies. They were adorable ladies, and very classy, and sometimes the women in the audience would get intimidated. It wasn't just men that came to see the show—it was couples! And the women would get intimidated because they were very beautiful, and they were wearing very little clothes. We met all of them and the Bunny Mothers as well, and my brother and I always treated them like the charming ladies that they were.

"We also made a lot of other lifelong connections — I met Freda

Payne there, and I later directed her in a play about Ella Fitzgerald. We met Dick Gregory; he was the first major African-American comedian, and he was the comic that really put the Playboy Club on the map. We worked with Flip Wilson and with Pat Morita, who was later in the Karate Kid movies—a wonderful person. When he was working as a comic he billed himself as the 'Hip Nip.' Ha!"

The experience of Hines, Hines, and Dad at the Playboy Clubs lasted only a year, during which time they worked the whole national circuit. "We went to New Orleans, Atlanta, St. Louis, back to Chicago, New York, Kansas City, Los Angeles—they were all over! Funny enough, we only met Hugh Hefner once during that time. But after a year, it was time to move on. It was thanks to Playboy that we got to do *The Tonight Show*, and now that was opening doors for us! Of course, the other thing that happened was Stanley. One night we were working in Atlanta, and that was a bigger club with a bigger stage, and more people could get in there. It was a very successful club. But this was the third show, the very late show, and, like the song says, it was a rainy night in Georgia. The weather was so bad that the room was completely empty, except for two men. It turned out that they were from the William Morris Agency, and one was Stanley Kay; he was an agent, and he had flown down from New York just to see us.

"From that day to this, I've never been able to figure out what Stanley could have possibly seen in us—under those conditions—a completely empty house, us out there with no energy in the middle of the night. But he saw something in us, he saw this magic, and he told the William Morris office, 'I'll take 'em!'"

The universally beloved Stanley Kay (who also managed Michele Lee, among others) got the act a booking at the famous Concord resort in the Catskills, where they were seen by Sammy Cahn, songwriter and personal friend of Frank Sinatra, who was then a part-owner of the Sands in Las Vegas. "He called the Sands and said, 'You've got to bring these guys there!' and we went from the

Playboy Club in Atlanta to the Sands lounge. It was rough at the Sands at first, because they put us on after Louis Prima. To this day, nobody could follow Louis Prima! The whole audience would just leave as soon as he was finished. So my mother would sit in the audience and applaud for us. That was wonderful. That was our last show, which was from five to six in the morning. It was a start!"

"But it was a great experience, because we got a lot of experience doing five shows a night. We worked very hard and very long and we were young and learning and making mistakes and learning from the mistakes. Our humor got especially polished in that year; it was a big step forward. We were very Dean Martin and Jerry Lee Lewis for a while, although Gregory wasn't quite as wild. It was more sophisticated. That year at the Playboy Club was one of my favorites. It seemed rough at the time—especially the last show of the night. The fourth show would end, and we would be exhausted. Gregory and I would just look at each other and say, 'We've got one more.' Ha ha! And we burst out laughing! You had to laugh—you can't say no!"

\* \* \*

Lou Alexander had a devil of time trying to book his all-important first gig at Playboy. "They became very important to my career, but for the longest time it seemed like I would never break in there." He told us, "the Chicago Club was brand new; it had only been open for less than a year, and there were all these hot guys working there, like Professor Irwin Corey, Jerry Van Dyke, Jackie Vernon, Jackie Gayle" [as Mel Brooks says, all the Jewish comics of the period seemed to be named "Jackie"—most famously, Jackie Mason]. One of the most important comics was Jackie Gayle, who counted Hefner among his personal friends. It was Jackie who finally interceded on Lou's behalf: "He told Hef that I was good and wondered why they weren't hiring me! So that was all it took!"

From that ignominious beginning, Lou began a long-running

career in comedy with a solid foundation of working the Playboy circuit even as it started to grow and mushroom around the country. "That was basically my bread and butter for two years," he said, "it was like a farm team for new comics. We could interface with each other—as the kids say—we could try out new material, we could break in new routines, like that. We all were getting ready for the really big breaks—the talk shows, the variety shows—that we were all certain were just around the corner for us."

Lou feels that gradually Playboy diluted its own value by opening so many clubs. "The original Chicago Club was the hippest place in history. People would line up to get in. Later on, they opened so many it seemed like any bozo could get a gig there; it seemed like every little jerkwater town eventually had a Playboy Club. But in the beginning, it was very special—all the high-line people would brag, 'I've got a key and a private club to go to.' You could impress girls by showing them your Playboy key!"

He remembers the original Chicago Club vividly, and most especially how the various rooms were steps in a ladder of advancement that corresponded to a particular kind of totem pole. The bigger rooms, logically enough, were the province of those comics and singers with the biggest names and the greatest following. "Jerry Van Dyke and both the Jackies—Gayle and Vernon—were always on TV at that time, so naturally enough they got the biggest rooms. The new guys like me got stuck playing the room they called 'The Library,' and believe you me, it was just as exciting as it sounds!" What was so terrible about the Library, we wanted to know. He told us, "The Library was the bottle-breaking room!"

This was an archaic law that had been in on the books since the end of Prohibition: Every bottle containing an alcoholic beverage of any kind had to carry a Federally-authorized seal clearly stating that said bottle could not legally be reused or resold. The idea, back in the day, was to close down all those home-made stills that continued to be used, especially in rural communities, even after spirits became legal again Somehow the Fed figured that fewer bottles around would lead to fewer bathtub distilleries, and less moonshine. Whatever the justification, every club or restaurant in the country was legally required to take the empty bottles and break them—or face a fine.

"The Library was already the shmuck room—it only held half of what the other rooms held—and that was the room where they broke the bottles! Imagine trying to tell jokes over the sound of glass breaking continually; it was like being at a million Jewish weddings all at the same time!" We could almost hear the "bada-bing!" "Victor Lownes sent me to work in that room so often that after a while I had a sneaking suspicion that he didn't like me. Soon the other guys, the comedians, would come around just to watch me squirm—it became a game to see how many punch lines would be ruined by all the flying glass and sound effects."

Lou suspected that Victor was biased against him because they both had eyes for the same Bunny, but in retrospect, this hardly seems likely, since Victor was the all-time Bunny-dating champion. "I'm not a jerk—if I had known that, I wouldn't have gone near her. You don't date the girlfriend of the guy who runs the club! He approached me one day and said, 'Look, you know you're not supposed to date the Bunnies, but we know the comedians do. However... stay away from that one.'

"I was a good sport about it, mainly because I didn't have any choice! Eventually Victor and the other guys who ran the rooms saw that I was a team player, and they figured if I could somehow get laughs in the Library, then I was ready for something better. As the other clubs opened, they sent me around to work in them, and I got to work in the non-bottle rooms. Thank God that law was finally repealed!" That wasn't until 1964, deep into the Playboy history.

If the bottles were the downside, there were significant perks that other clubs just didn't have—specifically, the Bunnies. "All the guys and I would chase the Bunnies, and we would hit all the different night spots together. There were rules against that kind of fraternization, but of course we never paid attention."

What was the proudest moment of Lou's association with Playboy? "I had enjoyed a long run in Chicago, and I was getting ready to move on to another stop in the circuit, when one of the girls presented me with a special trophy—a cup with a plaque that certified the fact that I established what was then the house record by dating twelve Bunnies." That was the kind of accomplishment that Hefner himself would have admired—and, as Lou adds, "fortunately, no one demanded a recount!"

One of Lou's closest friends is his brother comic John Regis, who tells us that he admired Lou's chutzpah. He and Lou and a third comedian would be strolling down State Street, and Lou would be constantly approaching pretty girls and telling them, "Hi! I'm the world-famous Lou Alexander! Surely you've heard of me! I'm headlining at the Playboy Club, and I would love to have you as my guest tonight." Comic number three would then turn to John and say, "Does that annoy you, him showing off like that?" And John would say, "No! Because I'm looking forward to picking up the leftovers." Bada-bing!

John still remembers the occasion when Lou walked up to this gorgeous girl, who turned out to be hearing-impaired. "So he took out pen and paper and wrote down his whole spiel. Believe it or not, the girl actually did show up that night. She brought her mother, which didn't bother anybody because the mother was equally gorgeous. I said to Lou, keep the young girl, I'd be satisfied if you'd just introduce me to her mother. But Lou had a great answer, he said, 'No, I need to keep both with me, I need the mother to translate!'"

Lou eventually said good-bye to the Playboy Clubs, moving up to the more elite nightclubs. He enjoyed his Playboy experience so much that even when he moved up to the super-high cover charge rooms, like the Copacabana, he stayed friendly with everyone in the Playboy organization and regularly visited the Mansion.

\* \* \*

So many entertainers have mentioned the generosity of fellow performers quick to lend a hand to an up-and-comer. Lou shared another wonderful anecdote involving Milton Berle. "Milton caught my act at the Interlude in Los Angeles, and after the show he said, 'I like your style. You're clean, and you talk about issues no one else talks about. I'm going to help you out.'

"'Wow,' I thought, 'this is my idol saying he's going to help me out. Great! Wonderful! I'm thinking he's going to put me in a movie or on a television show. Here's what he did. He said, 'I'm going to come in here once a week and I'm going to heckle you. But before the show, I'll go to your dressing room and tell you what I'm going to say. So you can think of snappy comebacks and you can top me.' That's what this man did for me. When you think about it, it's really amazing. He came in every week, heckled me savagely, and I'd be ready with all the toppers, and I would kill him. He'd then go into an act saying, 'Look at this kid, he's got me again. I'll be back and it won't be so easy next time.'

"After awhile, it was all over town that there was some schmucky kid killing Milton Berle up at the Interlude. It was a beautiful, beautiful thing that Milton did for me. I loved him. I loved Berle. We became good friends after that; he was a very kind, sweet man."

\* \* \*

The King of Jingles, Steve Karman, is most famous for his sharp melodic taglines, including, "Nationwide is on your side," "When you say Budweiser, you've said it all," "Aren't you glad you use Dial?" and "Wrigley's spearmint gum carries the big fresh flavor," among many others. But perhaps he's most proud of the jingle he created in 1977 for the New York State Tourism Board: "I Love New York." In 1980, Governor Hugh Carey declared that little ditty the state anthem. Steve responded by giving the song rights to the state as a gift!

Steve was one of the first—possibly the first—to copyright his commercial jingles, thereby providing himself with a royalty every time one of them aired. But before Steve developed into the savvy scribe of singable slogans, he did the rounds of the Playboy Clubs.

"I was a contestant on the Arthur Godfrey talent show, and lost, but that was when I thought I had a chance to make a good living from singing. I started working different small clubs all around the country. I remember the Purple Onion in Indianapolis, the Metropolitan Windsor in Ontario, The Lotus Club in Washington D.C., and even a club called The Gay Haven in Detroit. Then, one day, I was booked to play the Chicago Playboy Club. It was a lot of work—they needed three acts for each of two showrooms, so they hired six acts. You did your act in the first room, had a break, and you moved on to the second room, and finally you came back to the first one. You usually did four shows a night, sometimes five on weekends.

"The women I worked with were all okay singers. No one I worked with became a star, but the comics were great! Billy Falbo was wonderful to work with, and I loved Jackie Gayle. As a performer, I watched everyone's act every night—I didn't just go hang out in the dressing room. Jackie had some great lines. He'd get up on stage and say, 'At the Playboy Clubs everything is a buck and a half.' Then he'd look at a Bunny and say, 'Well, almost everything.' He was great and very sharp.

"Playboy was one of the great employers, and you didn't have to have a hit record, you didn't have to be a star. I was primarily a folk singer during that time—working with a guitar, doing Harry Belafonte sort of songs. I had a genius for *not* being in sync with the trends. Everyone wanted to hear songs similar to what Pat Boone and Bobby Darin had on the radio, so I worked up an act where I wore ties and jackets, and by the time I had it together, the trends had changed to folk singers.

"Every Friday night, all the entertainers in town—not only at the Playboy Club, but all over Chicago—were invited to the

Playboy Mansion, and that was a thrill. You had to take off your shoes, because the carpet was completely white all over—wall-to-wall—everywhere! The place had a swimming pool where you could sit around outside if you wanted, but if you went down a level, you could sit on couches and watch people swim from the inside. They also had these unbelievable things called 'headphones.' I mean, who knew from headphones then? And you could plug these things in and listen to great music and watch people swim. I never saw anyone nude, but I know that's what the big attraction was.

"On those Friday nights, Hef would lay out this huge buffet dinner for what must have been forty or fifty people. I recall Tony Bennett was there one of the times I was. He was working some joint in Chicago and came over to hang out. Hef was wonderfully hospitable. He had a small jazz trio playing, and we could tour his bedroom. He had a gigantic round bed, and again, everything was white—plush, white carpet; white, white, white, everywhere. You couldn't actually enter the bedroom, but you could look in—like you do in museums.

"I was a very happily married man, but, I must tell you, I worked with a lot of guys who professed to be very happily married and managed not to be alone at night. But I became the guy the Bunnies would look to for advice. They always had questions: 'Do you think he's telling me the truth, that he was using his body to warm her up because she had a chill?' Those kind of questions—that's a true story! I'm not kidding! I remember her face. She was an absolute knock-out, and if I had been a single guy, I would have made a move on her too, but it was different. I was the big-brother type....

"I had a great time working with Sam DeStefano. He was a superb musician, to be able to go in there and 'cut the show.' He had a tight band and a *wonderful* attitude, so much fun on stage.

"Billy Falbo did a joke about a musical saw and he had an actual saw. He would take out a bow and, using his mouth, go 'Mhhmmmm'—as if he was playing the saw. I would watch Sam—

he'd end up on the floor laughing! You know someone is a good comic when you've heard his act and you want to hear it again. Guys like Buddy Hackett can tell the same story fifty times, and it's funny every time. I would watch Sam and he'd fall off his piano when Billy Falbo played his musical saw. It was great.

"No one made a killing working there," Steve said, "but the idea that there was a place like the circuit to work was groundbreaking. Hef's genius was tapping into the times. His folly was not knowing when the times had changed, But for as long as they lasted, it was a great party. A great party, indeed!"

As Steve mentioned, he was married and had three small children, whom he used to, in his words, schlep around with him when he could, sometimes piling everyone into the car to drive to Florida, or wherever, for the next engagement. He told us he would write letters home and eventually got to the point where he could afford to phone instead. But, of course, it wasn't the same as being home. Eventually, he gave up the circuit—and judging from his trail of writing and business successes, it was a smart move!

\* \* \*

Pianist Ramsey Lewis feels that it was largely due to the exposure that he got working for Playboy that he became one of the major jazz stars of the 1960s and thereafter. A Chicago native, Lewis formed his celebrated trio with bassist Eldee Young and drummer Redd Holt in the mid-1950s.

"We used to play at a place called the Cloister Inn [the club where Hefner first heard Professor Irwin Corey], in the basement of the Maryland Hotel on Delaware and Rush Street. Shelly Kasten and Skip Krask ran it. Hefner used to come by several times a week to talk with them and show them blueprints of his first Playboy Club. He was so excited about it. I had played that first Playboy Jazz Festival in Chicago and then again later when they moved to

Los Angeles. I also performed at the New York Club in the mid '60s, once that opened."

In 1965, Ramsey achieved what was then almost unthinkable: He landed on the pop single charts with a piano instrumental entitled "The In Crowd," a funky, groove-driven number that was perfect for either dancing or socializing—it was pure Playboy ethos translated into notes and beats. Since then, Ramsey has racked up three Grammy Awards and seven gold records, as well as a slew of other honors.

* * *

"To get the real story of the clubs," Victor Lownes told us, "you have to talk to Arlyne. She booked everyone into the clubs. She knows it all." He was right.

Arlyne Rothberg, who later spent many years working with both Carly Simon and Dick Cavett, began her career working in supper clubs in Chicago, starting with Mr. Kelly's and the London House, which were both owned by George Marienthal. "George was primarily a restaurant guy. His brother, Oscar, was a music buff who loved jazz, so he persuaded George to start adding musicians, and before long they both were among the top jazz clubs in Chicago. Oscar originally did all the booking, and I did the PR for the club, but I learned a lot from him. Then, when Oscar died unexpectedly—he was only forty—I took over the booking.

"George mainly gave me that job because I was already working for him and I had worked closely with Oscar. Otherwise I was much too young to have such an important position. I remember we paid the same rate for everyone—this was the era when Woody Allen, The Smothers Brothers, and Barbra Streisand were all working clubs, and we got them all for $1,500 each. Hard to imagine, right?

"Oscar taught me most of what I knew about jazz, and I learned the rest from the musicians. They thought it was novel working with a very young girl, most of the clubs then were run by old men.

So they went out of their way to be helpful. George gave me a lot of support, by letting me do almost anything I wanted! As long as I got someone in the clubs that people wanted to see, he left me alone.

"That is, until we had a fight over Richard Pryor. The first time I hired Richard, he was doing a kind of a family act, sort of like Bill Cosby, but then when we brought him back again, he was starting to get more and more controversial, the way most people know him. A lot of people were offended by his act—and would be for decades to come—and one of them was George. In fact, George ordered me to fire him, but I thought he was fantastic and I refused. George then threatened to fire me, but I held my ground. I wound up quitting that very night. Victor called me the next day, and I wound up going to work for the Playboy Club immediately. The first act I booked was Richard. Victor was totally my hero! Playboy welcomed both Richard and myself with open arms.

"Within a short time, there were twenty-two Playboy Clubs across the country, and I was more or less in charge of booking all of them. They each had two or more rooms, so that was a minimum of forty-four different acts that I had to juggle. We would hold auditions, but it got to be overwhelming, and eventually we started running the operation like a 'circuit'—we would send the acts around from city to city. If you did well, you would always get booked again, but if you didn't, it was so long, Charlie!

"Before I got there, Hef had given the job of booking the rooms to various friends of his, but they didn't know what they were doing, so when I took over, he shifted their responsibilities around—some of those guys 'job' was playing poker with Hef on a regular basis.

"One thing I can't tell you is what my official title was, because it changed so often. Every few months they would send me a new box of business cards, always with a new job title! Let's just say that I was the 'entertainment director,' or whatever.

"I kept tabs on all the clubs, all over the country. They all had the same characters in the audience, no matter where the club was—it really was the *Mad Men* era. Those 1960s executive types really existed, they could be young guys or old men with bald heads, but they all had to have that famous 'three martini lunch.' That was the Playboy stock-in-trade! It's funny, but Playboy was known at the time for being daring and risqué, pushing the envelope, so to speak. But when I look back to the early 1960s, it all seems so innocent—even wholesome."

Arlyne has especially fond memories of the comedians she booked at the various Playboys: "Apart from Richard, George Carlin and Shecky Greene were probably my favorites. George was brilliant; he was a total package as an entertainer. I would love to watch Shecky especially when he had a tough audience. That meant he would really have to work to get the crowd in his corner, and that was something to see. He never failed.

"I eventually left the clubs to get into television. I could tell that the age of nightclubs had reached its climax, whereas TV was getting bigger and bigger. My friend Dick Cavett landed a morning show on ABC and asked me to help coordinate the talent—the guests and all that. I had never lived in New York, but I moved there, and I had never worked on television either, but I made the most of it. I told Hef what was happening, and he said, 'You know, don't forget that we have an office and a club in New York too! Why not work for Dick and keep on doing what you're doing for us at the same time?' I actually tried that for a while. I don't think I ever slept in that period. Eventually it got to be too much, and I had to move on from Playboy. I'm still working with Dick after all these years! But I really regretted having to leave Hef. He is a great guy, and a wonderful boss to work for. Not to mention a true American original.

"To this day, I have fond memories of the whole Playboy experience. Playboy was a time and a place unique in history. It will never come back again. It was an amazing moment and I was thrilled to be part of it."

\* \* \*

By the end of the first year, the Chicago Club had 106,000 members and had sold more food and drinks than any other club or restaurant in the city. During the last quarter of 1961, it was the busiest nightclub in the world—and the chain was destined to become the most famous in history, employing over a thousand Bunnies and hundreds of singers, musicians, comedians, and even magicians. Before the Chicago Club was a year old, Hef and Victor were envisioning a string of clubs in cities all over the U.S. To their surprise, the first opportunities to present themselves were not in New York or Los Angeles, but in the two major entertainment centers of the South: Miami and New Orleans.

Sarah Vaughn at the Chicago Playboy Club 1961.
Isaac Sutton. Ebony Collection via AP Images

# 7

# MIAMI HEAT

t's May 19, 1961, in Miami Beach, and the opening of the new Playboy Club is the biggest social event of the season. At the premiere of the first club in Chicago the previous winter, everyone had struggled to keep warm—but this occasion presents quite the opposite problem. No matter. In spite of the late-spring heat, the local ladies insist on wearing their finest furs. Accompanied by their nattily decked-out husbands and boyfriends, they wait in a seemingly endless line until finally given the opportunity to present their Playboy key to the Door Bunny.

Though the entire enterprise is little more than a year old, expectations are high. Some have already visited the Chicago location, and everyone else has been hearing and reading about it for months: the sophisticated, somewhat risqué atmosphere; the beautiful Bunnies serving classic cocktails and cuisine; and of course the top-notch entertainment. As the throng presses through the front door, hopes are high that the new club will live up to the hype—and when the consensus is in, it's clear that no one was disappointed.

With the successful opening of its second club, the Playboy juggernaut was launched and there was no turning back. A third

Bunnies welcome members at the front door of the Chicago Playboy Club. Bettmann CORBIS

club would open in 1961, in New Orleans, followed by three in 1962 (St. Louis, Phoenix, New York) and six in 1963-1964—and that was just the beginning.

While Playboy retained ownership of the flagship location in Chicago, the other clubs were set up as "franchise partnerships," a business model similar to that of the fast-food chains that were also expanding like crazy around the country. The advantage was that Playboy could move quickly into cities where they had no business connections, without having to bear the huge expense of underwriting each individual club.

But ceding control over the individual venues had its own cost. Almost immediately, Hefner sensed what he'd given up: quality assurance. He would soon begin buying back the clubs, at a huge dividend to the original owners.

Although Hefner did not end up owning all of the franchises, he and the corporation spared no expense to insure that each club was consistently first class. The same strict regulations regarding the appearance and behavior of the Bunnies were imposed nationwide. Seasoned Bunnies were flown from the Chicago headquarters to oversee and tutor the apprentice Bunnies at each new location. The program was so comprehensive that the supervisors spent a full three months at each new club—more if warranted. Many former

Bunnies have told us how much they valued this prized training assignment because it afforded them the chance to work the circuit just as the singers and comedians did.

Bass player Stan Musick remembers a time during the racially segregated '60s—prior to his association with the Playboy Club—when he was jailed for being seen in public with his black girlfriend. "Gay Perkins—who made quite a name for herself in the movie and music world—and I were going together, and late one evening we stopped at a little place in South Miami for a bite to eat and to listen to some jazz. All of a sudden, we heard sirens and a few minutes later we were arrested. They took us to jail! They were getting ready to put Gay in a cell when I said, 'There's no way that you're going to do that. I'll make the biggest fuss you ever heard.' I was livid. They didn't end up putting us in jail but they did impound my car, which made things miserable for a time. All because my girlfriend was 'colored'—or because I was white—however you want to look at it.

"Years later, when I was working at the Miami Playboy Plaza, Gay came to hang out at the club one day when Tony Bennett was performing. I still have a picture of the three of us, and I remember Tony asking, 'Stan where'd you find this girl?' He was really impressed; she was a beauty and could sing like an angel!

"I also recall that Tony's piano player and conductor, John Bunch, enjoyed the experience so much he said to me, 'Stan I know Playboy is opening clubs and resorts all over. Any chance you can help me get into one as a musical director?' Playboy was the hip place then!"

Early on, tension developed between Chicago and Miami when it became clear that the Miami franchise partners were not operating up to Hefner's high standards. In addition to the fact that they seemed willing to uphold local segration rules—which Hef was vehemently opposed to—there were other differences. One night in July, for example, a terrible thunderstorm hit the beach. The resulting power outage disabled the lights, sound system, cocktail blenders, and—worst of all—the air-conditioning. Had Hef or

Victor been in charge, they would have refunded everyone's money, paid off the talent and the wait staff, and taken a hit that night. But their franchise partners refused to give up a buck, insisting that the show go on as planned. Never mind the fact that audience and artists alike were sweating themselves into a coma.

I spoke to drummer Harold Harm the day after Christmas 2014, and he still remembered that night vividly. "Gabe Kaplan was performing and everyone was miserable. I was sweating so much that my glasses were falling off. The club manager made the poor Bunnies and the room manager hold huge candles at each side of the stage for the entire duration of the show. Gabe wasn't any more comfortable than we were. No one had a good time that night." It struck me that this was the first time I'd ever heard about an evening at a Playboy Club that was devoid of fun.

The Miami manager was such a skinflint that Professor Irwin Corey took particular delight in tormenting him. Irwin had an unusually generous arrangement with Playboy because of all the good publicity that had been generated by his 1960 mock presidential campaign. In appreciation, the home office agreed to pick up the Professor's entire tab when he entertained at the various clubs around the country. "I had carte blanche," he told us. "Anything I wanted at the clubs or resorts, Hefner picked up the bill. Almost everyone was fine with this except for the manager in the Florida Club. He didn't like me at all. If I was in the kitchen and asked a Bunny for a Coke, he'd say, 'Put that down, he's going to pay for everything.' Well, I had to annoy him some more, so I'd buy the Bunnies gifts from the shops, you know, whatever—maybe a tennis racquet, golf balls, candy—and at the end of my gig, I'd have a big receipt that said, 'Your bill has been picked up by Hugh Hefner.' That manager used to get so mad!"

Despite a few mishaps and unforeseen blasts of nature, South Miami, with its pristine beaches and opulent, laid-back lifestyle, turned out to be a perfect location for Playboy. The executives and entertainers thought so, anyway. Because the club was situated right on the channel between the Causeway and the Florida inland waterways, a number of key personnel and band members who had homes or apartments on the water simply jumped in their speedboats, docked them near the entrance to the club, jumped out, straightened their ties and dinner jackets, and went to work. Their delight at this arrangement surely added to the guests' enjoyment and the general merriment of the place.

\* \* \*

The late, great Joan Rivers needs no introduction—but perhaps only her most devoted fans knows that, in the early '60s, before she became a headliner on the Playboy circuit and elsewhere, she appeared at the Miami Club as part of a group called Jim, Jake, and Joan. The publicity posters for the act called them "a spirited trio." Shortly before her tragic death in 2014, we asked Joan *if we could talk*—and she told us all about it.

"The guys sang some folk songs, and I was the comic. Their names were Jim Connell and Jake Holmes and they were always arguing, so I was the glue that kept us together for as long as we were. The three of us didn't last long together, but we played at quite a few of the Playboy Clubs."

When describing the clubs, Joan used words like *hip, classy, elegant,* and *prestigious.* "They ran a tight ship," she said, "with a rule for everything. But I think that's probably what made it run so well. Nothing was left to chance."

When first asked to play the clubs, many entertainers brought preconceived ideas about the moral standards of the Bunnies. Joan didn't even wait for us to ask; she cut right to the chase and told us, "The Bunnies weren't sluts! They were pretty, wholesome young women. I thought they'd all be a 'certain type,' but they weren't. That surprised me. They were actually very good company. I liked to hang out with them more than anyone else between shows. Years later, after I had Melissa and she occasionally traveled with me, I was scheduled to do a show at Lake Geneva. The girls there made a tiny Bunny outfit for Melissa. I thought it was so sweet of them and I had to peel it off her. She was only two and she loved it."

Since Joan was one of only a handful of super-successful women comedians of the '60s and '70s (not that the odds are so much better today), we wanted to know how she had accomplished this feat. "To be a woman comic," she told us, "especially back then, you had to be very strong, stand up for yourself, and be a lion tamer. My idea of heaven is to be on stage with an audience laughing at me while their stomachs are full."

In parting, we asked Joan to identify the key thing about the clubs that had made a lasting impression on her. Her response was typically atypical. "The corn," she said without hesitation, as if this had been on her mind since the mid-sixties. "Don't ask me why, but Lake Geneva had the best fucking corn I've ever tasted in my life!"

\* \* \*

Impressionist, singer, and comic Rich Little began his career in his hometown of Ottawa, Canada, and was first inspired to mimic others as he sat in the Elgin Movie Theater as a boy. Completely captivated by the stories that unfolded on the screen, he'd go home and act out entire movies for his parents, complete with distinctive voices for each character.

"My mother finally said to her friends, 'We never go to the movies. My son does them for us,'" he told us when we spoke with him. "I could imitate most of the stars that were making movies back then."

After winning a local amateur acting contest, Rich went to work as a disc jockey, often incorporating his impressions of politicians and Hollywood stars into his show. One Aprils Fool's Day, he was hired by radio station CFRB in Toronto to do a series of shows, each as a different personality. As he tells it, "I did the news as David Brinkley, a talk show like John Wayne, another as Elvis Presley, women's commentary as Walter Winchell—and it went on for the whole day. I thought it was quite obvious that it was me impersonating them, but just like with Orson Welles's *War of the Worlds*, people really believed the real stars were there! They came from all over to the studio exit to try to meet their favorite celebrities. When I came out of the stage door and the station manager made an announcement that it had been me all the time, the crowd was not happy at all. They booed and threw things at me!"

In 1963, Mel Torméinvited Rich to audition for *The Judy Garland Show* and he easily won the gig, providing him with his debut on American TV. After that, he was off and running, performing on the top TV shows and in clubs around the world—including the Playboy Clubs.

"Miami was the best club in my opinion," Rich told us—but, from the naughty gleam in his eye, we were a little afraid to ask him, best for *what*? "During the day you'd go to the beach and at night you'd work for a few hours. There were a lot of performers who did all the clubs, worked the whole circuit. I did a bunch but not all of them."

By now, you know that it was against policy for the entertainers to fraternize with the Bunnies—and that the rule was flouted on a regular basis. Rich told us about one pretty young Bunny he met in Miami. "She was very nice and we talked after my shows, and eventually we started dating. We tried to keep it quiet. It turned out that she had also been a centerfold in the magazine—I don't know why that surprised me, because she was really lovely. Anyway, we thought we were keeping this big secret but soon everyone knew and they razzed me about it. And when I say 'everyone,' I mean it. One night, in the middle of the show, my drummer pulled out her centerfold, held it up to the audience, and asked them, 'What do you think?' Of course, they *ohh*-ed and *aah*-ed. I turned to him and said, 'We're trying to do a show here. Why are you showing everyone pictures of your wife?' Everyone kidded me about my centerfold girlfriend, including my parents. We didn't date long, but she was very nice.

"It's a small world," Rich continued. "Another of my drummers, Ray Price, had a side job retouching pictures for *Playboy* magazine. That's not a bad job. Playboy was great, it gave me a chance to break in new material because most people paid so much attention to the Bunnies that they couldn't tell when I wasn't hitting my mark. Once also down in Miami, I ran into a friend from home, and he said he had just been to the Playboy Club, 'What?' I said, 'I'm performing there—didn't you see me?' 'Oh no,' he said, 'I didn't pay attention to the show with all the Bunnies running around!' All in all, the audiences were fabulous.

"I was on Hef's *Playboy After Dark* with Otto Preminger. I vividly remember him because he was outspoken and quite a tough director, but when I started imitating some of the people he had directed, his reaction was pretty good. So I softened him up quite a bit. I did John Wayne for him because he'd directed him in *Harms Way*, and I also did a bad impersonation of Dana Andrews. It was all a good time.

"I went to the Mansion for movies a few times, which was a lot of fun, and we all—including Hef—went to Mel Tormé's house in Beverly Hills to watch films, too. Mel had a luminous house with theater chairs and posters outside the room that said, 'Tonight's Feature.' Back in the '60s, both Hef and Mel would show 35-millimeter movies with huge projectors—real movie theater-quality equipment."

Rich is still amazing audiences around the world with his spot-on impressions of celebrities, presidents, and superstars, but he clearly enjoyed reminiscing about his Playboy days. The gleam was still in his eye when we took our leave.

\* \* \*

The Miami Club attracted a host of loyal local patrons, snowbirds who spent the winter months in the area. And of course, the entertainers were more than happy to work in the city of eternal sunshine. In the spirit of "more is better," it seemed to Playboy that a second location couldn't miss—so they opened the Playboy Plaza Hotel in 1970, making Miami the only city ever to have two active clubs.

The new, larger venue featured the usual four live-entertainment spaces: the Penthouse for headliners; the Playmate Bar for well-known lounge acts; the VIP Room for intimate dining, accompanied by an orchestra for dancing; and the Celebrity Bar for cocktails and more dancing. The musical director of the whole shebang was Stan Musick, who at that time was playing bass in Sam DeStefano's band at the original Miami Club. "I had no ambition to run the Miami Plaza, but Sam was very persuasive, so I figured I'd at least interview for the position. Arlyne Rothberg was conducting the search and I guess she liked the fact that Sam recommended me, because a short time after I met her, she offered me the job."

Arylne was also impressed with Stan's résumé. Not only had he been doing a stellar job with the DeStefano orchestra, he had also played the Fender bass on the historic 1960 television special *Welcome Home Elvis*, filmed at the Fontainebleau. That show paired the King with the Chairman—Frank Sinatra—and was Elvis's first appearance after coming home from military service.

About that gig, Stan told us, "Since I was a new addition to the band, Elvis asked me to come up in the afternoon to talk about his music and say hi. I spent an hour or more with him and he was a really likeable guy and true gentleman. Since he had just returned from overseas, he called every man 'sir.' I was in my 30s and felt even older when he said that so I reminded him he was no longer in the army. He got a real good laugh out of that! I had just a wonderful time with him. I told him I had played a USO tour in Germany and actually appeared at his army base, and he actually remembered the show."

Getting back to the topic at hand, Stan told us, "The Playboy gig was supposed to just be a few weeks; Sam had originally asked Conti Milano to play, but he had another job to finish. Now, Conti and I were close friends, and he asked me to do a favor for him and pinch hit for him at the Playboy Club for a few weeks while he finished this other job. Conti kept putting off his arrival until finally he just asked if I want the job permanently. It was a wonderful job—especially working with Sam—who had beautiful piano voicings. I later found out he was in the service with the legendary jazz piano player Bill Evans, who had a huge influence on his music.

"I was only too happy to work there; playing with Sam and Harold Harms on drums was exceptional. The club was jumping with local and visiting personalities constantly hanging out there, and then there were the Bunnies... I only sometimes wonder if that wasn't Sam and Conti's plan to get me in there all along."

Even as Las Vegas was becoming a mecca for high-rollers, Miami held its own as a destination for live entertainment, second only to New York and New Orleans on the East Coast. It offered a whole strip of clubs and hotels, which meant plenty of employment for union musicians. During high season, which ran from October to May, every saxophone player and bassist in the city could count on a job at one of the two Playboy Clubs or at hotels such as the Fontainebleau, the Diplomat, and the Americana. During the summer months, when things quieted down a bit and the snowbirds flew back up north, the musicians either went elsewhere or bided their time at the beach. Dozens of top stars played the Playboy Plaza, including Tony Bennett, Sammy Davis Jr., Liza Minnelli, Diahann Carroll, and Mr. Television himself—Milton Berle. The artist that Stan Musick wanted to tell us about, however, was Marlene Dietrich, who was already in her 70s when she appeared at Playboy. I have spoken to Stan many times over the years, and he always brings the subject around to Marlene.

Miami Musical Director Stan Musick and Tony Bennett. Courtesy Stan Musick

"A lot of fuss was made when Ms. Dietrich performed," he told us. "Her audiences waited for hours to get the best seats, and went absolutely crazy when she made her entrance. She wasn't the typical Playboy entertainer, so when she came to town it was quite a treat for everyone, staff and patrons alike. She had her devotees, many who actually followed her from town to town, and they adored her! She brought her own, very select group of musicians with her. Her guitar player was from London, and in his early career worked with the Beatles. I'd hang out with him and we had a lot of fun. She also had her own drummer. At the end of the show, she had more bouquets of flowers than I've ever seen. She was very elegant and refined in the way she walked and presented herself— just like the glamorous movie star she was—and yet she made you feel as if she wanted to be there

Miami Musical Director Stan Musick and Steve Lawrence. Courtesy Stan Musick

just for *you*. She was so friendly; we all loved it when she came to visit us."

Arlyne Rothberg mused, "The first big headliner at the Miami Plaza was Marlene Dietrich—at the time Burt Bacharach was her musical director. Up until then, I knew Marlene only by her reputation as a very grand, imperious diva. But in person, she was very warm and down-to-earth—a real

Miami Musical Director Stan Musick and Mitzi Gaynor. Courtesy Stan Musick

earth mother type. I grew to love her very quickly. She cooked dinner for everyone every night—for me, for Burt, and for the whole band. I was supposed to be looking after her, but instead she would continually come up to me and ask, 'Are you okay? Can I get you anything?' Can you imagine—Dietrich!

"Marlene would leave her door open—she had no secrets—she had a way of making her skin tighter with a headband. It looked great on stage, but she didn't care who

Miami Musical Director Stan Musick and Liza Minnelli. Courtesy Stan Musick

Miami Musical Director Stan Musick and Mitzi Gaynor. Courtesy Stan Musick

knew. She was in her seventies then, but she still had a great body and was still beautiful. And very, very high-class. She was an excellent singer, but what really made her special was the way she communicated with the audience. I never saw another performer who had that same kind of relationship with the crowd. She was grand and regal but she made you believe that she was singing just to you. The audience just loved her, couldn't get enough of her. And neither could I.

"I have strong memories of the Miami Playboy Plaza Hotel," Arlyne told us, "I had been doing this for a while then, but I was still young and naïve. We were all working hard; we had to deal with a lot of performers, a lot of artists, a lot of agents, a lot of union officials. One day the phone rang and it was someone claiming to be from the stage hands union—the guy said, 'We're going to break both your legs!' I said 'Don't be silly! You must be joking!' and I hung up on them. That was the end of that. I can't believe I could have been so naïve—it never occurred to me that it might have been a real threat! Of course, the union stage-hands loved working there; it was such a pleasant place. So did everybody else. Hugh Hefner is what made everything work with this organization. It worked because of what he was—not his persona or perceived image—but the man himself. He's such a decent person who is incapable of lying—a typical Midwestern Methodist boy."

Stan remembered working with another ageless luminary—and living legend—the glamorous Mitzi Gaynor. Who wouldn't treasure memories of working with her? To this day, Mitzi possesses a peerless combination of seductiveness and wholesomeness, a smile that can light up a room, and legs that go on forever. But perhaps Mitzi's most enduring qualities are her contagious enthusiasm and irrepressible can-do spirit. Channeling her most famous role, Nellie Forbush in the 1959 film of *South Pacific*, Mitzi is a genuine cockeyed optimist and always has been—from the time she played the Miami Playboy Club forty years ago until today, at age eighty-four.

Mitzi had just turned seventeen when she landed in Hollywood and signed a long-term contract with 20$^{th}$ Century Fox as a singing, dancing, and acting triple threat. Her timing couldn't have been better: She'd arrived just in time to participate in the last great era of movie musicals, landing leads in classic films opposite legendary co-stars, including *There's No Business Like Show Business* (1954) with Donald O'Connor, Ethel Merman, and Marilyn Monroe; *Anything Goes* (1956) with Bing Crosby; *Les Girls* (1957) with Gene Kelly; and *The Joker Is Wild* (1957) with Frank Sinatra. But, as noted, if there's one role she's remembered for above all others, it's "Knucklehead Nellie" in *South Pacific*, in which she sang such classics as "Some Enchanted Evening" and "I'm Gonna Wash That Man Right Out of My Hair."

With the demise of the movie musical, Mitzi shifted her focus to live shows and television, which she conquered seamlessly with the aid of her manager, husband, and the love of her life, Jack Bean. (They were together for fifty-two years, until his death in 2006.) She became one of the first major movie-musical divas to headline in Las Vegas, as well as the opulent showrooms of Miami Beach—including the Fontainebleau and Deauville—back when lower Florida was the unofficial Vegas of the southeast. She also starred in two major television specials, titled, respectively, *Mitzi* and *Mitzi's Second Show—the Special.* ("Isn't that a clever title?" she asked us with a twinkle.)

"I first met Irving Berlin when I worked on *There's No Business Like Show Business,* many years ago," she said. "He called me once later on and asked me what I was working on, and I told him I was doing a TV special called *The Mitzi Gaynor Show.* And do you know what Irving's wry observation was? He said to me, 'Well, no one can steal that name!' He was right!"

Mitzi first headlined at Playboy's second Miami venue, the opulent Playboy Plaza in March 1971. "I've played dozens of clubs, from Vegas to Feinstein's at the Regency in New York," Mitzi recalled, "but this was something unique. There was a kind of an electric something in the air, a certain intangible feeling. It was everywhere: in the audience, among the hotel staff, and most important, on the stage. That was the last great era for Miami. The other old-school hotel showplaces like the Fontainebleau and the Americana were starting to dry up. Miami had been like the Vegas of the east for awhile, there was even gambling, though it wasn't legal. The Playboy Plaza was sort of like Miami's last stand, but it was a successful one. I remember that place firing on all cylinders! I was just part of a season that included the wonderful Diahann Carroll, who was an absolutely brilliant singer, plus Steve Lawrence and Eydie Gorme, who were terrifically funny in addition to being musically amazingly, and Sonny and Cher, a very different kind of marital team! I had to follow all of them that year and I don't think I did too badly, if I do say so myself.

"The club was always packed and my show was like a full-scale, one-act Broadway revue. I did seventy minutes with a full chorus of dancing boys and—this sounds amazing when I say it now—fifteen costume changes!

"I loved Miami. I worked in all the major spots up and down the beach but the Playboy was my favorite. Back in those days, everybody would dress to the nines—everybody but the Bunnies of course! We would refer to them as 'the best undressed women in town.' The Bunnies were so overwhelmingly beautiful that they raised the bar for all the other women. The only way that the wives and girlfriends could compete was by wearing their furs and jewelry. I think that I was the most competitive of them all. It was my job to outshine all the other ladies and keep the focus on myself.

"Even in spring, when there was obviously no need for fur coats, they wore them. The ladies would implore the club to crank up the air-conditioning as much as possible. A lot of the gentlemen were bald and the poor dears all had freezing-cold heads. So they adopted the custom of using the club's napkins—these pastel pink napkins—as head coverings. I looked out into the house one opening night and thought I was in some kind of strange reform synagogue, filled with men in crazy pink yarmulkes! It was Miami, after all, so you never know.

"My wonderful husband and I put together a great show we were very proud of. I loved my dancing boys. Usually, it was hard to draw the attention away from the Bunnies, but when my boys were on stage, all the ladies were looking at *them*. Jack was a sweet man but he knew how to get what he wanted out of the dancers and musicians."

Mitzi paused for a moment and then said, "I have to say a word about Stan Musick. He played our arrangements beautifully, I don't think our show ever sounded or looked better than at the Playboy Plaza. The organization was behind us 100 percent, we never lacked for anything. From Hef on down, everybody was amazingly supportive, and it was the kind of organization that made you want to give it your best.

"The only person that we ever met at the Club who was less than charming was a rather disagreeable janitor, who insisted on doing his job while we were in the middle of rehearsal. No matter what we said, he wasn't going to change his schedule to accommodate us. So in the end, we wound up dancing all around him as he mopped. It worked so well that we debated asking him to join the show.

"Those were different days. For one thing, it was before we were all terrified of skin cancer and we regarded the sun as our friend. We would lie out on the beach or by the pool as much as we could....I really loved those days. No self-respecting female would show up at a club or at any kind of a social event without a decent tan.

"Mornings were Jack's time to work. He'd make phone calls and argue with club owners while I relaxed in the sun for a few hours. Then, in the evenings, it would be the other way around. I would be up on stage working and he'd relax as best he could with a glass in his hand. He was just my sweet, darling Jack. Ella [Fitzgerald] and Peggy [Lee] asked him to work for them, but he turned them down as diplomatically as he could. He said, 'I married a great cook who sings and dances on the side.'

"When my run was over, the Playboy people presented me with a solid silver cocktail shaker, engraved, 'To Mitzi: many, many thanks, Hugh Hefner, Playboy Plaza, Miami Beach, Florida, March 1971.' That was one of those amazing moments that everybody should have in their lives, when everything was perfect.

"Jack was a perfectionist. If something was wrong with something, he'd let you know—but he couldn't find fault with anything at the Playboy Club. Our show went off perfectly. The chorus boys loved to gossip and complain whenever they could, but there was truly nothing to complain about at Playboy. The dressing rooms were spotless, the lighting cues all went off exactly when they should...you'd be amazed at how rare that is.

"It was just a perfect moment in time, one that I'll treasure it always."

\* \* \*

Before the Playboy Clubs, comedians primarily performed in strip clubs and burlesque houses. Some of the more prestigious hotels had showrooms with headliners, but there wasn't a mechanism in place for comedians to make a living while also getting to practice in front of live audiences.

"I started in Chicago," says veteran funnyman Jerry Van Dyke. "I worked at the Chicago Club until they began to open more clubs around the country, and then I traveled between the different cities. I opened Miami and New Orleans. I was the first act in Miami. I played the banjo and told jokes—did a few sketches where I portrayed different characters—but basically, I was your regular old standup comic. I had an act from high school, so I guess you could say that I'd been at it awhile.

"In my day, you had to have a perfected act and a recognizable name to get booked into a hotel showroom or one of the few big-bang nightclubs around. There weren't any places, other than the small little joints, for comics trying to break into the business— places where you could bomb and get away with it. In the beginning, there were only a few clubs, and Irwin Corey was also around, so I'd see him a lot, coming and going, and he was *hilarious*! He was one of the funniest—really offbeat. I'll never forget when we first saw him. We loved him.

"I always thought that Playboy was one of the best things that ever happened to showbiz. You could always count on a Playboy Club being nice—as opposed to all those seedy joints out there— and they were always very well run. They dotted their I's and crossed all their T's. They even respectfully asked patrons not to talk during the acts—can you imagine? No other club did that.

"I had a great break; I was working at the Miami Playboy [Club] when Earl Wilson, who was a New York columnist, happened to be in the house. I know, what are the odds? He put me in his column and that was a major break for me.

"After that, I got a part in *The Courtship of Eddie's Father*, with Glenn Ford and Shirley Jones, and that was my first movie. I started to get write-ups from these movie and TV appearances, and then I became a regular on *The Judy Garland Show*. Eventually Carl Reiner read one of those columns where I was mentioned. Of course, Carl was working with my big brother Dick on his show, and he says, to him, 'How come you never told me that your brother is funny too?' Everyone assumes that Dick got me the job on *The Dick Van Dyke Show*, but it really was Carl. Of course, Carl eventually became famous for being part of a big showbiz family as well!

"After I was on TV regularly, I had less time to play the clubs, so eventually that part of my life wound down. But really, I could never have done television without having worked in the trenches for Playboy; they gave me the chance to perfect my act and get it to the point where I could do movies and TV.

"I wasn't the only one," Jerry told us, "Playboy was a perfect opportunity for all of us, a whole generation of musicians and singers and comics—Playboy was like a huge finishing school for all of us. Just the comics alone would include Lonnie Shorr, Lou Alexander, Dick Lord, Howard Beder, John Regis, and me. Some of us stayed in the comedy racket, some of us moved on to greener pastures, but almost all of us owe our livings to Playboy. I miss those clubs. It was always a pleasure to work there, Bunnies and all! It's a shame that there's nothing like it around today."

\* \* \*

New Year's Eve is a raucous time anywhere, but in Miami—and especially at the Miami Playboy Club in its heyday—things could get out of hand! Starting in the early afternoon on December 31, 1970, the queue began forming around the block. To add to the excitement, the wildly popular singing duo of Steve Lawrence and Eydie Gorme were the headliners tasked with ushering in the New Year. Hours worth of drinking in the hot weather made the crowd rowdier than usual, and as the clock crawled closer to showtime, they surged against the glass doors—which promptly shattered!

To everyone's relief, no one was seriously injured. Admittance was finally granted, and the evening culminated in a classic singalong of "Auld Lang Syne" stylishly led by Steve and Eydie—but announced by Stan. "Steve was a very funny guy," said Stan, "my office was next to his dressing room and we talked every once in awhile. On New Year's Eve, he says, 'C'mon Stan, have a drink!' So, I'm enjoying a drink with him and I ask, 'When New Year's Eve strikes, what are you going to do, Steve?' He says mischievously, 'I'm not going to do anything, but you are!' I said, 'What do you mean?' And that's when he said, 'You're going to have to do the countdown and ring in the New Year!' I didn't usually get in *front* of the mic, but I did—and the band cracked up—but Steve said it came off well."

There were other dicey moments. Standard policy was to announce that almost all acts playing Miami would be accompanied by the house orchestra, directed by Stan Musick, and most of the time, that was the case. So, when Ike and Tina Turner were scheduled to appear, all of the posters and other publicity materials referred to the Stan Musick Orchestra, as usual. The two soul stars, however, were traveling with a full band and the Ikeettes, their leggy, fringe-clad backup singers. No house band was necessary when the Ike and Tina Turner Revue was in the house.

So the posters were wrong. Most artists wouldn't have minded the minor mix-up, but Ike was famously truculent and egotistical, and highly resented the implication that *somebody else's* orchestra might back him and his wife up. Furious, Turner called and demanded to speak with Musick—who had nothing to do with the PR and hadn't even been booked to work that weekend. "I was at home—not even scheduled to work that night—when I received a call from the night manager that they wouldn't go on with the show until the table cards and posters were changed.

This was an era well before Kinko's and desktop printers; it just wasn't possible to whip up new posters and table cards on a moment's notice, and Stan knew it. Fearing a conflagration, he took it upon himself to drive to the club and explain to Ike that the mistake had been made by the home office in Chicago—not the Miami staff. But Turner was seething; he refused to go on stage. The first show was already late getting started and the crowd was restless. Finally, thanks to Stan's careful diplomacy, the Turners agreed to go on. "They had to do an extra show because that one started so late, and that was great. Stan remembered it as the tensest moment in the history of the Miami Club. Mainly the celebrities and entertainers couldn't have been more of a pleasure; every once in awhile you have to be a diplomat," said Stan.

"Milton Berle treated us to a visit once," he recalled, "I loved his dry sense of humor but he was a real attention-to-detail kind of guy. Once, during rehearsal, he said, 'Stan, the band is wonderful, but get rid of the drummer.' Without any explanation. I told him that in order for me to get the top musicians for the season—which is what we always had—I had to guarantee them work for a certain length of time. 'If you have a problem,' I said to him, 'if he's not doing something you'd like him to do, just let me know and I'll work with him.'

"He just shook his head and walked out. Shecky Greene happened to be there and heard the whole [thing], and after Milton left he said to me, 'You talked that way to Milton Berle?' I said, 'I didn't talk to him out of disrespect, I just told him the truth; this is the man I hired to work with him. Milton ended up saying it was fine; he was just having a moment. He was funny like that. Another time we were on stage and I was in front of the band conducting, when he turned around to say something and noticed that I had a teeny, tiny rip on the seam of my tuxedo pants, only about an inch long. It was so small I don't know how in the world he could see it. But he put his mic down and walked over toward me to tell me about it! It wasn't in a mean way—he just couldn't let it pass without commenting on it."

A more cherished and agreeable memory was the time Stan greeted Frank Sinatra, who was in town for the 1972 Republican

Convention and brought his entourage to the Playboy VIP Room for dinner. But, in Stan's opinion, the single funniest thing that happened in Miami involved not a gathering of Republican elephants or Playboy Bunnies, but feline fanciers.

The club was pet-friendly, so one year, a big group of cat-lovers and breeders held its convention there—complete with their furry, purry friends. A special dinner and ceremony was planned, and somebody thought it would be a good idea to involve the orchestra. Each prize-winning show cat would be presented on a platform placed between the orchestra and the audience, and the band would strike up a tune for each animal. "Keep in mind," said Stan, "that these cats were pretty close to the band—facing away, but close. And they had no idea what was going to happen."

Apparently, when the orchestra hit the first chord, the flustered felines all jumped ten feet in the air and scattered throughout the room. "The audience was laughing like heck and scrambling around on their hands and knees to round them all up," recalled Stan. "Everything ended just fine, but the orchestra stayed quiet for the rest of the presentation."

That cat-tastrophe aside, Miami would be one of the most successful and longest-lived of all the Playboy venues, and one of the most fondly remembered by everyone who attended or performed there.

Decades later, memories of the clubs' special magic are still vivid. Stan told us about a recent conversation he had while at the gym. "I was working out at LA Fitness in Miami," he said, "and I struck up a conversation with another guy about this and that. I mentioned that I had once worked at the Playboy Club and he said, 'I remember the Playboy Plaza Hotel. On my first date with my wife, I took her to see Stan Musick and his orchestra.' 'That was my band!' I told him—and he freaked out. He couldn't wait to go home and tell his wife about it.

# 8

# THE BIG UNEASY

"New Orleans was the best and the worst Playboy Club. It was above a famous restaurant, Moran's, and a few doors down from Felix's Oyster Bar. Across the street was the Acme Bar, which supposedly had the best oysters in New Orleans. But here's the bad side. I had never been exposed to that kind of hatred. There was a big outcry when Hef opened the clubs to blacks—protests from local members that it wasn't right. He just said, 'Then leave. Just go. Forget it. Don't even come back here.' He was quite a man in that regard!"
—HOWARD BEDER, SINGER AND COMEDY WRITER

Well before the American Revolution, well before Thomas Jefferson and the Louisiana Purchase, well before Hugh Hefner even, New Orleans was America's original party city. It partied for centuries before the opening of the Playboy Club in 1961, and it has partied since its closing. Yet, somehow the Playboy Club, which lasted roughly twenty years in the Crescent City, represents a moment in the lives of those who were there that they remember vividly, if not

Dizzy Gillespie joins Richie Payne, Al Belletto [and Johnny Vidacovich behind the drums]
during a jam session as they rehearse at the New Orleans Playboy Club.
Courtesy of Al and Linda Bell

always fondly. The paradox is obvious; New Orleans is probably
the least serious city in the western hemisphere, but what happened
there during a pivotal time in race relations reverberated around the

country, and the world. For a man of Hugh Hefner's humanitarian principles, New Orleans was where the rubber met the road; it was where he would make his stand, even if it jeopardized the future of his empire.

On October 13, 1961, in a former carriage house strategically located at 727 Rue Iberville, in the legendary French Quarter section of New Orleans, the doors to a new Playboy Club opened. As expected—and as they had in Miami—crowds of keyholders waited eagerly to enter the lavish establishment and partake in the Playboy lifestyle. Even though New Orleans needed another party spot like Vegas needed another casino, the venue was an instant success. But Hefner was troubled. Playboy was more than a magazine with naked girls; it was an organization known for providing equal opportunities for men and women of all skin colors. The social realities of the American South in 1961 were like a slap in the face to him.

As Hef looked out over the crowd in the new franchise, he saw a sea of white faces—on stage, on the staff, and in the audience. Black Bunnies were out of the question, as were black entertainers, no matter how talented or well known. The application process was designed to discourage black members, and those who showed up with a key were refused admission. Truth be told, Florida wasn't exactly a bastion of enlightened thinking either, but it was certainly more flexible than Louisiana.)

National news coverage—a linchpin in the success of any new business—was depicting a situation that Hefner himself found abhorrent. He had pushed for desegregation in both the Miami and New Orleans clubs, but it was the franchisees—bolstered by state laws—that controlled hiring and membership policies. Hefner felt he had to do something, and he did. He bought back both franchises—at amazing speed, staggering cost, and unprecedented profit for their owners—so that he could manage them as he saw fit.

But if Hefner thought his problems were over, he was sorely mistaken. In 1961—which, coincidentally, also marked the opening of another French Quarter institution, Preservation Hall—segregation was still the law of the land throughout the South. The public school system had been officially integrated by the Supreme Court under President Eisenhower, but this decision wasn't federally enforced until President Nixon's administration. Louisiana State law forbade any kind of socializing between blacks and whites, including drinking or dancing. It would take a long time and a lot of fighting before the southern clubs were a true reflection of Hefner's ideals of equality and liberty for all.

The French Quarter Playboy Club will be eternally associated with saxophonist Al Belletto, who led the house band there throughout its history and eventually became a manager, responsible for booking all the talent. A New Orleans native, Al was probably best known, prior to that, for a series of albums he made for Capitol Records with his sextet in the mid-1950s, including one produced by Stan Kenton. He was thirty-one when the club opened.

"I was home visiting my parents," Al told us, "and I stopped in to see my friend Jimmy Moran. He ran a pretty well known restaurant at the time. Jimmy told me that Playboy had just opened a club next door and suggested that I come back to New Orleans and work there. I thought that was a pretty good idea, but I didn't really have any connections who could get me in. That's how things get done in New Orleans; it's all about who you know. Jimmy said not to worry, that he'd speak to them on my behalf. It turned out that Shelly Kasten [formerly of the Cloister in Chicago], who worked in the Chicago organization, had videotaped me when I recorded an album with the Kirby Stone Four, so he knew who I was. He was going to be in New Orleans the following week and we made plans to get together. That was the beginning of my association with Playboy.

"The arrangement was that my band would play in the club, but we'd still be able to accept national engagements. Eventually, I became musical director for eight of the clubs, which gave me the opportunity to hire jazz musicians from around the country. I hired a musical director for each new club and also local house trios and bands. It was a good feeling to give work to so many great musicians. Shelly and I would travel together and open clubs, and I was his ear when we had auditions. He'd also send entertainers to the French Quarter and have them work for me for a few weeks so I could evaluate them before they went on the circuit.

"In the New Orleans Club, we offered music six days a week, which was unheard of. I always had at least three full-time bands. Kenny Rogers came through New Orleans a few times and he was really great. He'd hang out and play with the band when he wasn't performing. He was with The First Edition when he played with us, and then later, of course, he went out on his own, and that's music history. He became a fabulous entertainer.

"Irwin Corey, the comedian, was like a fox. We enjoyed having him at the club, and the people who worked there were even bigger fans than the audience. Jackie Gayle was a dynamite comedian, too, and a Playboy favorite. Charlie Callas and Dick Gregory both came out to entertain. Dick might have been a mite political, but he sure made me laugh. Slappy White was there. Lurlean Hunter was the queen of Chicago at that time, and she came to sing for us, as did Teddi King.

"The club was closed on Sundays, and it was a routine for me to take the traveling entertainers, musicians, and band members home to my mother's house for a big dinner and family time. My little Italian mother, who was an excellent cook, spent the weekend preparing for and hosting these dinners, and she loved getting accolades for them. George Carlin came over once. He sat at the table and visited for a long time but, much to Mom's dismay, he didn't eat any of the food. In traditional cultures, it isn't nice to refuse someone's hospitality. It didn't make my second-generation mom feel any better when she found out he was a vegetarian. She never would have embarrassed one of her guests by making a scene in his presence, but when George left—well... maybe you remember the scene from *My Big Fat Greek Wedding*: 'What? He don't eat no meat?' Mom always remembered George as the guy who wouldn't eat her cooking!"

If you are surprised that Al Belletto talked to us for a long time before mentioning the issue of segregation, perhaps it's because he paid it very little mind—he was colorblind in his hiring practices. Thanks to him, preeminent jazz pianist Ellis Marsalis, patriarch of the most famous family in contemporary jazz, played at the New Orleans Playboy Club well before the laws were changed in 1964.

Marsalis recalled, "My trio consisted of Marshall Smith on bass, Jan Black on drums, and me on piano. We were hired mainly to back up the black performers, but pretty soon, all the black artists quit coming there and we were playing in the main room as a stand-alone trio. We were pretty good and working six nights a week, so I had a chance to develop some nice things out of that.

"I remember that the audience wasn't always so sophisticated in their behavior. I saw guys pull the tails off the Bunnies and pour drinks down their tops. That was Louisiana in the 'good old days!' Those girls worked hard in their high-heeled shoes. They'd sneak off to take a rest for a minute or two and the floor director would chase them right back onto the floor. More than a few tears flowed back there."

"Ellis had his own band, and a very popular one, too," Al added, "and sometimes I'd take my horn from the Penthouse, where we played, and go down to the Living Room and sit in with them."

From the start, Al had an integrated band, featuring such musicians as Richard Payne. "I don't recall having any trouble about including musicians of color at the Playboy Club," he said, "although I was once arrested, or almost arrested, when I sat in with a black group at the Texas Lounge on Canal Street. Earl Palmer was just an incredible drummer and—I couldn't help it—I took my horn up and played with him. I sat in for a few nights and then one night, the uniforms came at closing and they wanted to arrest me. It just so happened that my second-favorite uncle was a major on a neighboring police force. As they were getting ready to put me in the back of the police car, one of them said, 'I'm going to have to cuff you.' I was holding my horn and didn't want to let go, so I said, 'Do what you have to do, but my uncle is going to be so pissed when this hits the fan.' One of the cops asked who my uncle was. I said, 'Major Allie Franzella.' The other cop said, 'Jesus Christ, take your horn and get out of here!'

"I do remember one ugly incident at the Playboy Club. Richie Payne was my bass player. One night, this Alabama politician, who was in the audience with a patrolman escort, yelled out the 'N' word. I got down off the stage to throw him out when the patrolman said 'Maybe we should go.' I said, 'That'd be a good idea.'

"The building itself was unusual. Attached to it were some old slave quarters, with lots of hallways and passageways. Even the garage was interesting. I'd go through a small driveway, where they'd take my car to park, and I'd come up the back stairs that led to Moran's kitchen, and then go through their back entrance to a door that led to the club. Every once in a while, Momma Moran would make me something special and I'd have to sneak it in the back way so I wouldn't have to share with everyone."

When we asked Al whether the New Orleans Club was his favorite of them all, his answer surprised us. "Not necessarily," he said, "because no one was afraid of me there. Shelly Kasten would call me up and say, 'You've got to go to Kansas City. There's some trouble, and I want you to straighten it out. Well, the people in Kansas City weren't too happy to see me—but that was never true in New Orleans."

In 1968, along with Doug Ramsey, Al helped produce the New Orleans Jazz and Heritage Festival, the forerunner of George Wein's International New Orleans Jazz and Heritage Festival inaugurated two years later. Because of Al's connection to the jazz community, he was hired to book the entertainers. "Duke Ellington brought his band from New York to New Orleans for four thousand dollars," Al remembered, "which was incredible—but he did it to help us out. My sextet was the opening act of the festival, and I was so overwhelmed by the support of my friends and fellow musicians, I almost couldn't play. Gerry Mulligan, Dave Brubeck, Cannonball Adderley, Willie Tee [aka Wilson Turbinton, the New Orleans R&B star pianist], and Dizzy came—God bless Dizzy—I loved him so much. All of the popular folks came just because we asked them to."

Al's wife Linda recalled that a group of seats near her filled up when Ella Fitzgerald sang. After she finished, Ella introduced one of the people near Linda as an up-and-coming star. It was Stevie Wonder with his entourage!

In 1970, George Wein took over the local festival and made it into the international gathering that it remains to this day.

* * *

Dr. Bruce Raeburn is a professional drummer as well as one of the world's pre-eminent jazz historians. He fits in well in New Orleans, where everything is about family (from the Batistes to the Marsalises), because he, too, is the scion of a famous jazz family. Bruce's father was the great modern jazz bandleader Boyd Raeburn, a contemporary of Stan Kenton's, and his mother was the band's vocalist, Ginnie Powell.

In 1973, while Bruce was working on his Ph.D. in history at Tulane University, Al hired him to play drums with the house band at the New Orleans Club. Today, Bruce is a noted expert on cultural history and the curator of Tulane's Hogan Jazz Archives, as well as its director of special collections. Those roles, along with his personal experience of the Playboy Club, make him the perfect person to provide some background on the issues of race in New Orleans music.

"Jazz was creating opportunities for interracial collaboration as early as 1910," he pointed out, "in spite of apartheid in New Orleans. For example, Achille Baquet, an Afro-French Creole, and Dave Perkins, an African American, worked in Papa Jack Laine's Reliance bands, which were perceived as 'white.' In the 1920s, mixed-race recording sessions were taking place, including one with Jelly Roll Morton [who was Afro-French Creole] with the New Orleans Rhythm Kings [a white band from New Orleans] in Richmond, Indiana, in 1923. Sidney Arodin [a white clarinetist] played with the Jones-Collins Astoria Hot Eight [a black band] in New Orleans in 1929.

"A lot had been accomplished by the 1950s, including the establishment of integrated swing-bands such as Benny Goodman's famous quartet, featuring Teddy Wilson and Lionel Hampton. Interracial collaborations among bebop musicians included my father's big bands and Dodo Marmarosa with Dizzy and Bird. But bringing racially mixed bands on tour in the South was still considered too risky for most bandleaders."

Some jazz icons dealt with the situation by, essentially, boycotting the city. Native son Louis Armstrong refused to play there, knowing that his band, the All Stars, which included white and black musicians, could not legally perform there. George Wein refused to produce a festival unless both the bands and audiences could be integrated.

"Resistance to desegregation was rife in New Orleans, but the New Orleans Jazz Club, which was accused by Martin Williams of being 'Jim Crow,' began showcasing mixed bands at private events before 1960. Some members, such as trumpeter Johnny Wiggs, were quite radical in advocating for civil rights. From the time of its founding in 1961, Preservation Hall was a bastion of traditional jazz, but was also predicated on a strong commitment to civil rights. From the start, it welcomed mixed audiences and bands as part of its basic philosophy.

"Transgressing the color line became an aspect of Playboy Club policy in the 1960s as well, as evidenced by the support Al Belletto got from Hefner in hiring Ellis Marsalis and others. They flouted the black-performer-white-audience-fetish approach that was still alive on Bourbon Street in that era. By the time I worked there in the early '70s, the fact that Al's band was racially mixed was not the least bit controversial—so progress *was* made, and I would attribute much of it to jazz. As an art form, jazz was symbolic of the viability of black music as national treasure. Multi-ethnic constituencies were built based on its value as art and because it made people feel good."

Bruce filled us in on how his personal and professional affiliation with the Playboy Club had begun. "I was playing with a band downtown, fronted by vocalist Joan Harmon, with Reggie Scanlan on bass, John Hidalgo on guitar, and a guy from Tulane, Billy McCarthy, on keyboard. We called ourselves Joan Harmon and the Different Strokes—a terrible name, but Joan liked it. Word spread that the band that had been playing the ground floor at the Playboy Club—the Post Raisin Band, it was called—was being replaced. So John said, 'Let's give it a shot,' and we asked Al Belletto to come to the Backstage and watch a set. We were on pins and needles for about a week, until we heard that we were hired. We felt as if we were on the threshold of becoming professionals. The club had a more elite clientele than any we had worked at, plus, we had to join the union. We even had to go shopping for suitable attire. We knew we couldn't show up looking like a rock band, so we bought velvet blazers and gabardine pants and really dressed up for the occasion.

"Lots of interesting people were regulars. One was called Uncle Charlie—he probably got his moniker from *My Three Sons*, because he looked like William Demarest. He was a professional gambler who spent a lot of time at the racetrack in New Orleans, and if he liked what you were playing, he would tip you with silver dollars. Needless to say, he became an instant favorite and was pretty much there every night."

The club was also frequented by Allen Toussaint, who, on the strength of such highly caffeinated recent hits as "Java," and "Whipped Cream," was easily the most successful songwriter in the Crescent City at the time. "Allen would periodically come out and show support for Joan," recalled Bruce, "usually with a new young lady. They'd wear matching outfits that included fringe down to the floor. When Allen enters a room, you know it! He's a pretty flamboyant dresser.

"It was exciting being able to perform six nights a week. There weren't that many places outside of Bourbon Street—which was a terrible grind that combined music with topless and bottomless dancers—where you could do that. The band gets very tight when you work together that much. You work up new material and your musical skills reach a pretty high level. We were essentially a cover band and did all the popular songs, from the Beatles to the Doobie Brothers, to Jimmy Cliff and Stevie Wonder."

Bruce told us that Joan Harmon was frequently expected to cover the hit songs of New Orleans soul diva Irma Thomas, which, for some reason, didn't sit well with her. "She didn't realize that Allen Toussaint had written a lot of those himself, under the pseudonym 'Naomi Neville.' More than once, she made disparaging remarks about having to do all of these Irma Thomas songs, thinking the mic was off when it wasn't, which didn't go over well with either the audience or Allen."

The club itself was unlike any other in the Playboy chain. It was a beautiful five-story structure built in the early nineteenth century. The former slave quarters Al Belletto mentioned were maze-like and unused, even for storage, but as Bruce explained, they provided a convenient hideaway for smoke breaks. "On the second floor," Bruce said, "there was a fire door, and we worked out a deal with the Bunny working the bar nearby that we could go out and smoke a little grass during our break and not get caught. She would prop open the door just a little bit so we could get back in.

"One time, though, we almost got ourselves into trouble. We were out there smoking and we noticed a light coming from the other side of a door down the hall. We decided to explore and discovered that it led to a restaurant three doors down. When our break was over, we hurried back—we were late—but we found that someone had closed the door that let us back into the club! We knocked and knocked, and fortunately the right person opened it or we probably would have been fired.

"All those buildings look perfectly lined up from the front entrance, but the backs are all up against each other every which way. It's really an interesting maze that you could get lost in for a long time. We learned our lesson and didn't explore anymore after that.

"The high point of the gig, in my opinion, was Mardi Gras. We usually had Sundays off, but during Carnival, we worked extra shifts, including on Sunday, and got overtime for it. Reggie's girlfriend was one of the Bunnies and she helped paint up our faces. We played all done up in feathers and sequins and beadwork—it was a real Doctor John kind of trip, totally New Orleans-style."

\* \* \*

Al Belletto regards Bill Huntington as one of the finest bass players ever, but when we repeated this remark to him, Bill responded with typical modesty. He grew up with a strong appreciation for music, taking up the banjo at twelve, switching to guitar by sixteen, and finally graduating to bass in the '60s. Bill became adept at both traditional and modern jazz, and has recorded with Percy Humphrey, Ken Colyer, Al Hirt, Harry Connick Jr., Pete Fountain, and scores of others. The roster of greats with whom he's performed live includes Cannonball Adderley, Herbie Hancock, Nicholas Payton, Mose Alison, and many more. In 1961, *Down Beat* magazine singled him out for praise as one of the major modern jazz musicians in the Crescent City, profiling him in the same article as Ed Blackwell, who would become an internationally known modern jazz drummer, famous for his work with Ornette Coleman.

Bill passed on his craft to young musicians by teaching Jazz Studies at the University of New Orleans and Loyola University for more than twenty-five years, before retiring in 2005.

"I played with great musicians," Bill told us. "One in particular was Buddy Prima [the son of Louis Prima's older brother, Leon], a great pianist, trumpeter, and composer. We were very close and worked together quite a bit at the Playboy Club. We had a trio there. Al had hired me to play bass in his quartet at a jazz club in Columbus, and after the gig ended, we drove back to New Orleans together. About a year later, Playboy opened a club there and Al was the perfect musical director for it, since he knew so many musicians and Hefner loved jazz. Al hired bands for each of the rooms, and we'd rotate and play in all of them.

"The time went by quickly, working with all those wonderful, iconic, musicians. Some came to New Orleans for the job and others were great local musicians. It was like music school, really inspirational—and I was getting paid!

"No one in New Orleans really liked modern jazz at all, and there was very little audience for it at the time, but Al and Playboy began to change that. The other important thing that Al did, besides giving all these good musicians work, was hiring a bass player named Richard Payne. Rich was a fine black musician and there were segregation laws at the time. This was a breakthrough. It was a big deal to hire a black man for a steady job, six nights a week. And in such a prominent place as the Playboy Club! The fine, fine pianist Ellis Marsalis, father of Wynton and Branford, also played there with his trio. So Al not only promoted good music and great musicians, but he advanced civil rights—which was really an unpopular thing to do down here, you know.

"So many fabulous comedians and entertainers came through the club, too. Jackie Paris and Anne Marie Moss stand out in my mind as a wonderful singing duo, and man, Charlie Callas was a funny, funny comedian. Irwin Corey, with his malaprops ....he used to introduce Al [Belletto] as 'Al Betterbelow' or 'Betterblow.' He had me on the floor. I don't recall seeing Hugh Hefner, but I met his brother Keith quite a few times. There was Mort Sahl, David Allen, and just a whole host of quality talent—no schlock.

"Al put together a club baseball team made up of all the musicians and staff, and we got into the habit of calling him 'coach.' That became his nickname long after the baseball ended. Those Playboy years were special for me for so many reasons. They were very good years."

\* \* \*

Today, Johnny Vidacovich is one of the most sought-after drummers in New Orleans, and a member of the contemporary jazz group Astral Project. He's been drumming professionally almost his entire life, starting out with traditional New Orleans Dixieland bands when he was barely thirteen. In high school, he took a detour into rock 'n' roll, switching back to jazz in order to qualify for two successive scholarships to Loyola University. Throughout his school years, he worked nights playing rock 'n' roll at clubs on Bourbon Street and made good money at it. Eventually, he left New Orleans for a job in Las Vegas.

"I had auditioned to play in Al's house band at the Playboy Club," Johnny said, "but another drummer got the gig. Al called me back about six months later to say he'd changed his mind. I said, 'Man, I'm out here in Las Vegas, and my plans are to move to California. But thanks anyway.' He called me back the next day with an even better offer, and I gave in. I went home to New Orleans.

"Prior to Al hiring me as a regular, I had substituted downstairs in the lounge with a funk-rock band with Ricky Grishillo called The Dead End Kids. He had also hired me to play with Willie Tee and

Chuck Bagley, two famous New Orleans musicians, in one of the showrooms. This time, I worked as a regular for five years. I met some incredibly great musicians and got to play with some great, great, great guys. Different singers and comedians showed up every two weeks, so I'd have to learn new repertoire on a Monday and perform it for the next two weeks. Some shows were easy, some slightly more difficult. Once I played for a belly dancer and the music was extremely hard.

"Richard Payne played bass. He died a few years ago, but he taught me a lot. He was older than I was so I listened to everything he said. He taught me what to do and what not to do, and he told me when I did something well. He was a very strong bass player and didn't use an amp; he played acoustically. Wonderful man.

"Bill Newkirk was a piano player who knew a million songs. During the day, when no one was there, we'd go upstairs and play song after song after song. He'd play piano and I would play drums. We went through a million songs—standards and popular stuff. That's where I learned a whole lot of my jazz and standard repertoire.

"Then the band evolved. In came a piano player from upstate New York named Frank Puzzullo. He was a hardcore-bop Italian-style piano player, and we became good friends. We wound up living in the same big house together—Frank and his wife and me and my girlfriend at the time, a singer in Al's band named Angelle Trosclair. Frank came up with a lot of tunes, and I would—quick—write them down on paper, so we'd have them. He wasn't so good at writing down what he was playing. And Al's band started shifting from what was basically a bebop-style quartet to a band that was playing some funk.

"It changed even further when Rodrigo Signs became the bass player. He turned me on to Bill Evans and all kinds of great music and changed my life. He switched between electric bass, acoustic bass, and trumpet. Through the years, there were more band evolutions, but Al and I always remained good friends. As a matter of fact, I owe him a call. He's the man. He's the *coach*.

"Tom Medley was the first comedian I met at the Playboy Club. He was a 'punch up' writer for *The Dean Martin [Celebrity] Roasts* and a bunch of television shows at the time, and was also doing standup. We stayed friends for a long time and whenever I went to L.A., I'd stay at his house. His manager was Lenny Bruce's mother. She managed a lot of the comedians.

"Another guy I befriended was Gabriel Kaplan. He later became famous for the television show *Welcome Back Kotter*, but when I met him, he was on the standup circuit. Whenever he came to New Orleans, which was about four times a year, he'd say, 'Come on Johnny, lets go party.' He had been a minor-league baseball player before he became a comedian.

"George Carlin was a funny, funny guy. He had been a circuit comedian before getting famous and doing a lot of college concerts. Whenever he was in New Orleans to play Tulane or LSU or any-where else nearby, he'd come and hang out at the Playboy Club. He and Al were twenty-year buddies and we would all hang out and party together. He was fun and crazy and liked to talk a lot. Sonny Mars, Kenny Mars's father, was a wonderful Jewish comedian—just a crazy old, Jewish-style comedian who never shut up. He would keep me on the floor. I'd be on the bandstand, and he'd do his best to crack me up and he always succeeded. I think Lenny's mother was his manager also.

"Kenny Rogers would come and hang out when The First Edi-tion was just a regular old rock 'n' roll touring band. Whenever Kenny was in town, we'd go jam in an empty room on our breaks. He would play upright bass, because he never got a chance to do that once he became famous. You know, he started out as more of a jazz-style player on upright bass and not a rock or country player, or whatever they label him today.

"I was pretty knocked out the night Gary Burton, the famous vibraphone player, came in. He stayed and listened and talked the whole night. That was a pretty high point in my life. There are many, many, many others, but that was a definite high for me. Allen Toussaint used to come around a lot and socialize, but the best was when Gary Burton came by. The great drummer Roy Burns came by and played. Carl Fontana stopped by and played trombone—he just blew everyone away! He was a genius, man.

"I knew all about the early days, about Al getting into trouble—and all the foolishness—for political reasons. Al was way ahead of his time. He integrated bands way before it was even legal. By the time I got to his band, it was well integrated. Al had a hard, hard head and that's what I loved about his Italian ass. He said, 'You can't tell me who to play with. You can't tell me about any *color*.'"

When the subject turned to segregation within the musician's union, Johnny grew even more animated. "I remember when they had two unions," he said. "I played gigs with the black guys and they had a separate union, 496. Today, our union is called 174-496, the numbers of both unions from the old days. There were two unions until 1970, even though cats weren't really going by that strict shit anymore. Everyone knew it was old and dumb, just some old white cracker-faced shit.

"The hippest thing to come out of working for Playboy was that I got to meet Al Belletto. He turned out to be way more than someone I worked for; we became very close friends—family. He was there for me at a very formative time, from when I was eighteen to twenty-six or so. I learned so much just being around him. We spent time together, which is not something guys in a band typically do. They do *not* spend their days off together. But we spent almost every Sunday together, always ending up at his mom's, eating her crazy-good Italian cooking."

* * *

Frank Puzzullo, the guy Johnny Vidacovich described as a "hard-core-bop Italian-style piano player," joined the band after a tragic boating accident on Lake Pontchartrain in which Al's pianist drowned. Both Johnny and Bill Huntington were familiar with Frank's style, which was different from what anyone else was playing in New Orleans at the time, and thought he'd bring a fresh quality to the band. Al agreed and invited Frank for a visit.

As Frank told us, "It was a long time before I went back home. There was a plethora of jazz in the Playboy Clubs—the music definitely tended toward jazz. I loved it. Stan Getz even played at the New York Club for a while. It was an interesting time for me because I was doing a lot of writing. Al played a lot of traditional jazz and not what I'd call '70s music. So the band as a whole—and Johnny Vidacovich and Angelle in particular—worked to update things and get him more involved with original music from that period, more of a New Orleans funk sound. They were all a lot younger than Al, and I think he appreciated the update to his repertoire. He was open to the transition, and I wrote a lot of things that we recorded on an album called *Coach's Choice*—after Al's nickname. It was really a term of endearment that began before my time, when there was a Playboy baseball team, and Al was literally the coach. Many of the guys in the band were students finishing up their studies at Loyola, and they looked on Al as a father figure.

"So, yes, there was an abundance of jazz being played, but of course, we also backed up the entertainers who came through. Playboy was pretty heavy with comedians. They'd come in and do a show and we'd play for them. We'd move upstairs and play a jazz set and then back downstairs to another room. We were always moving between the different showrooms.

"There were always national football and baseball stars in the place. If the Saints were playing home games, you'd have lots of people like Paul Harding from Green Bay and some of the other guys hanging around. A wide variety of different professional sports folks were in and out. It was great fun for all of us to be able to meet and talk with them."

Frank worked at various Playboy Clubs from 1971 through 1979, when he was offered a position as director of jazz studies at New Orleans's Loyola University. In addition to teaching there, he established the first-ever jazz major in the heart of the greatest jazz city of all time.

\* \* \*

Entertainers came from all over the world to work at the Playboy Clubs. As unlikely as it seems, one of Australia's most famous entertainers—Lana Cantrell—made her American debut very informally at the New Orleans Club.

The musical prodigy and Australian native was encouraged to sing and play the piano from a very young age by her jazz-musician father. By the time she was ten years old, she was giving concerts at the Sydney town hall. Just a year later, she was a regular on Australia's version of *American Bandstand*.

When we spoke with her, Lana told us, "You have to understand that while, in America, you had different people appearing on *Bandstand* each week, we Australians were still experimenting with television. There weren't that many performers, so the same few were on all the time, including me—at age twelve. It was Peter Allen, me, and a few others. Everyone in the country knew us and watched us grow up. I became very comfortable in front of a camera and a really big deal in Australia."

Lana continued to appear on *Bandstand* and another show called *In Melbourne Tonight* for four years; then it was off to the land of opportunity.

"When I came to America," she continued, "I visited my cousin, and he said, 'I'm driving to New Orleans. Do you want to come along?' So I said, yeah, that sounds like fun. As soon as we got there, he took me to the Playboy Club and got me a shot at singing with the band. He thought all show business was the same. I knew my way around a television camera, but had never been up on a stage! He said, 'Oh, c'mon, get up there. So I sang with the band and the audience liked what they saw. The New Orleans people contacted the people in Chicago who booked the clubs."

Shelly Kasten, Playboy's talent director at the time, auditioned Lana. He loved the way the quirky Australian belted out a song, as well as her fresh, wide-eyed look, but everyone agreed that her stage persona could use some polishing. "They were right," admitted Lana. I could get up on stage and sing, but I didn't know what else to do. I had trouble just saying hello.

"Shelly said he'd like to manage me as well as book me at the Playboy Clubs, and he gave me a choice. We could either hire someone to write an act for me or I could play the circuit and learn as I went along. I said, 'Let me go and learn.' The word got around that I would play all the clubs and no one could fire me, no matter how bad I was. It was like being sent to college, and I definitely got an education.

"I had no home, per se, in America. I was going from club to club to club, and if I had two or three weeks off and had nowhere to go, Shelly arranged for me to live at the Playboy Mansion in Chicago. I started opening for other people, doing ten minutes, and then graduated to fifteen, twenty, and finally, I told Shelly I felt pretty comfortable on stage and he started giving me headline positions. I traveled to all the clubs. I remember that in New Orleans, once Hef was able to hire black Bunnies a bunch of us went to a club after work together—a mixed group—and they wouldn't wait on us. They told us to leave.

"Hef supported civil liberties, civil rights, civil everything. He even helped me get my green card. Because I didn't have working papers, I was arrested in Kansas City and served with notices to get out of the country within three months. Hef hired a lawyer for me and helped get me my working visa.

"I remember, as I traveled from club to club, everyone wanted me to succeed. The piano players would help by doing arrangements for me to build my repertoire. Even Sam DeStefano wrote some charts for me to take away."

"I'm really a blessed person," she insists. "I work hard, but I'm blessed to have been in the right place at the right time more than once. I was playing in the New York Club, and Skitch Henderson, from *The Tonight Show*, came in to see me. He liked what he heard and got me on the show a few times. Then, someone called Johnny and asked, 'Who was the French girl you had on your show?' He couldn't think of anyone, but remembered I had sung a French song. Pretty soon, I was booked into the Sands in Las Vegas. I walked in and the show director said, 'You're not the girl!' But I was there, so they put me on. That night, Ed Sullivan came in, and he booked me on his show! When I say blessed, I really mean I've been very fortunate!"

By the end of the 1960s, Lana was a major star, particularly in clubs and on television. There's a 1967 clip of her singing on *The Hollywood Palace* that shows her as a slender songbird with a Twiggy hairdo and a musical and visual style very much out of the era of Streisand and Minnelli. She does an excellent job with the Irving Berlin/Fred Astaire standard "Isn't This a Lovely Day," as well as the more recent Bert Kaempfert hit "And We Were Lovers." Lana released seven albums with RCA Victor in those years, but, unfortunately, never really racked up the hit singles or signature songs that an artist needs to keep working over the long haul. In the mid-1980s, she began to transition out of music and into the law. Lana, who turned seventy in 2013, continues to practice law in New York.

* * *

No question, New Orleans has and always will be associated with music—especially jazz. But its unique entertainment culture has also always made plenty of room for comedians. Among the many great but lesser-known performers who stopped there along the Playboy circuit was Dick Lord.

Veteran comics refer to the Playboy clubs and other night spots that once crisscrossed the nation as "the trenches"—a rather military metaphor, to be sure, but for young comics in the 1960s, the trenches were where you paid your dues, where you rose through the ranks, and where you either killed or died.

Lonnie Shorr, Jerry Van Dyke, and others described the nightly grind of the clubs, the process of perfecting and polishing their sets, figuring out what worked and what didn't, learning to respond to hecklers and pause for big laughs—all of many details that make up their craft. And they agreed that the best place to master these and a million other things was the trenches.

Dick Lord started as a drummer in a small band that played private parties, business affairs, local events—even a party at a potato-salad factory (yes, he tells us, a potato—salad factory). He also worked extensively in the resorts of the Catskill Mountains—also known as the "Jewish Alps"—where one of his earliest professional associates was a fellow musician that everybody already knew as "Bobby" but whose full name was Walden Robert Cassetto. Within a short while, both young men shifted their focus: Dick switched to stand-up comedy while Bobby changed his last name to "Darin" and became a major, though sadly short-lived star.

Why the switch from drumming to comedy, we asked Dick. "I had a gig at a club called the Crystal Coronet, way up in the Bronx," he began. "It paid next to nothing. I would drive there in this cheap little car I owned, but one day it broke down and I couldn't afford to fix it. So I had to take my drums to the club via mass transit—one train, then another, and then a bus on top of that. And if that wasn't bad enough, while I was in the middle of carrying them, it started raining. So I gave in and called a cab, which ate up everything I was going to make playing drums all night. And to top it all off, when I got to the club, somehow there was a leak over my head and my trap kit got soaked anyhow. Talk about depressing!"

Dick began thinking about other ways to make a living on stage. He had attended the University of Vermont, where he earned degrees in marketing and television production, so he was confident that he could write. He'd also earned a reputation as a funnyman for making his fellow musicians laugh. But he knew there was a big difference between cracking up his friends and working in front of an audience.

"At the Coronet, we played for a belly dancer and a comic, who seemed ancient to us—he must have been all of 40! Anyhow, he was pretty lousy, he was bombing, he figured he couldn't do any worse, so he thought he'd get a cheap laugh by provoking me. He turned to me—the drummer—and challenged me to tell a joke. Now, the pianist had heard me tell jokes so he encouraged me. And there I sat, the water leaking onto my drums. I noticed some plastic flowers they had put around as low-budget decorations and for some reason, a joke about flowers popped into my head. I remember it to this day: 'Most of the time, I love flowers. Matter of fact, I have flowers at home, but it doesn't work out for me. Even my African violet calls me a *honky*.' This was at the beginning of people using that term. To my surprise, the audience actually laughed. So I told another joke and another. I actually had the stones to turn to the professional comic and say, 'You can leave now!' The crowd went wild at that point.

"It was such a thrill, making people laugh, much more of a kick than I'd gotten from my struggling career as a drummer. The club owner saw a chance to save some money, figuring that if he paid me a little extra he could save on the cost of a professional emcee. So he gave me an extra fifty bucks to host the show and do comedy. My pay went up to a hundred dollars for the three nights of a weekend!

"That week, I wrote an act for myself. I tried to come up with something appropriate for the club. I figured that since they were mainly there to see the belly dancer, no one wanted to hear me talk about voting rights or integration or anything heavy like that. I also started chasing after agents for work as a comic. A manager named Ruth Kaye told me how I could volunteer to do my routine at servicemen's hospitals, things like that, it was good training. I slowly built up ten minutes worth of good material. I would call clubs and agents and their first question was never 'Are you funny?' The first thing they always wanted to know was 'Do you have a car? Can you get here?' When I said yes, they'd sometimes make me chauffeur the musicians or the stripper around. In those cases, I'd try to hit them up for money for gas and tolls.

"B y this time, I had a family—a wife and little kids. My parents were starting to lay down the law. 'How can you work for so little and gallivant around the country when you have a family to support?' But they had faith in me and eventually it started to pay off. I moved up a notch or two when I was able to get into a spot called Number One Fifth Avenue, a very nice club. I did well enough that they held me over two extra weeks and I got a nice write-up in *Variety*. During the second week, I met a man named Murray Becker who worked at the New York Playboy Club, and not only did he want to book me there, he wanted to manage me in general. So, of course I said yes. From that point on, my career was off and running. Once you made it to the Playboy Club, you knew that you had achieved something.

"The first one I worked at was in Phoenix. At that time, the Playboy Clubs seemed like a miracle to me. A miracle! The conditions were great, they had dressing rooms, you could have dinner at the club, there was a place to relax between shows, and the shows were very professional. You did two, three, or four shows a night. People say, 'Oh, that must have been so tiring,' but, no, it was wonderful! Where else, at that point in my career, could I have performed every night? And that was without driving to Connecticut or upstate New York or wherever for one-nighters. This was being employed! Wow. By the end of the week, I felt as if I were really in show business. This was the way it was supposed to be.

"Every showroom had a room director who was kind of your boss. He watched the reaction of the audience. Of course, everyone can have a bad audience once in a while—but the director would say, 'There's no such thing as a bad audience!'

"The Playboy Clubs were genius. Every club was the *same*. If you were a tie salesman and one week you were at the club in Cincinnati and the next week you were in New Orleans, the clubs were exactly the same. There was the Playroom, the Pool Room, and the bar. Guests *immediately* felt at home. If you were a member of the club, you'd call ahead for reservations and when you walked in, they'd have your name up on the welcome board. I think it said 'Guests Tonight' or something like that. All the food was the same, too, whether you were in Cleveland or Atlanta. Everything was the same price and the Bunnies were always friendly. It was a wonderful feeling.

"The early shows were tougher, because the audience was mostly men. They weren't rowdy, exactly, but they were a lot more interested in hitting on the Bunnies than watching the shows. By nine or ten, there were more couples and the men didn't do as much turning around to ogle the girls.

"Many of the Bunnies were married. I got to know a lot of them because I worked all the clubs at least once or twice. They worked while their husbands stayed home watching the babies. If they were single, they had boyfriends. But, let me tell you, many of the guys became very childish around them.

"I only missed a show once. It was New Year's Eve and I was supposed to do five shows! The crowds were wild. I lost track and, after the fourth show, I thought I was finished and went home.

Dick played the circuit—almost every club—and he smiled as he remembered a favorite moment down south. "There was one time I was late. It was in New Orleans during Mardi Gras. We were staying at a little hotel across Canal Street. In order to get to the club, I had to cross Canal, which, during Mardi Gras, was impossible! You couldn't get across. There were police barricades and thousands of people marching down the street in costume, all drinking and dancing and playing instruments. It was like trying to cross a river. I walked down my side of the street until the crowds thinned a little. When I finally crossed over, I was *lost*. Totally lost. I finally made it, but I was late.

"So many wonderful things came from working at Playboy but there was one experience I wasn't prepared for, especially having grown up in New York. It happened in New Orleans. The act 'Hines, Hines, and Dad' was opening for me. They were great—a father and his sons, Gregory and Maurice. The father played the drums and the guys did their stuff, dancing and singing. They were just great—I mean, a *great* act. I became very friendly with all of them. Well, one night, I was watching the show and as part of the act, Gregory stepped off the stage and circulated around the audience, doing his dance.

"Now, I'm going to say a word that I don't want to say, but it's part of the story. Gregory put his hand on a guy's shoulder, and the guy said, 'I don't let no niggers touch me.' I was shocked. I'd never heard that—or anything like it—before working in the South. That was the worst thing I had ever heard inside of a club! At the end of the show, Maurice and Gregory called me up on stage with them to take a bow, and as I stood between them, I said, 'I feel like an Oreo cookie.' Of course, everyone laughed and it broke the tension.

"Two nights after that incident, we all wanted to get out of the club after our show. I think even Maurice and Gregory's mother, Alma, came along. It's hard to go from the club right to bed, even though we had been working for five hours. So we went to a place called the King's Room, right next door, to have a drink and unwind a little. Well ... we didn't get to relax, because someone got shot right before our eyes! There was no confrontation or argument or anything, just a guy pulling a gun—maybe twelve feet from us—and killing another guy. Shot him right in the chest. The four of us were just paralyzed. The police came and took everyone's statements and we went home. We didn't get to unwind *that* night.

To sum things up, Dick told us, "Playboy was fantastic for us guys in the trenches—the good, hard-working comedians—and there were many, many of us. Sometimes, two comedians played a club at the same time, one in the Playroom and one in the Penthouse. When your show wasn't on, you'd go watch the other guy work. We could hang out together and learn from one another, which was great. We'd talk about the business and see what other comedians were doing. Even the traveling was great. I saw places I probably never would have seen. I'd never been to New Orleans before I played the club there and don't know if I'd have stopped in Detroit on my own. I learned a lot about people and saw a lot of the country. It was good."

Playboy encountered its share of tensions in New Orleans, but nothing would prepare Hefner and his colleagues for the cold bite of politics that awaited them in the Big Apple.

# 9

# TAKING A BITE OF THE APPLE

Victor Lownes, it turns out, was one of those restless souls who grow bored with their own successes. As the 1960s wore on, Playboy was fast becoming a corporate giant, complete with all of the bureaucracy that Victor had already begun to find stifling years earlier. In 1954, he and Hefner could knock around ideas for a few hours and then implement them immediately. In 1962, new initiatives had to be filtered through layers of management. Even worse, communicating directly with his old friend meant making an appointment and being allotted a set amount of time. After one such meeting, Victor decided to retire from the organization.

He officially resigned in June of 1962, but not wanting to end his involvement altogether, he negotiated a yearly fee of $75,000 for his services as an exclusive Playboy consultant—contracting, in essence, to do what he had always done for them. With that and the money he made by cashing in a portion of his Playboy stock and equity, he was in good shape financially. He immediately set up his own head-quarters in the swanky St. Moritz Hotel in Manhattan, complete with staff, and went to work creating a Playboy Club in New York.

Victor explored every street and avenue in Manhattan, searching for a first-class location. He soon found an ideal, six-story building on 59th Street, near the Sherry Netherland Hotel, just east of elegant Fifth Avenue. As soon as the deal was done, Playboy began renovations. As Victor told us, "Playboy immediately invested almost two million dollars to get the building in top shape and open as expeditiously as possible. Additional funds for the finish-out, furnishings, decorations, licenses, and all other sundries associated with a new business brought the total cost close to seven million dollars. The advertising budget was also extended to entice new 'charter keyholders' to enroll."

Hef and Victor were warned that they might have trouble procuring a liquor license if they weren't prepared to pay off a few key figures in the State Liquor Authority, including its Commissioner, Martin Epstein. Through an emissary, they were informed that Commissioner Epstein required a $50,000 cash fee to guarantee that their application would go through smoothly. Playboy agreed to pay, but months went by before they got any news about the application.

Then came the bombshell. In addition to their agreement with Commissioner Epstein, they would have to come to an "understanding" with L. Judson Morhouse, a lawyer and the chairman of the New York Republican State Committee. In a meeting between Playboy representatives and Morhouse, he gave assurances that he foresaw no difficulty in the company securing their coveted license for an additional fee of $100,000. Epstein received his payout and arrangements were made to accommodate Morhouse as well. After almost a year of frustration, anxiety, and expense, Playboy was finally awarded a liquor license.

Unbeknownst to anyone involved, the New York District Attorney was investigating extortion and corruption within the State Liquor Authority at the time. With Playboy's cooperation and assistance, Morhouse was indicted and found guilty. Epstein was deemed too sick to stand trial. No charges were leveled against any of the Playboy executives.

Victor and Hef thought that their troubles were finally behind them, until they received word that they had been denied a cabaret license. City License Commissioner Bernard O'Connell had ruled that because the Bunnies were allowed to do the "twist"—the latest dance trend—with keyholders, the club's proposed activities were not in the best public interest. Ironically, the twist was the first social dance in which the partners didn't touch each other, making it perhaps the least salacious dance of its time. Playboy appealed and ultimately triumphed, but the 59th Street club would be deprived of entertainment for a long time. "Eventually, it was full steam ahead," Victor said. "Even with all our delays and setbacks, we sold sixty thousand new keyholder memberships before we even opened."

December 10, 1962 Comedian Joey Adams gives Hugh Hefner some pointers at the New York Playboy Club. Image by Bettmann CORBIS

* * *

More than any other Playboy Club, the New York venue employed a remarkable roster of young musicians who were almost completely unknown at the time but would go on to major careers in jazz, and on the New York studio scene. Kai Winding, who was already one of the top trombonists and arrangers in the jazz world, was the musical director of the club and he had a remarkable ear for finding new musicians. Some of his "discoveries" were pianists Walter Norris and Larry Willis; bassists Bob Cranshaw (who would work at the 59th Street venue when he wasn't on the road with Sonny Rollins), Earl May, and Bill Crow; guitarists Gene Bertoncini and Al Gafa; and drummer Al Foster. The drummers came after the rest because, in the beginning, no drummers were allowed in the club, according to licensing rules.

Of all the new players who spent many happy nights working for Playboy, none would become a bigger star in the jazz world than Monty Alexander. Born in Kingston, Jamaica, in 1944, Monty became a headliner in the 1970s and a leading figure in what was sometimes called the bebop revival. In addition to leading his own top-notch trios (the most famous of which was based in Los Angeles, with bassist John Clayton and drummer Jeff Hamilton), he was the most frequent collaborator of the pioneering jazz vibraphonist Milt Jackson, of the Modern Jazz Quartet. Today, Monty's great renown comes from having returned to his roots; his band, Harlem-Kingston Express, is widely recognized as the most successful synthesis of North American jazz and Jamaican roots music (ska, mento, calypso, reggae) on the scene, and, as such, is one of the era's most popular jazz ensembles. Monty's group sells out concert halls and clubs across the country and around the world, and has been nominated for a Grammy Award in the reggae category—though many feel he should be in a category of his own.

What is generally overlooked is Monty's passion for the Great American Songbook, which blossomed in those early years in New

York. To this day, he never hesitates to wave the flag for the two figures that he believes to be the greatest interpreters in all of American
music: Frank Sinatra and Nat King Cole. He has performed and
recorded many tributes to both men, and, in fact, Sinatra played
a key role in his career. In the early 1960s, when Monty arrived in
the United States, his first stop was Miami Beach; he was playing
piano at one of the hotels when he came to the attention of Sinatra
and the singer's aide-de-camp, Jilly Rizzo. Sinatra was so impressed
that he immediately hired Monty to come play at Jilly's saloon in
Manhattan; he would go on to serve as the house pianist at Jilly's
for most of that bar's existence.

"That's how I came to New York," Monty affirmed, "to play at
Jilly's and at parties at Frank's apartment. One night Kai Winding
came into Jilly's. He was a monster trombone player, a fantastic
musician—what he did with J.J. Johnson! He was also a sharp
cookie, and on top of all of that, a very nicely dressed guy. He heard
me playing and said, 'Hey this guy is alright.' He came right up
to me and first thing he said was, 'I want you to come play at the
Playboy Club.' I had been to the Playboy in Miami, just hanging
out, checking out the Bunnies, you know? You know, they had them
all over the place. I knew the room directors in Miami, I knew the
managers, they all knew me.

"I said, 'Man, yeah, sure!' because I wasn't always at Jilly's. I
would be there for roughly two months and then I would be off
for a little while. So I started to work at Playboy. The thing was, at
the beginning, they didn't have a cabaret license. The New York
political 'thing' would not give Hefner a cabaret card. So among
the things they could not have were drums, trumpets, and vocalists! They could only have combos of stringed instruments. That
was the set up.

"I was the first piano player there and I asked for two guys who
had played with me a lot at Jilly's—Bob Cranshaw and Gene Bertoncini. This was at the very beginning of the New York Club and

the whole scene in New York. We had no drummer."

Ironically, although Kai Winding was the musical director for a time, he was not legally allowed to play his trombone in the club.

"I don't remember last week too well," Monty continued, "but I remember fifty years ago. It was an exciting time. That's when I met Quincy [Jones]. Quincy had just come back from Europe after his so called 'failed' big band tour, and he got a job at Mercury Records. He used to come hang out at the Playboy [Club], checking out the chicks.

"Our trio was in the Living Room. When they finally got the cabaret license, the entertainers would work upstairs in the Playroom, although the regular pianist up there was Ross Tompkins—who later played on *The Tonight Show* with Doc Severinsen. Russell George was on bass. Then you'd have singers like Jack Jones. I think Jack came later on when they had the full trio, when you could have the drums. But it took awhile before they got the drums, and by then Gene Bertoncini had left, also to play in *The Tonight Show* band, so we got Al Gafa. The other room upstairs, at the top of the club, was the Penthouse. For that room, they hired Milt Buckner with his B3 organ. He'd come in there and rock the house. Wonderful, Milt—who I loved. All by himself, he could rock the house."

Al Gafa, who later became known as a guitarist-accompanist for such iconic vocalists as Sammy Davis Jr. and Johnny Hartman, remembered the general layout of the club. "There was music on nearly all of the floor,s and we were in a room called the Living Room; that was the first room as you came in. Our group was very strong. We used to have a lot of trouble, in fact. The original idea was that we would just play for the people as they walked in, but we were so strong that a lot of times they never went to the other rooms. They would just stick in that front room. This group was just dynamite!

"The Playroom was where the comics and singers worked, but there was always a trio, too—piano, bass, and drums," said Al. "And then there was another floor where they had a trio on weekends.

Walter Norris was the pianist and Bill Crow was the bass player, and myself. So there were a lot of musicians working there. If I had to guess, I would say there were somewhere around nine or ten working at the Playboy Club all the time."

Monty continued, "When we got the license, our first drummer was Dick Berk. We all called him 'Dick Sputnik' because he was a heavy-set guy. He passed away last year. He's the drummer on a record we made called *That's the Way It Is,* recorded at Shelly's Manne Hole. It was Dick, myself, Ray Brown, and Milt Jackson. Dick was a swinging drummer. Then we got a very young drummer, Al Foster. It was one of his first jobs. We got to be very friendly, and I remember Al saying to me that his life's ambition was to play for two of his heroes, Miles Davis and Sonny Rollins. I said, 'Really?' And look what happened. He sure did play with both Sonny Rollins and Miles Davis!

"For awhile, we had Les Spann, who had played with Quincy and Dizzy's band. He was a tremendous guitar player, and also played the flute. One night, his good friend Wes Montgomery came into the club with his guitar. And Wes and Les plugged into the same amp together while I played the piano. What a session!

"So that was my life in the mid-'60s, switching between Jilly's and the Playboy [Club], with a little 'off gig' here and there—some party or bar mitzvah or wedding. But Jilly's and the Playboy Club were my two jobs. Playboy had its laws and rules, one of which was that you had to play 'Playboy's Theme' by Cy Coleman.

"I admire Hugh Hefner tremendously. He did a lot of good for jazz—made it part of the lifestyle. The message was, 'If you're a playboy, you've got to have a beautiful motor car, a convertible with the top down; you've got to smoke the best pipe; and you've got to have a good jazz album collection.' He started a jazz poll so people would recognize the best musicians.

"Hef came into the club occasionally, but it was Keith Hefner who looked after a lot of things. They had these guys called room directors who were watching over the situation, too. And then there were the Bunnies! Well, I won't go into the ladies—we won't go there. But, boy, it was a party—let's put it that way. The official policy was, 'Don't talk to the Bunnies, don't touch.' It was like a dormitory with these beautiful ladies. But it didn't go like that. There was talking and there was touching.

"Lauren Hutton was a Bunny there for awhile, and I knew Gloria Steinem when she was working there as well." For those few of you who didn't know, the feminist firebrand worked as a Bunny for awhile in 1962, under the name "Marie Ochs." She wrote a two-part article about the experience that was published in *Show* magazine the following year.

"I had a close friend named Bunny Maxine," Monty went on, "who married Joe Zawinul from the group Weather Report. I remember I went with Joe to the hospital when their first child was born. There was another Bunny who went to Hollywood and married the famous arranger Phil Moore, and another who got a role in a James Bond movie. One night, Gene Bertoncini and I took a couple of the ladies to Forest Hills to see Sinatra with Basie, Quincy, and Ella Fitzgerald. It was a hell of a show at Forest Hills Stadium.

"I mostly played in the Living Room, though I might have played for the singers once or twice. Anything could happen there. One of my favorites to listen to was a singer who is often forgotten, named Damita Jo. Unfortunately, she was managed by her husband, who didn't help her get to the place she should have gotten to, but everybody loved this woman. They would compare her to Ella in terms of her vocal dynamics—she had an incredible, *incredible* gift. She worked a lot with Steve Gibbs and the Red Caps, and also with Milt Trenier and the Treniers.

"I also remember the funny guys who would come in to work—the comics. It was at the Playboy Club that I first saw Steve Martin put the arrow through his head. Professor Irwin Corey would come through and I'd be laughing my head off. One night, when some guy in the audience was hassling him, Corey walked up and knocked him out with one punch—bam! Ha! Then there was Jackie Vernon... and Larry Storch, who is alive and well, and I talk to now and then—the great funny man from the *F Troop* series."

Al Gafa has his own memories of the comics and singers he met while working at the New York Club: "Playboy was a stepping stone for a lot of comedians. People like Woody Allen, Charlie Callas, Pete Barbutti, Lily Tomlin, [and] Nipsey Russell. On one of the upper floors, they had revues. Lily Tomlin was part of an improvisational group that worked there. There were fewer singers who became big stars after working there, but Lana Cantrell was one of them.

Two Bunnies-to-be training at Kenny's Steak Pub, in anticipation of the opening of the New York Playboy Club on October 11, 1962. Image by BettmannCORBIS

"Anyway, a lot of the big names who were working at the Copa would come into the Living Room, just to sit in with our group or hang out just for a set or two. I'm talking about Tony Bennett, Dionne Warwick, Damita Jo....

"In New York, there were always the best guys playing. Kai Winding hired the musicians. After awhile, I started going out in the world, getting hired to play on the road, so I gradually stopped playing at the Playboy Clubs—I just wasn't there anymore. I can't remember how much longer it lasted, but it was one hell of a thing, that L.A. Club... so many memories of jazz people and Bunnies and weirdos and excitement—you know, good times! You can look back with a smile, you know?"

* * *

After Monty moved on, the New York Living Room featured a quartet with pianist Larry Willis, bassist Earl May, guitarist Al Gafa, and drummer Al Foster. Al remembers the era well. "Whenever Larry would get another gig, he'd send a dynamite piano player, somebody like Chick Corea, Herbie Hancock, Albert Dailey, or Roland Hanna. The band was always loaded there, so that was a pleasant situation for me.

"I still have a menu from the New York Playboy Club, 'Filet Mignon: $ 2.00.' You know it's a long time ago! 'Roast Rib Eye Beef: $2.00.' 'Gourmet Dinner: $12.50.' It's way back there. 'Whole Maine Lobster: $6.00.' This was between '65 and '68. At that time in my career, I was focused on practicing and playing—it was great. It was the right time for me to be there and the right time for everything else. I was twenty-four years old in 1964, busy in the studios in the daytime about five days a week, Monday through Friday, and then playing the Playboy Club Tuesday through Saturday nights. When things were overloaded, I would be sleeping on the subway going back and forth from my house, between working in the daytime and working at night. It was crazy, but that was what my situation was at the time. I was very busy in New York.

"About two weeks after that job came to an end, I got a call to go on the road with Sammy Davis and I just took it. I'd wanted to get out of New York for awhile, so I went out with Sammy for about nine months. While we were working in Chicago, we were invited to the Playboy Mansion. We went after a show and had a drink or two and that was it. But later we did go on the TV show in Los Angeles, *Playboy After Dark*. It was great working with Sammy; he was wonderful to the musicians. I only left him because he went off to do a movie and I got an offer from Kai Winding to join his band. Remember, it had been Kai who hired me to work at Playboy in the first place."

* * *

Elaine Trebek-Kares—or Bunny Teddy, as she was known when she was one of the first New York Bunnies—later became co-host of Canada's National Morning News show *Canada AM*, launched her own advertising agency, created the Scent Seal, a hi-tech fragrance and skincare sampling system with offices in New York, Los Angeles and Paris, and is now the owner of Gallery Go, a successful contemporary art gallery in West Hollywood. Gallery Go targets the younger collector, specializing in celebrity art and the creative endeavors of many actors and top recording artists.

But in 1963, Elaine competed with thousands of other young women for one of the 125 highly coveted Bunny slots at the brand-new New York Playboy Club.

Fresh out of Columbus, Ohio, she had been working for about a year as a model at the Garment Center on Seventh Avenue. "One of the other models saw an ad in the *New York Post* saying that Playboy was hiring Bunnies," she told us. "We had heard that the Chicago Bunnies were earning much more money than we were as models, so we decided to see what it was all about.

"We were interviewed by Bunny Mother Alice Nichols and Keith Hefner. We'd been instructed to bring a bathing suit to the interview, so about 200 of us slouched around for hours in our bathing suits, waiting to be called. A few weeks later, I got a call back for another interview, and after more 'cross-examination,' Keith jumped up, threw up his arms, and yelled, 'So you really want to be a Bunny?' I yelled back enthusiastically, 'YES, YES, YES!'

"When they'd finally picked 125 of us, we met and were handed a forty-page Bunny Manual to memorize and told to familiarize ourselves with club rules. We had to learn to take drink orders, organize our serving trays so the bartenders could be speedy, and—hardest of all, since most of us were clueless—learn the names of all the liquor brands and ingredients in a variety of cocktails offered by the club. Up until that point, the only drink I knew was Cherry-Herring on the rocks.

"We had to go through two full weeks of intensive training, where we learned how to deal with club members and how to do the perfect 'Bunny Dip,' an exaggerated way to arch our backs and bend over backwards while serving drinks. I still sometimes re-enact this for my friends!

"The club was overly meticulous in our training. There was a rule for everything, including emptying Playboy logo ash trays by putting a clean ash tray over the dirty one, removing it from the table to our tray, then returning the clean one to the table. Its weird looking back to when everyplace allowed smoking, but with all these rules and regulations, we became excellent waitresses. Maybe that doesn't sound like something to aspire to, but we were young, in the limelight, and having fun—no matter how much our feet hurt from eight-hour shifts in three-and-a-half-inch heels, and no matter how numb our legs got from the tight Bunny costumes with all the stiff metal stays.

"Depending on how well we did in the two-week training session, we were assigned to different positions: Door Bunny, Table Bunny, Gift Shop Bunny, Camera Bunny, or Cigarette Bunny. The Cigarette Bunny had a tray holding cigars and cigarettes strapped around her neck, just like in one of those nightclub scenes in *The Thin Man* movies! Of course, everyone wanted to be a Table or Serving Bunny, as that's where the money was.

"Bunnies worked for minimum wage (about $6 an hour), and we had to contribute a certain sum daily to the busboys and bartenders. But on a good day, we raked in from $60 to $200 a day in tips… mostly cash that we stored in the bra area of our costumes… so needless to say our busts got bigger toward the end of our shift. Some of us stuffed our costumes with dry cleaning bags and gym socks to enhance our cleavage, until Playboy created 'push-up' foam pads that made even the flattest of us look like Kate Upton.

"Opening night of the New York Playboy Club was like the grandest theater opening, with limousines, Rolls Royces, and klieg lights on 59th Street and Fifth Avenue. A line of members holding up their Playboy Club keys stretched around the block, and a special 'no-wait' line was created for VIPs, celebrities, and press. All five floors of the New York Club were buzzing with excitement. 'Please don't touch the Bunnies, sir' was all you heard throughout the evening.

"All of us were made-up and coiffed in our sorbet- and jewel-colored satin costumes. We were the stars that all these people were coming to see. It was a real non-drug-related high!

"I was assigned as a Table Bunny to the second-floor Living Room area where I had a good view of the Door Bunny, China Lee, who later married Mort Sahl. She was in one of the few black-satin costumes reserved for former Playmates or Door Bunnies. I could also see the Kai Winding trio at the piano bar and people going upstairs to the Playroom or the Penthouse.

"The third floor was the VIP Room, mainly staffed by very exotic foreign Bunnies rather than us 'all-American' girls. That room also offered gourmet dining and a more diverse menu than the Playmate Bar, Living Room, or showrooms. All the food was handled by the busboys, by the way. The Bunnies were above slinging food and clearing tables—thank God!

"After I celebrated my twenty-first birthday, I was allowed to work the night shift. The executives were vigilant about maintaining all the rules, including not allowing underage girls on the floor after 7:30 PM or dating customers. Dating customers was a fireable offense! Playboy had to protect their valuable liquor and cabaret licenses, so they were super careful about how we behaved.

"At one point, Hef hired these guys from the Wilmark Detective Agency to pose as keyholders and flirt with us and try to get us to meet them—so we were always on our guard, never knowing who was a Wilmark guy or who was just one of the members. Bunnies were very much in demand and the velvet rope to every club in town was opened to us without a wait, and on any given night, there were limos parked outside the club to take us to Playboy Exec. V.P. Victor Lownes's penthouse at the St. Moritz Hotel on Central Park West for parties attended by his cronies.

"I made a huge mistake of attending a party at Victor Lownes's penthouse at the St. Moritz one night and walked into a virtual orgy of the older 'night-shift' Bunnies and real playboys. I drank a little too much and stood at the bar, talking to a young lawyer—I remember he went to Dartmouth—about everything but what was going on around us. Then, all of a sudden, I leaned over the bar and threw up in the sink! The lawyer was so sweet—he took me to my apartment, which I shared with two other Bunnies, tucked me in bed, and left."

Perhaps because Elaine was the epitome of the American dream girl and spoke with a proper Midwestern accent, she was chosen to be a Bunny spokesperson. She gave interviews and went on a number of TV shows and radio call-in shows where listeners got to talk to a Bunny.

"I was personally coached by Hef," Elaine told us. "He schooled me on how to answer certain questions and what topics to avoid. I would always try to diffuse things with humor.

"Once, Hef asked me to attend a court hearing with him about Playboy's cabaret license. The judge wanted to inspect the Bunny costume to make sure it didn't fall outside of the city's moral code. Of course, prior to the hearing, I was fitted into a new, more modest lavender satin costume, and you can bet I didn't stuff it with gym socks or dry cleaner bags!"

Elaine made appearances on Johnny Carson's, David Frost's, and David Susskind's shows, as well as others, to promote the merits and mystique of the Playboy Clubs. Typically, she wore the Playboy promotional costume, which consisted of a white pleated mini-skirt and black turtleneck with the Playboy Bunny logo on the front... and of course those three-and-a-half-inch heels. "We looked like cheerleaders in those outfits," said Elaine.

"When Playboy was finally granted the cabaret license, we started to fill the showrooms with more than just music. We had popular singers and comics every night. Paul Anka and Rich Little were early performers; so was Tony Bennett. Everyone loved Tony. If he wasn't performing, he still came to see the shows or just hang out into the wee hours. He brought lots of other famous people with him, including Lena Horn, Ella Fitzgerald, Tony Curtis, Dean Martin, Eddie Fisher, Frank Sinatra, Sammy Davis Jr., Steve Lawrence and Eydie Gorme; even Elizabeth Taylor stopped in.

"Don Rickles used to make cracks at us from the stage; not *mean* ones, but funny things, as part of his act. This was New York; we were the hottest club in the city, so it attracted a lot of celebrities and recognizable faces. Anyone who was anyone came to party there.

"But being a glorified waitress in a screaming-tight outfit and high heels was hard work, so when 3:00 AM came and we turned in our Bunny ears, we were exhausted and only wanted to sit down someplace quiet with some scrambled eggs and a bagel before heading home to bed. Most of us frequented a 24/7 eatery called Sixties East just a short walk from the club, where we were usually left alone. One night, about eight of us were sitting at a table quietly chatting about the evening, when Frank Sinatra and his Vegas friend Jilly Rizzo and his wife sat down in a booth on the other side of the room. They were all drunk and got very loud, throwing comments our way. They tried to buy us drinks, said they knew we were Bunnies—but we all just ignored them. We were too tired and could not have cared less about a very drunk Frank Sinatra. Well, he and Jilly started lighting lady-finger fire crackers and tossing them toward us, but we still ignored them. Then, Sinatra got up and came toward our table and threw a lighted cherry-bomb under it! It went off with a loud bang, burning the legs of the girls sitting nearest to where he threw it. Luckily, I was on the far side, so I wasn't burned.

"Some of the girls couldn't work because they had open sores on their legs. When Hef found out what had happened, Playboy sued on behalf of the girls, and Sinatra and Jilly settled very quickly. The girls got a few thousand dollars apiece, which helped compensate for the lost wages. It wasn't a comfortable position for Playboy to be in—suing Sinatra—but they went the distance for us."

All these years later, Elaine remembers playing second base on the Bunnies softball team in Central Park. "Our team was part of the Broadway Show League—all the summer Broadway actors played on teams against each other, and the Bunnies always won! We were very athletic, with particularly strong arms from balancing heavy trays loaded down with drinks. So we could really whack those balls. Plus, we had a star pitcher in China Lee, who pitched several no-hit games that summer.

"The games attracted huge crowds. One Tuesday, we were playing an exhibition game against the WMCA Good Guys, radio disc jockeys who promo'd the game on the air every day for weeks. So many people came out to watch that game that it became riotous. The mounted police were called in and had to hoist the Bunnies up on their horses to escort us out of the park. It was quite frightening until the boys in blue came to the rescue.

"Most men made the same remarks to their Bunny servers: 'I'll have… and my brother will have…' 'I'll give you $10 bucks for your tail…' My name was Teddy, .so they'd say, "I thought Teddy was a bear," and I'd answer, 'I'm almost bare!' About fifty percent of them asked for our phone numbers, or asked us out—but suffice it to say, we identified them as 'Chivas on the rocks,' or 'JB straight-up with a soda chaser'… we didn't even know their names. But there was one man none of us could forget: Giles Copeland. He had been married to one of the Billy Rose 'Long-Stemmed Roses' chorus girls, who had passed away after a long illness. Giles came in every day for a few months with a pocket full of $100 bills. The girls went crazy over him, as he would give $100 bills to whomever he had contact with. Even today, that's a lot of money, but in the '60s, it was a windfall. In a way, it was unfortunate, because it brought out the greed in many of the girls. They'd be tripping over themselves to light his cigarette or pull out his chair. Everyone wanted to take care of Mr. Copeland. I don't think he went out with any of us—he just seemed lonely and very generous, and loved beautiful women. He was known to ask a Bunny who served him lunch what she really wanted as a present. I know he sent at least one girl a mink coat—right to the

Rock Hudson autographs the cuff of a New York Bunny on November 19, 1962 Donaldson CollectionMichael Ochs Archives Getty Images

club. It was all very innocent, though. He sent flowers to us on our birthdays and was just very sweet to all the girls."

When Elaine moved to California, she was often invited to events at the Los Angeles Playboy Mansion. Occasionally, she would go for Sunday Movie Night. On one such visit, she told me, she strolled through the gardens with Hef and Victor. "I liked both of them," she said. "They were creative, charming, and intelligent. Hef was a legend and Victor—still the naughty boy.

"As we entered the aviary, Hef said, 'So Teddy, how do you like the Mansion?' I said, 'It's the same scene it was thirty years ago. Lots of beautiful young twenty-something girls, but you guys were in your early thirties and now you're in your sixties! We had the best of you.' Then I told them, 'Gentlemen, I think I've outgrown this.' Victor looked at me and said, 'Teddy, you're no fun anymore!'"

As we wrapped up our talk, Elaine grew a little wistful. "Those were memorable days; there's nothing to compare it with today. Most of the Bunnies were young, ambitious, adventurous, pretty normal, wholesome girls. I didn't tell my family about my stint as a Bunny until years later. I was from a strong Catholic family and had five younger brothers. When they did find out about Playboy, my brother Ray said that had he known, he would have come to New York, thrown his coat over me, and dragged me home. We were really the first scantily clad waitresses to be accepted as mainstream. I've heard some of the girls claim, 'I was only a Bunny to work my way through college,' but I think that was just an excuse. Many of them made up excuses for why they decided to become Bunnies. As for me, I knew it was a valuable experience and I've retained a lot of good memories."

\* \* \*

Just prior to landing the engagement at the New York Playboy Club, Lily Tomlin was performing at a club called Upstairs at the Downstairs, in a chic cabaret revue directed and choreographed by

Sandra Devlin. The show portrayed the company as a tiny band of counterculture people who had broken into the showroom and taken over. The room was the size of a postage stamp, seating fewer than a hundred people.

As Lily explained, "The audience consisted of midtown New Yorkers who were used to going to this cabaret and seeing shows with songs that rhymed words with *Oedipus Rex* and the like, and instead, we'd come in and take over like guerillas. As part of the act, one of the guys in the revue set fire to his arm, and we swarmed him to put it out."

Apparently, nothing was off-limits or sacred with this bunch. Robert Kennedy had just been assassinated, and even he was worked into a skit.

"I would never have played the Playboy Club in those days," Lily went on. "I was too much of a feminist. But Sandy Devlin said, 'I got us a job. We're going to take our show to the Playboy Club.' I said, 'What? *This* show?' And she said, 'No, I'm putting together something new and it's going to be great.'"

There were no blazing arms in the Playboy revue, and although Lily had been reluctant to perform there, she went along out of her legendary sense of loyalty. And that's how Lily got her start at Playboy.

The show started with Lily out front, playing an all-around goofy hostess seating people, who had no idea they were part of the entertainment, as they came into the room. Then, as Bunny Lisa Aromi (whom you'll hear more from later in the chapter) told us, she'd clean tables, empty ashtrays, and engage in all manner of zaniness before the other performers hit the stage.

"There were four or five of us," Lily continued, "and we did monologues, sang songs, and carried on. Lyrics to certain songs were changed. There were a few songs where we altered the chorus. There was a litany of verses about *muff diving* and *beat your meat* that, in the songs, really wasn't as overt as it sounds. A song about a pig farmer had a twist—it was that sort of thing. We had to play to what we conceived the club was, right? I'm not saying everything was like that, but a good part of it was. And, of course, I threw my lot in with the rest. Once I go, I go all the way!

"I did a couple of monologues on my own and, as a result, got a big review from the New York newsman, Chauncey Howell. I did have fun. I lived in Yonkers at the time and had to catch the last train, so I would under-dress for the final number and leave right off the front of the stage and run for the exit to catch the train.

"What I loved most of all was eating in the kitchen with the Bunnies and the cook. The woman who cooked was sort of like everyone's mom, and all the Bunnies were there in their wrappers. We'd all sit around a huge table with oilcloth on it—it was a regular down-home kitchen and the exact opposite of what was going on in the showroom. I was hooking a rug at the time and I'd be at the table eating and hooking my rug and having a great time! Oh my God, I have very heavy memories of it—it was the antithesis of what I would have done, politically."

Like Victor and others, Lily loved the music of Mabel Mercer. Using almost the same words to describe her feelings as Victor had, she told us, "I was *mad* for her, and such a huge fan that we'd go to listen to her at the Bon Soir every chance we got. We went as a group and never had any money, but we'd scrounge up a quarter for the coat check. We could go without eating or drinking, but whatever boys we were with would have to check their coats. We'd just stand there and listen to Mabel. Joanie [Rivers] was getting famous and she had the room on weekends, and Mabel played there Monday, Tuesday, and Wednesday. When I was asked to open for Mabel, I was in seventh heaven! I'd drive down from Yonkers, pick her up in Harlem, and we'd go down to the club together. Heaven."

Lily was soon faced with choosing between two TV offers in Los Angeles—*Laugh-In* and *Music Scene*. "I chose *Music Scene*, because I was foolish enough to think that it was hipper, and—of course—we were canceled mid-season," said Lily. "Luckily, the offer for *Laugh-In* was still on the table. I went on in the third year, and as soon as my sketches with 'Ernestine' aired, I exploded. *She*—I should say—*she* exploded!"

* * *

So… why have we chosen to include some comedians—and an impressionist—in a book about music? Because, at the Playboy Clubs, they were inseparable. Comics tended to open for the musical acts and had an enormous impact on the mood of the crowd. Plus—as you can imagine—comedians told us the very best stories about those days. Here are a few more of them, all guaranteed 100 percent reliable. Or, at least as reliable as a comic can be.

John Regis grew up in Forsyth, Missouri, where the population was 292, and children from even smaller neighboring towns were sent there for school. His stepfather was a vaudevillian and taught him a standup routine that set him on the road to show biz.

Fast forward a little, and John found himself in the Air Force as a drill sergeant, trying, through humor, to get the recruits to *want* to do what he wanted them to do, without—as John put it—"having to beat them over the head with it."

"One day, a certain Sergeant Gavin asked me to take over Special Services, because the commanding general was upset about the AWOL rate. I said, 'What do you suppose I can do about it?' He said, 'That's up to you—just do it!' Special Services was supposed to entertain the troops and keep morale high, while giving the talented guys something to do. But they weren't doing anything. No shows, no nothing.

"Before you know it, I was the director of entertainment and we started having talent shows. For the finals, we borrowed a local schoolhouse auditorium because a lot of civilians wanted to come. The contestants could rack up points—twenty-five for this, twenty-five for that—in four different areas: material, costume, presentation, and cleanliness.

"I really pulled off a coup when I got Dan Dailey to act as one of the judges. Frank Gorshin was in the service at the time, and he was one of the contenders. That's where his great career as an impressionist started. Dan gave Frank a one-hundredpercent ranking. No one else had ever gotten a perfect score. On the score card he wrote, 'I'd love to have ten percent of this guy.' When I told Dan that Frank was being discharged in two weeks, he agreed to help him get started in Hollywood. He gave me his card, with his agency number on the back, and I gave it to Frank, and he was on his way.

"Jerry Van Dyke was also at Lowes with me, and he was a pain in the ass ,but a friend. So that's how I met Jerry and Frank. Sadly, we've lost Frank, but I see Jerry all the time, and we *all* entertained at the Playboy Clubs!

"Lenny Bruce, Sally Marr [his mother], Frankie Raye, and Jackie Gayle were also all real tight friends of mine. Jackie was the star of the Playboy Clubs and like a brother. We even shared a house for five years. I was performing at the Body Shop, a high-class strip joint in Los Angeles, and Jackie heard me, and we connected and became very close.

"Well, I hit a bad stretch where I had to quit show business, which is unpredictable," he told us. "My mother was sick and needed help, so I got a steady job selling cars. I hated it. So Jackie called the booker at the Playboy Clubs, Billy Rizzo, and said, 'Give John Regis some work.' Jackie knew that, if I did a good job there, I could work Playboy on a regular basis. Billy said, 'Who's John Regis?' which was a perfectly natural reaction. Jackie said, 'Look, I'll tell you what. Give him six weeks—two weeks at three different clubs—and give him some decent money. If he doesn't cut it, I'll come in and finish the job for what you're paying him!'

"Jackie was making $1,500 a week then, so he was really being a pal. Billy called me and said, 'John, I hear you're doing well, and we'd like to have you come over and work here,' like he hadn't heard from Jackie."

John was slotted to work the clubs in Baltimore, Kansas City, and finally Boston. He made them laugh in Baltimore and got good reports—but Kansas City was a disaster. "Al Frazier, a very gifted black singer, opened for me there," remembered John. "The night started out badly, with only six people in the audience because Dwight Eisenhower was being buried, and the funeral procession was going right through Kansas City. Then, while Al was singing, a woman pulled out a cigarette. He went in his pocket, came out with a lighter, and leaned over to light it for her—and she slapped it out of his hand! 'Okay,' he said, 'All right. That's it. Good night.' And he walked off the stage.... And then came, 'Here's the comedy star of our show, John Regis!'

"Of course, I *bombed*. It was a nightmare—one that probably wouldn't have mattered if the manager hadn't been there to see it. Al Frazier was an old timer, been around a long time with Playboy, but I hadn't. The manager wrote a scathing letter to Billy Rizzo and all the other managers on the circuit saying, 'This is the worst act I've ever seen. Don't book him.' After the show, I went down to Al's dressing room and said, 'Al, I can't follow that. You can't do that to me.' He apologized saying, 'You're right, man, I was wrong, but you saw what happened.... We have to deal with these things sometimes.'

"I killed in the second show, but the manager wasn't there to see it. Later, I get a call from Billy Rizzo. I explained what had happened, but he said, 'Man, you really got the wrong manager. He sent a letter to everyone on the circuit. I'll try to get you some other gigs, but as of now, after you do Boston, it's over.'

"In Boston, I was supposed to open for this Spanish guitar player and singer that they were really hot for, but at the last minute, they couldn't get the visas for him. Instead, they brought in an act from New York and decided I should close the show. Either way was fine with me. After the first show, which went very well, the manager came and asked me about Kansas City. I told him the story and he showed me the famous letter. It said, 'Don't ever book this guy. He's the worst.' So the Boston manager wrote his own letter that said, 'Not only is he not the worst guy I've ever seen, he's one of the best, and he can work for me anytime.' He was a very nice man—and I liked that club, though it was supposedly owned by the mob.

"Sally Marr was one of the funniest human beings I ever knew. She was incredibly comical, just off the top of her head. She did some standup under her real name, Sadie Kitchenburg. She didn't know how to handle an audience, but she was funny—at least to Lenny, Jackie, and me. Sally had carte blanche at the Playboy Mansion, and she was my favorite date. She knew everyone in the business. We had an arrangement that if I 'got lucky,' she'd take a cab home.

"After that crazy trial by fire, I worked the circuit forty weeks a year for seven and a half years. It was like going to college for comedy!"

* * *

Howard Beder spent the first nine years of his Playboy career as a singer before segueing into comedy for his final year in the trenches.

"I never thought I knew it all," he told us. "I took advice whenever it presented itself. The entertainment community is tremendously encouraging to young talent—you just have to be smart enough to listen. I was the lead singer in a group called the Mello Mates—two guys and a girl. We were performing down in Greenwich Village when Sammy Davis Jr. came in. He liked us and took us on the road with him.

"Our first engagement with Sammy was at a place in Buffalo, and after the show ended one night, he said to me, 'Don't leave right away.' As soon as everyone had cleared out, he took me back up on stage and worked with me for thirty or forty minutes. He really helped me hone my skills. For instance, he said, 'You're blocking your face with your hands. The people on the wing side can't even see you. Maybe you should do this...' He was very, very kind to me and became my friend and mentor till the end."

Frank Sinatra also felt compelled to cheer Howard on, going as far as complimenting him on stage. "I was singing solo at a supper club in Florida," said Howard, "After three or four songs, Mr. Sinatra walked on stage, took the microphone from me, and said to the audience—as a joke, I'm sure—'If my kid could sing like this guy, I'd be the happiest guy in the world.' *And it gets better*—he invited me to his table after I finished! So I went over to thank him, and audience members circled his table to hear what he had to say to me. 'You know, you have great breathing,' he said and went on to comment on a few other technical aspects of my performance. Then he asked me how I liked show business. I said, 'It's good—even at the bottom.' He couldn't believe it. 'The bottom?' he said. 'You're at the Fontainebleau, in Miami; this is one of the top places to work in America!' I said, 'Well Mr. Sinatra, on payday, you take my check and I'll take yours. We'll see who's at the bottom.' He liked that. He had parties every night in a private room, and he told his bodyguards, 'Howard is welcome anytime he wants to come. Just let him in.' So, every night during that engagement, I went to a party. Wouldn't you?

"During the mid '60s, I had a hit record called *Tumbling Tumbleweeds*. It had originally been recorded by the Sons of the Pioneers, but I had a great arranger put a rock beat behind it. It hit the *Billboard* charts in 1965 and I went around promoting it, which was a little tough because the payola scandal had made everyone afraid to push a new artist.

"After that, I was working in Winnipeg and I wanted to get on the Playboy circuit. My agent did a lot of the booking for the Chicago Club, so he got me a date there. I took a Greyhound bus from Winnipeg to New York, and then on to Chicago.

"The first night, I was waiting my turn to go on after another singer and a comedian. That was the typical lineup in those days.

They were not doing well with the audience. A bunch of wise guys were yelling things. So when I was introduced, I came from the back of the showroom and shook hands with people and talked a little to them as I walked towards the stage. I felt I had put them at ease, so I told them to calm down, quiet down—which they did. I got up on stage and my act went great. That's how they started to use me. That was how I got onto the circuit.

"When I was starting out, Larry Storch, the great comedian, told me, 'If you're on stage and your material isn't going like you want—if you're not getting the reaction you expect—*do not* let the audience know it's bothering you. They're like sharks smelling blood in the water, and they will deliberately climb up on you just to see you sweat!'"

Howard was booked as a singer but he was also a good writer, and very funny. At the Playboy Clubs, he was paired with a comedian and, as was typical, they hung out together—sometimes for breakfast, lunch, and dinner. Howard would write down snippets of their chit-chat and other things that came to mind during the day, and in the evening, he'd hand his notes to the comedian.

"It was just stuff we'd say at the table, but it was amusing and the comics sometimes put it in their acts. They all told me the same thing: 'What the hell are you doing singing? *Do you have any idea how funny you are?*'"

Eventually, Howard did add comedy writing to his résumé, providing material for many of the recording comedians in addition to writing a television script for Walter Matthau.

"I used to open for Flip Wilson at the Playboy Clubs," he told us, "before he was famous. And we became very good friends. In fact, he would stay up late working on material and I'd keep him company. Flip told me, 'Oh my God, you have such a comic mind that you've given me a million good ideas without even trying.' I remember saying, 'Thanks, but what are you talking about?' I didn't realize what I'd said.

"Playboy was my life for ten years, so I made many close friends there—including Pat Morita. We were on the road together a lot. I have to digress a minute here and explain that, when I was very young, I used to play cards really well; I had an incredibly good memory. Sometimes, I'd even be set up by backers, who'd stake me and then we'd split the money. Back to the story. One day, Pat Morita told me that he was a gin rummy player, and suggested we play for a quarter a point. After the first night, I realized that he didn't have a clue. He couldn't even shuffle—he was showing me the bottom card every time!

"So, the next night, I came in and gave him a letter, and I said to him, 'Do me a favor. Don't open this until the end of our engagement.' So he put it in his room and forgot about it. By the end of the run, he owed me hundreds and hundreds of dollars. *He was really bad at cards*! He said to me, 'I'll have to pay you over time... my wife... I have two kids....' I said, 'Remember, I gave you a letter? Read the letter.' So he went and got it and opened it, and in the letter, I said, 'Pat, you are the worst gin rummy player I have ever run into. I would not take your money. It would be stealing. You are terrible.' It's the truth!

"I met George Carlin down in New Orleans. The first time he opened for me, he was still part of Burns and Carlin. All the acts stayed in the same hotel and we'd eat our meals together, so we all became very friendly. George's wife even became good friends with my wife. George could do voices well, and once, he called me, got my answering machine, and pretended to be Victor Lownes: 'Hey, Howard, this is Victor. We have a new policy now. We're going to do at least four shows a day, maybe five. And you'll have to work Sundays, and you're going to work all the lounges....' He went on for a while, and then, in his own voice, he said, 'Hey, this is George Carlin, how ya doing?' I still have that recording. I'll play it for you sometime. He was a very nice man.

"New Orleans was the best and the worst Playboy Club. It was above a famous restaurant, Moran's, and a few doors down from Felix's Oyster Bar. Across the street was the Acme Bar, which supposedly had the best oysters in New Orleans. I'm a big oyster guy, so I was in heaven. They had the best seafood down there.

"As I said, I worked at Playboy for ten years—nine as a singer. We all hung around the mansion, and every comic used to tell Hefner how I'd helped him with his material. I was really a comic all along, masquerading as a singer. So one day, I was at the airport and I got a page. It was the director of entertainment at Playboy, and he said, 'Look, you have to go to Cincinnati right away. Their comic got sick, and he can't go on.' And I said, 'This is Howard Beder. I'm the singer.' He said, 'Listen to me. Hefner says every comic you ever worked with tells him how you could be a comedian. He said to give you one year as a comedian with a free pass—no matter what the room manager's report says, you're okay. So go be a comedian, but go to Cincinnati now!'

"Hef did that for me. I had a guaranteed job at Playboy for a year to work on comedic timing and audience reaction and important things like that. It was a gift—but once in a while, it didn't go so well. One time, I was on stage and a man with a portable iron lung decided to sit ringside. They ran his electrical cord in between my legs, across the stage, to the outlet at the far end. The lung was going 'whoosh, whoosh, whoosh,' and no one was laughing at the jokes because they were so disturbed by it. So I stopped and said, 'Sir, one of us is going to die here. It better not be me.' And I reached down and acted as if I was going to put the plug out... and the place went nuts! They started screaming with laughter. The nurse had to hold the poor guy down because she thought he might have an attack—he was laughing harder than anyone else.

"Another time, I did a show where everyone was deaf and mute—I'm not kidding! So they put a lady on stage to sign my act for them. No one was laughing, so after five minutes, I stopped the show, walked over to her, and said, 'Please sign exactly what I say.

Please tell them I don't think your fingers are funny!' She signed that to the audience and they roared with laughter."

Howard worked at all the Playboy Clubs, including the ones in London and Jamaica. "Hefner was fantastic," Howard said. "Every year, he would tell them to book me for a month at the Jamaica Club during my children's Easter break. My family came down for a good portion of the time and we'd have two suites on the ocean! I was one of the highest-ranking acts during all those years, both as a singer and a comedian, and I'm very appreciative for all they did for me. It was a great job.

"Playboy put out a monthly magazine, *The VIP*, and they had caricatures of different entertainers. Naturally, I have the issue with my caricature in it. I'm standing with Gabe Kaplan, Mickey Sharp, Bobby Sargent, Bobby Wig, Allen Kent.... These are great Playboy names—real Playboy people."

\* \* \*

We wanted to hear more about the inner workings of the clubs from the point of view of the girls who worked in them, so I looked a few of them up. Lisa Aromi worked in the New York Club from 1963 to 1974, and offered to give us a Bunny's-eye view of life there at the time.

"First of all," said Lisa, "we were the first club to stay open until four in the morning. I remember going up in the elevator, and this old-time burlesque comedian, Joey Faye, got in on his way to perform in the Penthouse and said, 'This is like a theatrical concentration camp! Three shows a night!'

"The singer Damita Jo opened the Penthouse. The Penthouse really had wonderful revues; you'd see Patti LaBelle, Chubby Checker, and others, all in one show. The Kai Winding Quartet played every night and Kai was the club's musical director.

"One of the first entertainers to play the club was Peter Allen, who was married to Liza Minnelli at the time. He had an act with another young guy and they called themselves Chris and Peter Allen, as if they were brothers—but they weren't. Well, Liza was appearing at the Persian Room in the Plaza across the street, and she would come over when she finished her show. Peter would be on stage at that point, so she'd wave a white handkerchief in the dark so he'd see she was there. They were both so young and seemed almost shy. He was really a great entertainer. Peter and Chris sang together and did some ad-libbing, very conservatively dressed in suits and ties. This was a far cry from the image Peter developed later on, when he was this great big star, wearing Hawaiian shirts and jumping around.

"Flip Wilson was very quiet and nervous and just sat at one of the tables after he got off stage. Once, I went over to see if he wanted something to drink, and he told me, 'I'm waiting for some people from *The Tonight Show*, to find out what they thought of my act and if they want to book me.' He was very jittery until they came in, and of course, the rest is history."

The Playroom operated differently. For one thing, it was available to rent for catered events. In 1968, Roman Polanski held an opening-night party there for *Rosemary's Baby*. The cast and crew, as well as local luminaries and show-business movers and groovers, were in attendance. Lisa recalled happening upon the eccentric actress Hermione Gingold as she was exiting Polanski's party. Hermione peered into the main showroom, shook her head, and mumbled to Andy Warhol, "Tacky, tacky, tacky."

When Lisa was done reminiscing about the memorable performers from those days, she turned to the subject of the Bunnies. "Keith Hefner was the director of training for all the girls. We had to learn so much: how to carry the drinks, the famous 'Bunny Dip,' how to walk, how to converse. But Keith was wonderful. He really wanted us all to succeed."

Lisa chalks up some of her good fortune to timing. "When I went for my first interview with the Bunny mother, Keith happened to be there. I had done some modeling and had my portfolio with me, and he asked me to try a Bunny costume on. He okayed it, and I was hired. He was just wonderful. I was very young and shy and nervous. I really needed the job because I wasn't married and had a child to support. Keith was so encouraging to me and everyone.

"We had to memorize all the liquors, drinks, and garnishes they sold at the club, and we were tested on them. The only drink I had ever had in my entire life was a brandy alexander, and that was when someone took me to see Katrina Valenti at the Persian Room. I didn't know what to drink, so my date suggested that a brandy alexander was a nice drink for young ladies. Needless to say, I didn't pass Playboy's drink test at first, but Keith made a game out of it to help me learn. He took me to the employee lounge and quizzed me about the garnishes. He'd ask, 'Does a cherry go with this drink or an olive?' There was a drink called a Cuba libre, and he'd say, 'Now what is that?' I knew it was rum and coke, but I was also supposed to remember the lime, because the garnish was important. We also had to know how to pronounce the liquors. We had to basically know everything, every detail, which is something I find lacking in restaurant services now.

"With Keith's help, I passed the test. He helped all the girls, and our training made the club that much better.

"There was also a system of merits and demerits. If we were late or did something wrong or showed up to work looking messy, we'd get demerits and couldn't go out on the floor until we'd pulled ourselves together. We had to pass inspection every day; our nails and makeup had to be perfect, our stockings straight, our shoes perfectly polished. I lived in Brooklyn, so between commuting and taking care of my daughter, sometimes I'd be late for work. But we could volunteer for different jobs and earn merits to offset the demerits—I volunteered to announce the acts in the showroom."

To this interviewer, that sounded like a prize job.

"I know," said Lisa, "but I was nervous about it. I thought it would be a good way for me to build up my confidence, and it worked. The more I did it, the better I felt. It also enhanced my tips, because the people who were at my tables would say, 'Oh, that's our Bunny announcing the show.'

"If you had more merits than demerits, you could actually cash them in for money. There was a hat in a store on 57$^{th}$ Street—just this fun, turn-of-the-century straw hat with roses—that I'd been eyeing for a while. It was thirty-five dollars, which was a lot of money to me at the time. Then it hit me. I had one hundred merits, which was equal to about thirty-five dollars. I could get that hat! I still have it. It's pretty dilapidated, but I can't bring myself to throw it away.

"My parents were big fans of Professor Irwin Corey, and when I told them he was scheduled to appear, they couldn't wait to make reservations. My father loved to sing, and was also a come-

New York Bunny Lisa Aromi. Courtesy Lisa Aromi

dian of sorts, so when the Professor came over to their table and started kibitzing with them, Dad was in heaven. Mr. Corey said to me, 'You make sure they don't pay for this. I can sign for it.' And he did. He was so funny. He'd call the Camera Bunnies, 'Bunny Snappy.'

"Sadly, I wasn't assigned to work the Party Room the night Woody Allen was there with his Dixieland Band. I'm a big fan. But I did ride in an elevator with him and his wife at the time, Louise Lasser. We exchanged a few words.

"Gerry Mulligan played in the Living Room with a jazz trio. At the time, he was dating Sandy Dennis, the actress, and she'd come and listen to him play.

"Cindy Adams came in one night with her husband Joey, to see Soupy Sales. That was a fun night, because I got to go on stage and introduce him. In her column, Cindy could sometimes be snippy and mean—but I remember that when her husband left the table to go talk to Soupy, she was concerned about keeping his coffee warm until he came back. She put the saucer over the cup as a cover. I only mention this because it made me see her in another light. I met her years later and told her that story, and she said, 'Thank you for telling me that. It means a lot to me.' Joey was apparently quite ill at the time.

"As Bunnies, we had to follow so many rules and regulations, but we liked it that way. The rules protected us. No one was allowed to touch us, and if someone tried, we'd call a room director who would step in and deal with it. The only time I had an incident was in the Playroom, when someone pulled off my tail. It happened to be a woman who did it. Looking back on it, it seems funny. I was serving drinks and she said, 'Bye Bunny,' and ripped the tail clean off my costume. The tray of drinks crashed to the floor—and on some patrons, I'm afraid—and I yelled, 'Stop that woman! She's got my tail!' People were yelling and pointing at her. She ran the whole length of the room before the room director stopped her. Then she looked at me and said, 'You lousy Bunny! I wanted this for my Halloween costume.' I told her I was sorry, that maybe they would sell her one, but that I had to turn mine in at the end of the night. It was part of my costume; I was responsible for that tail!

"The only other time I remember someone trying to steal anything was when a group of men took a huge painting of Frank Sinatra. It was by LeRoy Neiman, who did a lot of the paintings that were in the clubs. They took it right off the wall, put their overcoats over it, and tried to smuggle it out of the club. They were caught as they scrambled to get it out of the elevator. After that, Tony Roma, the manager, hung Frank in his upstairs office and had the rest of the paintings bolted to the walls.

"After work, I'd usually go straight home to Brooklyn and my daughter. The first time I went out after work was when a group of us went to a restaurant to celebrate someone's birthday. Carol Bongiovi [Jon "Bon Jovi," the rock star's, mother] was a Bunny, and she came out with us that night. She was married and lived in New Jersey, and her nickname was Bonji. As the two of us were leaving the restaurant, Frank was coming out of the back room and Bonji, who was a huge fan, said, 'Oh my God, we have to get his autograph! So we took doilies from the restaurant over to his limo to have him sign them.

"He was very nice to both of us, and Bonji was so excited! As we stood there *ooh*ing and *aah*ing over our autographs, a man got out of the limo and said, 'Frank would like to invite you girls back to the Waldorf; he's having a little get-together there.' Well, we just fell apart. Bonji said, 'Oh, no, I'm married… I have to go home… I live in New Jersey….' And I said, 'My daughter has school in the morning….' We were just babbling and probably sounded pretty silly. So we didn't go to the party—but it was sure fun being asked!

"The Bunnies did a lot of publicity for the club. Our uniform for those occasions was white pleated short skirts with pretty black tops that had the Playboy logo on them, and our bunny ears. We'd go to charity events, conventions, visit sick children, all manner of things. During the Vietnam War, we visited the soldiers and sailors in the hospitals. Once, we presented Sammy Davis Jr. with the Entertainer of the Year Award at the Astor Hotel. We even had a softball team, although I didn't get to play much. Once, when I did, a ball hit me right in the face. That was my last game.

"The ten years I worked there flew by. It was a wonderful job.

I made a nice salary that enabled me to support my daughter, saw great entertainers and musicians, and made lifelong friends. I was never able to take advantage of it, but many of my Bunny sisters went through college on Playboy scholarships."

\* \* \*

In 1968, after capturing the top prize in a talent show in the Catskills, twelve-year-old "little" Julie Budd astounded Merv Griffin's audience with her anything-but-pint-size voice. By the end of her song, they were on their feet in an ovation. She would appear forty more times on Merv's show. He guided and mentored her, and she went on to appear as a regular on virtually every variety show of that era, including *The Tonight Show*, *Entertainment Tonight*, *The Kraft Music Hall*, *The Jim Nabors Show*, *The Carol Burnett Show*, and *The Ed Sullivan Show*. The following year, she signed a recording contract with MGM and released her first album, *Child of Plenty*.

Julie smoothly made the transition from child prodigy to adult star and performed in all the top venues stateside and abroad, including Lincoln Center, Carnegie Hall, and London's Palladium, as well as multiple Las Vegas showrooms. We met up with her at the New York Friars Club, where she shared her Playboy stories over lunch.

Maybe it was because Julie was still a teenager when she first performed at the clubs that she received special treatment, such as a security detail to escort her to and from the showrooms. "The clubs were all about the allure of the good life," she began. "The major clubs looked expensive—when you walked in, you felt as if something was going to *happen*. A guy could walk into a club and imagine what it was like to be Hugh Hefner for a night, and Hef didn't want that illusion shattered by any of us messing with anybody from the audience. That's why I think he had someone to watch over me. My appearances, and everyone else's, were heavily advertised—my pictures were all over the place—and he didn't want any of the patrons to start something with me. You know, sometimes guys have too much to drink and they think they're something that they're not. So I always had security pick me up from my room and escort me to the dressing room and then the stage. If I wanted to walk around, I could, but someone always trailed behind. I never had any problems, but I believe that's because I always had my angels close by. If anyone caused problems, they were bounced out real fast. There weren't too many places that were that well run and thought out.

"In general, the Playboy publicity department was just fantastic. When you opened there, you were on every TV show and got the lead article in the show-biz section of every paper. They made sure you were covered—which was not the case everywhere. God, Playboy was incredible!

"They had wonderful musicians in all the clubs—really top notch. Herb Bernstein wasn't with Playboy, but he went on the road with me and played for me at almost all the clubs. Art Weiss, a great musician, played for me in New York.

"You've probably heard about the regulations the Bunnies had to follow. Well, the same—but not as stringent—went for the performers. The place was run very tightly and if your clothes didn't look right or if you didn't fit the image—maybe you had on too much makeup or not enough makeup, whatever—they advised you. They kept everything very classy. When a girl hit the stage to do the show, they wanted a little glamour.

"I always wanted to know what it felt like to put on the Bunny costume. I became friendly with one of the girls—this was at the Chicago Club—and I thought, wouldn't it be hilarious if I went out on stage with the costume on and did my show? In the end, I didn't have the nerve to do it, because I thought they'd fire me.

"This wasn't anyone's fault, but I did have one kind of bad experience. I was set to perform at the New York Club on a Saturday night, and we had full house. I did my first show and was just waiting around in my dressing room, getting ready for the second.

The shows were pretty close together, and the late show had already been pushed back an hour because of the crowds and the time it took to get the room cleared for the second seating. I was putting on my eye makeup, and all of a sudden, I looked in the mirror, and—I guess because of my allergies—my eye was all blown up! Out of nowhere. I looked like *the eye that ate New York*—really horrible. I tried to flush whatever was going on out with cold water. I put eye drops in. I did everything I could think of, but it just kept getting worse. Irvin Arthur, who did a lot of the bookings there, came backstage and almost fell over. *'What the hell happened to you?!'* he shrieked. Then the maître d' came in, took one look, and said, 'You can't go on stage like that.'

Alfred Hitchcock enjoying dinner at the New York Playboy Club.
Donaldson Collection Michael Ochs Archives Getty Images

"They had to take me to the hospital, the Manhattan Eye and Ear. This was about a half hour before curtain, and the audience was already starting to come in as I was being taken to the hospital in a taxi! When we got there, Irvin said to the nurse in charge, 'You have to take her right away. There are three hundred people waiting for her.'

"It was like a Marx Brothers movie—I was in my evening gown as they wheeled me right into the exam room, and the doctor irrigated my eye and put some goo in—I don't know exactly what, maybe an antibiotic or an antihistamine ointment. He told me that I couldn't put any makeup on that night, and then he said, 'You should wear a patch; I'm putting one on for you'! I said, *'Are you kidding me?'* I yelled, *'I gotta go out and do a show! I can't go on looking like Moshe Dayan!'* Then I looked at my watch and said, 'Goddammit, I should be on stage right now. Hurry up and finish irrigating my eye—and *no* patch.'

"Meanwhile, back at the club, they announced: 'Julie Budd fell ill but—don't go anywhere—she might be coming back! They said that even though they weren't sure if I'd make it. All they knew was that I was at the hospital.

"The nurses all tried to help me with my makeup, but I couldn't wear any on that one eye—which was awful. I was powdering my face, and the stuff was still dripping down. Everyone was trying to get me ready. We got back in a car and raced back to the club to my dressing room, so I could fix my hair Veronica Lake—style to hide the fact I couldn't make up my one eye. All of a sudden, I hear *knock, knock, knock*—the audience had all waited and they had heard I was back and okay, so they were banging their silverware on the table for me to get the show going.

"I went out and they cheered! They had waited! I was almost an hour late and no one had left. One o'clock in the morning, I started my show, and the audience was *wonderful,* the best crowd ever. We all had a good time over the whole incident. I'll never forget that.

"The doctors confirmed that I'd had an allergic reaction to whatever makeup I was using, or that maybe something had gotten into it. I had to throw away every mascara, powder, shadow, and liner I had.

"Things usually went smoothly, though, except for that one night. Entertaining at the Playboy Clubs made me more of an adult act in the eyes of the bookers, because it was a sophisticated club. And if they liked you, you played year after year after year."

\* \* \*

In 1966, pianist Art Weiss walked through the door of the New York Playboy Club. He was there to audition for a brief job as a sub for the then-house pianist. First, they hired him for what he was told was a two-week engagement. Sixteen years later, he was still playing there—and loving it. "I outlasted everyone!" Art proudly declares. "They swapped managers in and out, right and left. By 1982, I had made it through twenty-one general managers!

"I can't even tell you how many musicians and singers and other performers I worked with in that time. Initially, each show was an hour, including two singers separated by a comedian; the first singer would do twelve minutes, the comic would be on for a half hour, and then the second singer would take us to the end of the hour. That was four shows a week, for at least six nights a week—sometimes all seven, without a night off. The first thing working they did was to help me build up my chops as a musician—that's a lot of practice time! Then there was always a new act coming in that we had to rehearse. You can't imagine how busy the New York Club was in the late 1960s—and how glamorous. I played for Freda Payne, Marlena Shaw, Julie Budd, Donna Theodore, Blackstone the magician, and too many others to name over sixteen years. After I left the club, I traveled with Harry Blackstone for a while.

"There were two main full-time showrooms, the Playroom and the Penthouse, and a 'weekend' room. That's where I got to hear one of my piano heroes, the great Teddy Wilson, and his trio. Kai Winding, who was the first musical director for the club, led an all-star quintet in the Living Room in the early days. For a while there was also a VIP Room featuring a solo harpist. We were really jumping!

"In the 1960s, it was a big deal to be a Bunny! Today, they just seem like waitresses in sexy outfits, but there was a lot of competition for those jobs; they took their work very seriously. Word got out that some of the Bunnies were taking in a thousand dollars a week in tips, and that was huge fifty years ago. We weren't supposed to fraternize with the Bunnies, but, of course no one paid

Gregory Peck and singer Bobby Darin take a break away from all the excitement of the Motion Picture Pioneer Association dinner at the New York Playboy Club.
Donaldson CollectionMichael Ochs

any attention to that rule—least of all me! We were an after-hours 'joint' of course, so there was no place to go after we closed. There weren't many places to unwind that didn't involve Bunnies. I dated a Bunny named Shakira, and that turned out to be another long-term relationship—we moved in together, got married, and were together for twenty-five years.

"I rarely ever saw Victor Lownes or Hefner. Victor was living in London by then, and when he came through New York he would move through town pretty quickly. Likewise, Hef was in Chicago or later Los Angeles, I only remember him being in the New York Club less than half-a-dozen times. My most memorable encounter with Hef was kind of funny—although it didn't seem so at the time. I was dating Bunny Shakira, and she had a friend, an actress, who was dating Hef. Well, once they came into New York together, and Hef's girlfriend recognized me and started waving at me on the bandstand. Hef was not pleased! He could be very possessive!

"There were lots of stars who came through, to hang out as much as to work. Tony Bennett was there all the time—he loved the Playboy Club, he loved Hef, and he was very supportive of all the acts. Truly a great guy. Likewise Bill Cosby; he was very, very hot at the time, yet he worked for the clubs out of loyalty to Hef. We couldn't have afforded to pay him his usual rate!

"They kept giving me more and important titles. I started just as a pianist in the trio in 1966, and four years later I was officially musical director. Arylne Rothberg was initially booking the room, and she put me in charge of all the music. Eventually, I became entertainment director as well." When Arlyne left to produce *The Dick Cavett Show*, she recommended Irvin Arthur to fill her shoes.

How long did the good times last? "In the beginning, it was the hip, chic place to be, and brought in the high rollers, so to speak. But by the late 70s it was starting to decline," says Art. "Eventually there were fewer A-list celebrities, and more and more bachelor parties from the outer boroughs. I noticed that things were changing with the basic wardrobe of the women in the club, and I don't mean the Bunnies, I mean the paying customers! In the disco era, the girls were wearing bikini halter-tops and hot pants—the Bunnies were covered up rather conservatively by comparison. A lady named

Mosello, who worked in the lunch room, started a side-business going; she knitted custom hot-pants ensembles, and they were so popular that she couldn't turn them out fast enough.

"The times were changing. Downstairs, there was a little alcove—the floor was sort of shaped like a champagne glass. In the 1960s, we had a jazz quintet playing there. In the disco era, they put in a *Saturday Night Fever*-type layout—a glass floor, a mirrored ball, a deejay, the whole works. It was successful for a few years, but we couldn't compete with Studio 54, a few blocks away. To me, that just wasn't what Playboy was. Compared to what was going on on 54th Street, Playboy was like Disneyland.

"By the end things had changed; comedians still worked the circuit and toured the country, but we tried to save money by only hiring singers and musicians from the local area. Fortunately, this was New York, so that wasn't a problem, but you could see that things weren't the same.

"But when the clubs were at their peak, there was nothing like them. I realized that when I was on a two-week vacation, on the other side of the country. I was in the middle of the Muir Woods, near San Francisco, and a guy came up to me and said, 'Hey! I saw you at the Playboy Club, in New York!' There we were in the middle of California and someone recognized me. That made me realize how truly iconic those clubs were.

"I worked there for sixteen years and don't regret a moment of it. I played for some great stars, met some very wonderful friends, found a girlfriend and a wife. I wouldn't change any of it."

\* \* \*

Singer, comedian, and actress Dana Lorge told us that, by the time she'd started playing the Playboy Clubs, she already knew what she was doing. "Before that," she said, "I did all of these horrible jobs to learn how to work an audience with snappy comebacks. That's the way you learn. People talk to you from the audience, and they're not always complimenting you, so you become quick with the zingers.

"I played the Boston Playboy Club, and they had an open mic set up later in the evening, for comic wannabes, after the main shows were done. Well, I have to say, they were tough. I'm a singing comedian, and I'd be on stage and doing well with the regular audience—except for the kids in the back, who had their arms crossed. These were the ones who were waiting for the show to end so they could go on. But in the meantime, they were criticizing every move I made, saying things like, 'Oh my God, I can do so much better,' 'That's a horrible joke,' and on and on. I'd stay to watch them, and each one was worse than the next! One of them got up on stage and said, 'Good evening, ladies and gentlemen...' looked at the audience, said, 'Thank you,' and left the stage. I think he realized it wasn't as easy as it looked from the audience. That's the difference between amateurs and professionals. We all know what it takes to get up on a stage and deliver a show that's worth what the audience paid—and we *support* each other.

"Well, *mostly* we support each other. Once, I opened for Henny Youngman—this was just before I worked my first Playboy Club, but it illustrates how I segued from straight singing to comedy. I had a seven-piece band that didn't read music. We'd talk over everything in rehearsal, and it seemed as if it was all in order, but when I introduced a song, they'd play something else completely. I wouldn't know the song they were playing, plus, it would be in the wrong key. So I started joking around about the situation and telling funny stories, because I was determined that I wasn't going to mess up Henny's opening. Oops. It turned into a disaster, because Henny was furious. He called the agent and said never to hire me again. He was jealous that I was being funny when he was the comedian.

"The New York Playboy Club was wonderful. Art Weiss played piano, and I wore a gown that gave the illusion of being see-through, and the guys in the audience went crazy! I got a standing ovation—

February 9, 1964 Beatle John Lennon and his wife Cynthia stop by the New York Playboy Club after their whirlwind appearance on the Ed Sullivan Show.
Image by Michael Ochs Archives Corbis

just for walking onto the stage—before I said a word! Can you imagine? I thought, wow, they like me, and I didn't do anything yet!

"Great Gorge was a beautiful club—just dazzling. I played there shortly after it opened, and I was rehearsing, and Myron Cohen walked in with his wife. God was he great, and so gracious. He walked over to me and introduced himself and his wife and said, 'I'll be working with you, and I'm looking forward to it.' You don't hear that much, and I thought, 'Wow, what a gentleman.' He was also an elegant dresser. I worked with so many great people, but some really stand out in my mind, and he was one of them."

After Playboy, Dana continued to entertain and amuse crowds around the world, and today, she produces a variety show presented in New York nightclubs.

*  *  *

Julie Budd wasn't the only one who found the celebrated Bunny outfit irresistible. Fabulous Lorna Luft, singer and stage actress, remembers a day when she was just starting out that one of her girlfriends—who was a New York Bunny—called her. "We were just girl-talking, and she complained that she was sick, and that nobody could take her shift, on and on. Well, I had been to many of the clubs, including the New York one, and I really admired how the Bunny costumes made a girl look. They were like wonderfully engineered bathing suits made with really good taste—absolutely adorable and form-fitted to each girl. Nothing was going to fall out that wasn't supposed to fall out.

"I had waited tables before, so I thought, maybe I can make a few bucks and help my friend out! I got as far as the Bunny dressing room before someone saw me and said I couldn't be a Bunny just like that—that I had to be trained. It wasn't like filling in for another waitress! Apparently, you had to go through months of training, and I don't think a lot of people realize that. Those girls were really, really, tested.

*  *  *

In 1966, when Marlena Shaw first auditioned to perform at the New York Club, she wasn't yet a full-time professional singer. But when Pete Barbutti, the comedian who was then serving as entertainment director at the New York venue, heard her, she began her career in earnest. Shaw credits her uncle, trumpet player Jimmy Burgess, with inspiring her love of music.

"There was great music playing whenever he was around," she told us. "He introduced me to the recordings of all the wonderful musicians. I adored listening to Miles Davis and Dizzy Gillespie and just a ton of others. I never had any formal singing lessons but I always sang. Everywhere I went, I was singing."

Once, when Burgess was performing at the Apollo Theater in Harlem, he brought Marlena on stage with him. After that, she became passionate about building a career in music. Her mother had other ideas, and influenced her to pursue a more stable profession, so she registered at the Columbia University Teachers College.

Discovering quickly that teaching wasn't for her, Marlena dropped out of school, got married, and started a family—all the while harboring dreams of becoming a professional singer. Eventually, she found herself divorced with five children to support. She sang at neighborhood jazz clubs whenever she could find the work, but it was a struggle. In 1966, fate stepped in when she went to the New York Playboy Club to support two of her friends, who were auditioning there.

"I wanted to be there for my friends, who sang as a duo, and, as usual, I was singing. I sang before we left the house and in the cab on the way to the club. By the time the car pulled up to the door, I was singing at the top of my lungs. I remember there was a blond guy who smiled at us as he waited to grab our cab. After we composed ourselves, we went inside and waited. There were a lot of people auditioning so we had to hang around for a while.

"After everyone had sung their special pieces, the guy running the session said, 'Is there anyone else who wants to audition?' Just at that moment, through the door came the blond guy we'd seen waiting for our cab. He was Shelly Kasten, the talent director! Shelly said, 'I want to hear that girl over there,' and he pointed to me. So I sang a song—I forget which one—and within a very short time, I got a call to work at the Chicago Club.

"Within the first few days that I was there, someone who worked for Cadet Records came in, heard me, liked me, and signed me to a recording contract. While I was with Cadet, I did a cover of Ramsey Lewis's "Wade in the Water," and all these years later, I'm still getting royalty checks for it.

"Not long after that, I was back in New York, singing at the Playboy Club, and Al Gaines—who was with Count Basie's band and also a Playboy keyholder—came to the club, caught my show, and asked if I had any records with me. Of course I did, because I always carried some. I gave him one that he played for Basie, and a couple of days later, I received a call asking if I wanted to work with him in Las Vegas.

"We played the Sands Hotel—Basie on piano and me on the stage next to him! That was what my Playboy experience led to. I think I played at all the clubs they had. They kept opening new ones so I might have missed one or two. It was a very good period and I did great, even though I never had formal lessons or an agent."

\* \* \*

Marlena was just one of the many artists and entertainers whose careers were launched or revolutionized by exposure and experience at the Playboy Clubs. By 1966, there were fourteen clubs in the United States, employing over a thousand musicians and performers, Bunnies, and club personnel on a monthly basis.

What had begun as an idea in the fertile minds of Victor Lownes and Hugh Hefner had become a cultural revolution—and made them very wealthy in the process.

# 10

# WELCOME TO L.A.

"The United States has a new bunny—it's the Playboy Bunny!"

Ironically, Los Angeles was the last major city to get its own Playboy Club, the irony being that just about a decade later, Hollywood would become the center of the Playboy Empire. But in 1964, L.A. was just another stop on the circuit. As a center for live entertainment and nightlife, it has always lagged far behind New York, Chicago, New Orleans, Las Vegas—and even smaller cities such as Kansas City, Atlantic City, and Boston. But, perhaps because of its proximity to all those moviemakers, the Los Angeles Club had one thing that the earlier Playboy outposts did not: a film crew at its opening-night festivities. The resulting footage, which can be found easily on YouTube, is priceless as an artifact of that moment in time.

Personally, having spent the better part of two years talking to as many veterans of the Playboy organization as we could find, it was a delight to see what one of the most famous original Playboy Clubs—and some of the key members of the behind-the-scenes team—looked like "in the flesh." The footage, which ran on local

TV news on December 31, 1964, depicts a swanky affair that turned the opening into an A-list New Year's Eve party.

The biggest star present, by far, was Milton Berle, television's "Uncle Miltie," who can be seen getting his bow tie straightened by a very happy, sandy-haired Bunny. Hugh O'Brian, better known as television's Wyatt Earp, walked the carpet, as did Julie Newmar, years before she became Catwoman. Was her leopard-print a coincidence or a spooky foreshadowing? Don Murray, best known for playing Marilyn Monroe's leading man in the 1956 film *Bus Stop*, made the scene (now *there's* a *Playboy* connection); and Barbara Rush showed up, fresh from playing opposite Frank Sinatra, in *Come Blow Your Horn* and *Robin and the Seven Hoods*. Shirley Jones looked resplendent in white ermine.

Watching it today, it's fascinating to see such candid moments as an eager Bunny bopping up and down to the music in her little white heels (we can't help wondering who was playing). Keith Hefner took center stage in a sequence obviously filmed before the actual opening itself, putting the girls through a rigorous course of training that included a demonstration of the famous "Bunny Dip," and the proper method of emptying an ashtray. The Bunnies practiced their bartending skills, too, selecting the proper glass and garnish for each concoction while a few male attendants hovered about, dressed as if serving dinner at the White House.

We also get a tour of some of the rooms in the Los Angeles Club, including the Playroom and Penthouse. We learn, via a voiceover, that the hard-working Bunnies had to go up and down the stairs as many as a dozen times every hour and, though it was hard on their feet, the sight of them doing so was "easy on our eyes." We see one Bunny lighting a customer's cigar in front of a wall of LeRoy Neiman's drawings of his famous "Femlin"—that now-iconic little minx garbed in long boots, long gloves, and… there's no "and." We even catch a glimpse of an unidentified Neiman, who could never be mistaken for anyone else, thanks to his signature facial hair.

Near the end of the ten-minute featurette (broken into two parts on YouTube), the New Year's festivities reached a climax. Cost of admission per couple? A whopping $65! We can see the hands and instruments of the drummer and bassist, though not their faces, alas, followed by a rather amazing shot of three Bunnies dancing on top of the bar, in front of an appreciative crowd in tuxedos, gowns, and party hats.

What contemporary viewers probably take for granted is the degree to which the club was integrated. The patrons were all white, it's true, but a number of African-Americans can be seen working at the club, and at least one member of the band and one Bunny were black. Like it or not, the term bandied about in those days was "Chocolate Bunny." It's difficult to appreciate today, but the casual integration of the Los Angeles Club was groundbreaking.

Let's face it, it's hard to keep one's mind on politics when watching three beautiful girls in Bunny suits and high heels dance on top of a bar on New Year's Eve, clearly having the time of their lives along with the rest of the crowd. "Our cameras have visited countless openings and parties," says the unidentified narrator, "but this one looks like it's New Year's Eve every night."

* * *

Many Bunnies and other club veterans from Los Angeles and elsewhere fondly remember the original Neiman paintings that festooned the clubs. The famed artist's association with Playboy began well before the clubs—or even the magazine—were more than glimmers in Hef's imagination. The two men had become friends when both were working at the Carson Pirie Scott department store in Chicago, LeRoy as a fashion illustrator and Hef a copywriter. Some time after Hef left that job, they renewed their friendship when Hef asked LeRoy to provide some catchy illustrations for a new venture of his, not yet named *Playboy* magazine.

LeRoy loved the concept of the publication, accepted many assignments, and quickly secured the distinctive title of *Playboy*'s artist in residence. He was soon granted his own segment in the magazine, dubbed "Man at His Leisure," for which he visited and sketched various nightclubs around town. Over his long tenure, he provided the magazine with hundreds of memorable illustrations that, even now, hold the power to transport people of a certain age back to their younger days.

Dick Van Dyke admires the shapely assets of a California Bunny during a McCarthy Fund Raising dinner at the Los Angeles Playboy Club.
Ron GallelaRon Gallela CollectionGetty Images

"Femlins," erotically dreamed up by LeRoy in 1956 at Hef's request to spice up the "Party Jokes" page, are nearly nude, sprite-like creatures—inspired by the folklore of World War II pilots—whose name derives from a combination of *female* and *gremlin*. They have been popping up throughout the magazine ever since, and one pushy Femlin even made it onto the cover of the August 1960 issue. Faithful readers definitely believe in Femlins; one told us with great certainty that they weigh about five pounds and stand about six inches high—give or take an inch. *Imp* and *pixie* are words often used to describe the mini minx. The owner of the Carousel Club in Dallas appropriated their familiar—not to mention copyrighted—image for his business card in the early 1960s. His name was Jack Ruby, and he would go on to be universally remembered for a crime slightly more serious than trademark infringement.

At the height of the Playboy era, the distinctive Neiman paintings could be seen in clubs all over the world. Victor Lownes told us, "One of my most prized pieces of art is an oil painting that LeRoy did of me. Marilyn and I have it prominently displayed in our house in London."When we first opened the clubs," Victor continued, "LeRoy came and painted a great many pictures. He was an amazingly fast painter and would work on three or four large paintings at a time. He loved drawing the artists—the performers—and many times would sketch their images and then present the results to them. When I was opening the London Casino, he came over and sketched and painted so many wonderful pieces. As his popularity rose and the value of his work increased, we had to secure them to the walls. Many are worth millions today. Hef still has a lot of them that aren't on display to the public."

According to LeRoy's book *All Told*, just a year after the Miami Club opened, a five-by- four-foot oil painting of sunbathers was snatched from the VIP Room. Even though the culprits were swiftly spotted and a high-speed pursuit ensued, the painting was never recovered. For all anyone knows, it is still in the hands of a private admirer.

Another famous painter with Playboy connections was the Peruvian pin-up artist Alberto Vargas. In the early 1960s, Alberto was struggling to make ends meet when *Playboy* began to feature his work—soon known as "Vargas Girls." During his decades-long association with the magazine, Vargas produced monthly pinups, usually accompanied by witty captions chosen in a contest—with a $50 dollar prize—among the employees in the editorial department. Because of this exposure and backing, Vargas's career took flight, and he was soon showing his work at galleries worldwide. Today, he is widely regarded as the most famous "pin-up artist" of all time.

* * *

The Jamaican jazz pianist, Monty Alexander, became so popular in New York that the Playboy management asked him to help get their newest club off the ground. "They asked me to go to Los Angeles to work at the Playboy Club on Sunset, not long after it opened," Monty said. "So I was there for like two months. I worked with Ralph Peña, the bass player who had worked with Sinatra and later got killed in a car accident. I also got to know [pianist] Les McCann, who also played the club out there, and we became good friends. He was a real character—still is. Les recorded for Pacific Jazz Records, which was run by Dick Bock, who came in to hear me and eventually recorded my first album.

"Dick was a big, big man and he was the first guy I ever met who was into Eastern religion—and music, too. One night, he came into the club with Ravi Shankar. I had actually heard Shankar the weekend before, at Shelly's Manne Hole. It was a Sunday afternoon and this man came out with his sitar and bare feet, burning incense on the stage, and I said, 'What the hell is this?' Anyhow, Dick brought him into the Playboy Club! Believe me, it was somewhat incongruous to see him in the midst of the place, with the Bunnies walking around.

"In Jamaica, we have a strong connection with India since we were all part of the British Commonwealth. We all played cricket together—India, Jamaica, the West Indies—so I felt very comfortable, and I was talking to Ravi Shankar and I asked him, 'Do you like jazz, Ravi?' What a stupid question! He said, 'Oh, yes, I like jazz music.' He asked me, 'Do you know Mr. John Coltrane?' I said, 'I don't know him, but he's one of the great musicians.' He said, 'He comes to my house for lessons.' I had no idea that Coltrane studied Indian music with Ravi Shankar!"

* * *

Pat Lacey (who likes to be known as Lacey) has worked with the Playboy organization most of her adult life. She started as a Bunny in 1965 at the Los Angeles Club, then transitioned to Bunny Mother, working in that position until the club closed in 1986. Eventually, Lacey parlayed her Playboy experience into a career in promotions at Playboy headquarters. She still works in the Playmate Promotions department.

"The club opened New Year's Eve, 1964," Lacey told us, "and, as soon as I was old enough—which was March 1965—I applied to be a Bunny. The training and experiences were something that, as a young woman from South Central Los Angeles, I didn't even know existed! The L.A. Club had a VIP Room where you could order a fabulous five-course, gourmet meal. But in the showroom, where I worked, there was a limited menu consisting of a fillet, a New York steak, Chicken Kiev, or trout—and they all came with the same sides—French fries and a little baked apple.

"Starting out, I didn't even know the difference between a fillet and a New York steak—Chicken Kiev was certainly nothing I had ever tasted prior to walking in there—but I sure liked it once I tried it! That's the kind of door that Playboy opened for me. The entertainment was the thing—and not the food—in that room, but the steaks were so good. They were flown in from someplace in Chicago.

"They didn't just put the Bunnies out on the floor—we went through a very involved training program. We were never given anything to do that hadn't been thoroughly researched and thought out. Everything had a purpose; the questions had all been asked: 'How are we going to entertain our keyholders?' 'How are we going to make them comfortable?' 'How are we going to make them laugh?' 'How are we going to keep the customers and Bunnies from getting too friendly?' Someone made the decision to have in-house trios perform. A concern at a lot of the clubs was whether the musicians coming in were any good. Having a trio of local talent made the management feel comfortable that they'd have really good musicians available for each room.

"I love tooting Playboy's horn, because there wasn't anything that wasn't done with care, clarity, and, yes, practical sense. You already know about the training that we got in identifying drinks and garnishes, and all the rules laid out in the Bunny manual—but do you know why we wore our nametags on our hip? The Bunny costume included a small, very pretty ribbon rosette with our first name on it, and we wore it on our hip, because that was eye-level for the customers. People sitting down to dinner didn't have to look up to see our names! So simple, but brilliant.

"Did you ever wonder why it was that Bunnies didn't wear any jewelry other than their cufflinks? Well, jewelry tells a story, and Mr. Hefner wanted the Bunnies to have some mystique. What if one girl wore diamond earrings and another had dangling Christmas trees? That would give clues to our personalities. What if one wore a wedding or engagement ring? Then, when we walked up to a table, everyone would be reading us—the mystery would be gone! That's also one of the reasons we never told our last names.

"The whole Playboy Club atmosphere was sold as a package, but the business model was straightforward and uncomplicated: to cater to the businessman's fantasies with pretty girls, good food and drink, and great entertainment.

"As a Bunny in the showroom, I got to enjoy all the great entertainment. The jazz was cool—Les McCann was big in those days, and there was Ray Brown, Roy McCurdy, Thelma Houston, the Cannonball Adderley Jazz Trio, Sammy Shore, and Rodney Dangerfield. I remember Freda Payne singing 'Band of Gold' while she was pregnant. Esther Phillips, who was very big in the jazz community, played that club. She wasn't the prettiest woman in the world, but every night, she was made up immaculately. She was a tiny little woman but had style that went beyond style, and on stage, she had such a fabulously distinctive voice. As a young woman, I learned a lot from her.

"Johnny Carson came in a few times to catch Rodney, and Bob Hope would frequent the Sunset Club for dinner and a show. So not all of the celebrities were on stage—they were in the audience, too. I made so much money off Irwin Corey, Lainie Kazan, Jackie Gayle, and a few others, because they packed the house every time they were there—and that meant a lot of extra tips!

"Whenever I run into Pauly Shore, I tease him by saying, 'Your Dad [Sammy Shore] made me a lot of money!' Jackie Gayle had a funny bit he did a lot about the Bunnies. He'd tell the audience that when a Bunny retired, Playboy would send her off to the Bunny Ranch—not the kind they have in Nevada, but a retirement ranch—and as entertainment, they were shown slides of big tippers! No matter how often we heard that, we'd laugh as if we were hearing it for the first time.

"Jackie was just the funniest man—no wonder he was Hef's favorite. One night, he was working in the Penthouse. During the week, the last show usually wasn't as full as the first one, and I remember sitting—well we weren't allowed to sit, but 'perching'— on the back of a tall bar chair and putting my feet up on the rungs of another chair. I was just taking a break for a minute in the corner, holding my tray, and Jackie was on stage doing an impersonation of Jimmy Durante in which he said that Jimmy reminded him of a windshield wiper and he wiped his head back and forth to illustrate. I thought that was so funny that I started laughing and my feet slipped! I went up and over and my tray fell, making the biggest noise—clack, clunk, clunk! Jackie never flinched; he just said, 'Will someone make sure this Bunny is charged a cover charge?' He never skipped a beat. Obviously, I was back on my feet real fast. I always equated him and the other good entertainment with money, because that's what we were all there for. We'd say, 'Oh, Jackie's coming back, that's wonderful!'

"An act called Hines, Hines, and Dad did very well. Maurice and Gregory danced and their father played the drums. Talk about

Rick James is all smiles with Playboy Bunny. James FortuneRexREX USA

good—they performed on a stage no bigger than a postage stamp and were just fantastic. The showroom was very intimate, very small. It held a little over a hundred people and had small tables with straight-back chairs and narrow aisles.

"During my Bunny years, I had the opportunity to work on the second go-round of Playboy on TV, *Playboy After Dark*. A lot of the entertainers who performed in the clubs were on the show, plus about seventy-five extras—you could actually be an extra or a featured extra and I was lucky enough to be both. A featured extra was cast to be one of the celebrities' date for his part of the show. All it meant, usually, was that you got to sit on the couch next to him. I was selected to be Sammy Davis Jr.'s date. That was a lot of fun, but also, that's when Hef became familiar with my face. Later, when he bought his plane called the Big Bunny, he asked if I would be a Bunny stewardess. So I flew on the jet for a few years."

\* \* \*

The Big Bunny was more than just transportation. Originally designed to hold 125 passengers, Hef had it reconfigured, removing all the seats and replacing them with ultra-plush seating for twelve. It was essentially a flying luxury bachelor pad, complete with Hef's customary round bed, which was appointed with black Himalayan goat leather and white silk sheets. The exterior was painted black with the Playboy Bunny-head logo proudly illuminated on the tail.

Select Bunnies served as stewardesses and cooks and were trained at the Continental Airline School to comply with safety regulations. The Big Bunny's maiden voyage was from Chicago O'Hare to the Burbank airport in southern California, and took four-and-a-half hours. Select members of the press were invited along, and they shared in the then-unheard-of luxury of in-flight movies.

"When I said that Playboy opened the world to me," Lacey continued, "I wasn't exaggerating. After thirteen years as a Bunny, I went on to be a Bunny Mother until the Los Angeles Club closed. Then I moved over to the corporate office and, after a few promotions, I landed in my current position in Playmate Promotions."

When the 2011 TV show *The Playboy Club* was in the planning stages, Lacey became very proprietary about the Playboy image. She expressed her concerns repeatedly to Dick Rosenzweig, until he invited her to go with him to a meeting with the producers and writers at 20th Century Fox.

"I was so passionate about the brand," Lacey told us. "I wanted people to see exactly how it was. It had to be authentic—not a joke! The Bunnies and the entertainment at the clubs all created a certain rhythm. Everything had to be done with a stylized pace and rhythm. I felt the TV show had to capture that feel. There couldn't be a show with a Bunny leaning over a table."

The top brass took her seriously and ended up bringing her on board as an advisor, putting her in charge of training the four main actresses in Playboy's ways. Steve Martinez, Hef's senior archivist (and a big help to us with this book), was also very instrumental in providing the producers of *The Playboy Club* photos of the actual clubs and even copies of the artwork that hung on the walls.

\* \* \*

The Playboy Clubs were always glamorous, especially in their glory years. The New York location, in particular, was within a block of some of the most prestigious addresses in the worlds of entertainment and hospitality: the Plaza Hotel, the Sherry Netherland, the Pierre Hotel, and the Copacabana. Yet, everyone who spent any time working at any of the clubs invariably talks about their homey, nurturing, familial atmosphere.

Jazz great Al Jarreau told us, "Playboy was like the 'I think I can' engine. Everyone was young and had dreams and thought anything was possible. Lots of folks were getting big breaks because scouts from TV shows and other clubs would come around to find new and interesting talent. In addition to the scouts, the bigger-name entertainers who played there were on the lookout for good opening acts. That happened to Julio and me when Jackie Gayle asked us to open for him on the road for four weeks."

Al's musical partner, guitarist Julio Martinez, was born in New York City, the son of Puerto Rican Americans. "They met in New York and became a dance team in the '30s," Julio told us. "They did very well, dancing with the Xavier Cugat Orchestra. My dad was also the orchestra accountant. In the early 1940s, he had an opportunity to go to Hollywood with Cugat to help him out with some contracts for an MGM movie. They arrived in L.A. in January, leaving behind a New York blizzard. Dad took one look at the L.A. sunshine, quit dancing, brought the whole family out, and opened a restaurant."

Julio took up the trumpet in junior high school and soon became part of a jazz orchestra. "It was then that I decided I wanted to make music my life," he said. He majored in music at L.A. College and received a scholarship to the University of Michigan. "Somehow, I was pulled into the army at the beginning of the Berlin Crisis in the early '60s, but they made me a music instructor, so I spent the majority of my time in the army doing that."

After his release from the military, he began graduate school at the University of California, Berkeley, and became absorbed in the atmosphere of radical politics there. "The fall of '64 was a very interesting time," he said. "I was surrounded by radicals like Bettina Aptheker, Mario Savio, and Michael Rossman. It was then that I switched from trumpet to guitar. I auditioned for, and became the musical director of, the San Francisco Mime Troupe—this guerrilla theatre company in the Bay Area that was so radical [that] I got arrested quite a few times.

"This was at the start of what they now call the 'San Francisco Sound.' I played acoustic guitar in coffee houses with people like Jerry Garcia, Marty Balin, and Michael Conan. All these folks played sort of pseudo-folk, folk-rock, folk-hillbilly music, and I was a mere beginner—but, since I had a degree in music and knew a lot about theory, I was able to do a lot of things on the guitar. I couldn't execute well but I sounded impressive, because I knew all these advanced chords."

By the end of 1967, Julio was music director for a play called *High Mass* being produced at the Old Broadway Theater in San Francisco and starring a young Italian-American actor named

Michael Procaccino. He later changed his name to Michael Cristofer and became fairly well known as both a playwright and an actor.

"The Old Broadway Theatre," said Julio, "looked like an old-fashioned opera house, and it had this lovely lounge. To force myself to get comfortable playing the guitar in front of an audience, I used to get up and just sit and play on this modified stage. I only knew four songs, but I played them well and they sounded good, because I knew all these very interesting jazz chords. On December 30, 1967, I was playing my four songs and this woman came up and introduced herself to me. She had brought this young man along with her to audition for the club. He had asked who the pianist would be and they said they didn't have one—they just had this hippie kid sitting on a stool with a guitar. That was the first time I met Al Jarreau."

Al picked up the story from there. "I had a full-time day job working as a rehabilitation counselor. I had graduated from Iowa University with a Masters degree in occupational rehab, but was singing jazz three nights a week with the George Duke Trio at the High Note, because jazz and music were my passions. I was an up-and-coming little jazz singer and San Francisco was a real hotbed of music at the time. We were the flower-power generation people, like the Grateful Dead and Grace Slick and Janis Joplin, Big Brother and the Holding Company, Jefferson Airplane—I could go on and on. So it wasn't too farfetched to think that a local guy like me might find his way to a record company, just as those other local flower-power children had.

"That night at the Old Broadway, I sat in with Julio, singing and playing the four songs he knew, and the owner of the club, Keith Rockwell, said, 'Would you two like to play here tomorrow night?' It was New Year's Eve. And we did."

Julio continued, "We played the gig and then met the next day, New Year's Day, and worked out a set of eight songs. We started playing two sets, but played the same songs for both. Al said, 'I know I need to make some changes, because there's a whole lot of stuff happening musically, and I'm still caught in the 1950s jazz scene, but I don't really have anyone to work with.' He was quite frank. 'There's a lot of times, on the guitar, where it looks like you're fumbling to find what you're looking for, and I'm not used to that.' So I said, 'Well, I think you're a great singer, so if you want to do this thing, I'll dedicate myself to being your accompanist, and the one thing I can do is learn. I'm probably fumbling around on the guitar because I've only been playing it for a year and a half.' This seemed to surprise him. He told me he'd think about it.

"Within two weeks we were practicing steadily, and in March we auditioned for a club in Sausalito called Gatsby's. They loved us there, and we did really, really well. I learned what to do on the guitar, but Al decided we should stick to playing music that I knew, rather than my learning music that he knew, because I was into all the new composers like James Taylor, Carole King, and Laura Nyro. I also knew a lot of bossa nova, because it fit well with the type of guitar I played—an amplified classical."

Al said, "I just got bowled over by the wave out of Brazil. There were some songs, including 'The Look of Love,' that came along at that time that were so Brazilian-influenced that I wanted in! Even today, a lot of my sound is either Brazilian or taken from Brazilian music.

"We billed ourselves as Al and Julio, and it turned out to be the perfect combination," Julio said. "My chord style resembled the way a pianist played. And we became very popular. Sometimes the line to see us would wind around the block. People wanted to manage us—some earnest, some not so earnest—and there was a lawyer in town, an up-and-comer named Bill Straw, who was an amateur musician himself and on staff at Capitol Records. He said, 'I can arrange for you to audition at a club where some of the Capitol artists have performed.' It was Dino's Lodge on the Sunset Strip, partially owned by Dean Martin. Bill told us that if we wanted to come to L.A., we could stay at his house. He lived with three other lawyers from Capitol Records. So we did; we got the job at Dino's and played there for a few weeks. We traveled back and forth between Dino's in L.A. and Gatsby's in Sausalito for a few months.

"The Playboy Club was just a stone's throw from Dino's," Al continued, "and everyone came over to see us after their shows there. Julio and I became friendly with a lot of the artists, especially the comedians. Lou Alexander and a few of the other guys asked us what else we were doing, and we told them about Gatsby's."

"Jackie Gayle," said Julio, "was sort of the head honcho comedian at the Playboy Club at the time, and he asked us to come open for him. We did it for four weeks that May. Then we spent the summer back at Gatsby's, and when we returned to L.A., the booking agent for the Playboy Clubs said he wanted to book us on the Playboy circuit—or an abbreviated circuit—L.A., Chicago, and New York.

"No matter which city we were in, the inside of the Playboy Clubs looked the same. They were designed and decorated exactly alike, modeled after the Chicago Club. The first time we played Chicago, Hefner was still using it as his headquarters. He hadn't moved to L.A. yet. After our opening show, which was on a Monday, J. C. Curtis, the comedian we worked with, took us to the Playboy Mansion. It must have been a tradition or rite of passage for first-timers. We saw the legendary Hugh Hefner in his pajamas, holding a Pepsi-Cola and playing backgammon with his girlfriend, Barbi Benton, who was also in her pajamas. At some point during our engagement at the Chicago Club, Al got involved with a Bunny. This would become a recurring theme throughout our time on the circuit.

"Musically, playing at Playboy was never that challenging. Al and I always opened for the headliner. On weeknights, we did two twenty-minute sets, and then the comedian came on for forty minutes. It was pretty formulaic. Those audiences didn't want to hear a lot of obscure music like Joni Mitchell; they wanted to hear the pop tunes of the day and Broadway stuff. Al could do all of it very well, and I wrote out the arrangements. We'd open with something like 'For Once in My Life,' the Stevie Wonder hit, or Burt Bacharach's 'Promises, Promises.' Then we'd go on to a combo, and every once in a while, we'd throw something new in. They liked bossa nova, so we did some of that. They loved to hear jazz. Al could do all sorts of things with his voice—turn it into a flute, a trumpet, a harmonica, even a conga drum.

"Fridays we did three sets, and Saturdays we did four twenty-minute sets. Al worked extremely hard and sometimes he'd strain his voice because, even though each set was only twenty, the entire evening stretched out from eight until one in the morning. Meantime, we played a lot; the other kind of play." He winked at that.

"You have to understand," Julio went on, "Al was six-foot-two, an immensely handsome, all-American, black, athletic-looking intellectual. He'd gone to college on a baseball scholarship and was recruited by the Milwaukee Braves. His parents wouldn't let him play football, although he would have been great, so he ran cross-country. He even ran for student-body president, but was beaten out by an even more charismatic young man named Harrison Ford. So you can see why he was a favorite among the Bunnies.

"During the day, I worked on arrangements. Al wasn't writing music then, but we were always working on new tunes because we wanted to keep things fresh. I'd write out easy charts for a trio consisting of, piano, bass, and drums. Al usually didn't get up before noon or one, but I'd get up around eight or nine and try to catch my wife in L.A. when she was waking up.

"The New York Club was memorable from the start because we arrived in town on the first day of the big New York garbage strike, and it lasted the whole time we were there. I'd call that aromatically memorable!

"Wherever we went," said Julio, "the Bunnies immediately fell in love with Al. Chicago was the Bunny training center, and there was one young trainee who fell in love with him, but the feeling wasn't exactly mutual. Well, this girl wanted to take Al and me out to dinner after work, so we all went out. Then came the uncomfortable moment of where to go and what to do next. She was living at the Mansion so she couldn't take Al home, and we were sharing a room at a hotel downtown. So she leaned over and whispered to me, 'Julio, would you mind disappearing for a few hours?' Now, this was Chicago in January, but I said, 'Um, okay.' When she excused herself to go to the ladies' room, Al asked me what she'd whispered.

"I said, 'She wants me to disappear so she can screw you for two hours, and he said, 'Oh, God, I just want to go to sleep.' And I said, 'Well, for the sake of harmony amongst the cottontails, will you just do this?' Mind you, I was the one suffering. It was freezing out, so I couldn't take a walk. I actually stayed in the restaurant until I'd had it. I went back to the hotel at three in the morning, knocked on the door, and she came out beaming and smiling and thanked me. Al said, 'Next time, it's you who's going to have to do this!' *Yeah, like that was going to happen,* I thought.

"The next day, one of the really tough Bunny Mothers came up to me while I was eating my pudding in the lounge and said, 'Did you actually sit at the restaurant while Al got shanked?' I said, 'Yeah.' And she said, 'Well, it's your turn.' Sure enough, at the end of the evening, this very nice young lady took me by the hand and said, 'You're coming with me!'

"One of the great things about the Playboy Clubs—they fed you. They had a second kitchen for the help, especially the musicians and entertainers. We were sitting there eating at the New York Club one night and a woman came up and told us she was with *The Tonight Show.* She told us that Fred de Cordova wanted us to audition for the show—which was a pretty big deal. I said, 'When? Our run ends on Saturday, and then we're heading back to L.A. I don't think we'll be back in New York for six months.' Al jumped in and said, 'We'll be here if there's a chance we can get on *The Tonight Show.*' Back then, Carson's show was based in New York and it was ninety minutes long, so they needed a lot of musical talent to play in between the name people. If you were playing in a legitimate venue in New York and you were any good, you stood a good chance of getting on. The lady said, 'Fred would like to audition you Friday at eight thirty.' Al said, 'But I'll be on stage at that time.' 'No,' she said, 'that's eight thirty in the *morning*.'

"You have to understand, Al slept until one in the afternoon to rest his voice. If he had to get up at eight or nine or ten, he sounded like a demon from the grave—he could barely get anything out. I asked him how he was going to pull this off, and he said, 'The same way I did it when I had an early vocal class in college.' As soon as we finished the show, Al went straight to bed. He got up at five thirty the next morning and spent close to two hours in the shower doing nothing but vocalizing, 'Me, oh, my, oh, my,' and all of those vocal exercises. He sounded terrible at first, but by seven thirty, his speaking voice was normal.

"So we went to the audition with the music they asked for and charts for the pianist. Al explained that I was the only accompanist he needed. We did 'Say a Little Prayer for You,' and 'The Look of Love' by Bacharach and [Hal] David. Cordova looked at Al and then looked at me and said, 'Book 'em,' and he walked away. So our manager worked out the details and told us we were hired, but that it might be weeks before we'd get on. Al said that was fine; we'd stay in New York and hustle a gig somewhere while we waited.

"My problem was that I hadn't seen my wife for awhile and she was threatening to divorce me. She was a stewardess and could fly me around for free, so I wanted to spend the weekend in L.A. with her. Everyone was cool with that idea.

'I was getting ready to return to New York on Monday morning when I got a frantic call from Shelly, our manager. They wanted us on that night! The first thing I thought of was that I had all our arrangements and Al couldn't read music. Shelly was yelling, 'Get back here; get back here!' There was no way I could make it, especially with the time difference. So I said, 'Look, take a tune that anyone can do, like 'The Look of Love,' and tell Al to do it with the pianist and rhythm section. It will be very easy.

"I was missing out on my big chance to be on *The Tonight Show*! That evening, my wife and I watched from three thousand miles away as my partner sang 'The Look of Love' in the wrong key. He was almost a fourth too high—but Al is such a genius that he kept flipping his register back and forth, and he was great. They gave him a standing ovation and Doc Severinsen, the leader of the orchestra, invited Al to go on tour with him to the New England colleges.

"I came back to New York and we did other gigs, including opening for the rock bands Three Dog Night and Steppenwolf. The following year, we played Rodney Dangerfield's new club and met other up-and-comers including John Belushi, Bette Midler, and Jimmy Walker. Then Al and I discovered the Improv in New York and a whole new world of adventures."

Al closed by saying, "Working at Playboy in New York, I felt anything was possible, and I found the music that would define me. It was a wonderful time, filled with good music and good friends." He would go on to win seven Grammys, in addition to a number of international jazz awards and accolades in virtually every country he played in.

Julio performed with Sarah Vaughan at the Hollywood Bowl and toured with Helen Reddy to many of the capitals of Europe. By the end of the '70s, he'd begun to make the transition to journalism, writing about jazz and cabaret in *Daily Variety* and elsewhere. Today, he says he's enjoying life and trying to stay out of trouble.

\* \* \*

What was the most frightening thing that ever happened to anyone at a Playboy Club? You might have thought that it was making a pass at a Bunny and then turning around and finding out that her husband happened to be a prizefighter. But the famous comic Lonnie Shorr had the best answer. He was working in the San Francisco Club, where the house trio at the time included the pianist Al Plank and the bassist "Puzzy" Firth, best known for his work with Vince Guaraldi on the famous *Charlie Brown* TV Specials. Lonnie started to introduce the trio, but, unbeknownst to anyone, Puzzy's amplifier had some kind of a short in it. Puzzy was holding his equipment, Lonnie was holding his mic, and in the middle of the introduction, the two spontaneously fist-bumped each other. The bumping fists caused an electrical connection, and they both felt a charge running through their bodies. "We were both almost electrocuted!" says Lonnie. They were then both visibly shaken by the sensation and were unable to move for a few moments. "All I could think of," says Lonnie, "was that if I had to die, it might as well be at the Playboy Club!"

August 23, 1973 Los Angeles mayor Tom Bradley autographs Bunny Gloria's cuff as Mrs. Bradley looks on. Image by BettmannCorbis

* * *

By now, the basic *modus operandi* of the Playboy Clubs has surely become clear; these were relatively small clubs, laid out in a circuit across the country (and, eventually, the world), each featuring several showrooms of different configurations. Compared to the Playboy Clubs, more traditional nightclubs such as the Persian Room or the Copacabana in New York were gigantic venues with correspondingly gargantuan cover charges. The Playboy rooms were more in the spirit of the Village Vanguard or the Blue Angel and priced within the range of the average Joe. In describing the clubs, the word that comes up most often is "intimate."

Another phrase that everyone seems to use in reference to the Playboy circuit is "up-and-coming talent"—today's equivalent might be "emerging artists." Because the rooms and cover charges were small, Playboy couldn't outbid the Copa for superstar head-liners such as Nat King Cole, Frank Sinatra, or Judy Garland. Of necessity, they became places where new talent was discovered and nurtured. Both Aretha Franklin and Barbra Streisand worked there before they were famous, as did a raft of other entertainers consid-ered household names today. Eventually, when the Playboy Empire expanded to include large resorts with Vegas-style showrooms, they began to attract iconic, high-priced names such Bob Hope and Sammy Davis Jr.

Tony Bennett was an exception. He was probably the single biggest name ever to work the bread-and-butter Playboy Clubs, and the only Playboy regular to travel the circuit at the height of his career, having logged a ten-year run of hit singles.

It was at the zenith of the Playboy era, in 1962, that Tony scored the biggest hit of his life with "I Left My Heart in San Francisco." This heralded a new lucky streak for the crooner, who went on to rack up number-one hits with "I Wanna Be Around," "The Good Life," "Watch What Happens," and "If I Ruled the World." Tony was a mainstay on the pop charts throughout the 1960s, and he worked the clubs all the while. Why? Not because he needed money or a break. It was because of his deep, enduring friendship with Hugh Hefner.

In the mid-1960s, Tony and his piano player, Ralph Sharon, were enjoying working the Playboy Clubs so much that Ralph was moved to take a rather unexpected step. The London-born pianist was living in New York with his wife at the time, and she was tired of her husband being continually on the road. She was pressuring Ralph to part company with Tony and take a more stable job. The situation came to head around 1965, when Tony took on what would be his only acting role in a major motion picture, playing the secondary lead in the Hollywood behind-the-scenes drama *The Oscar,* with Stephen Boyd and Jill St. John. While filming in the daytime, Tony accepted a long-running evening gig at the Playboy Club in Los Angeles.

To the surprise of both Tony and his pianist, Playboy made Ralph an offer as well. As Ralph describes it, "The Playboy people came to me and said, 'We're opening a place in San Francisco, and you can be the musical director. It will be four trios on different floors and you'll be in charge of the whole thing.' They weren't offering a great deal of money but, while I was there, I got a local TV show with my trio that was on 5 days a week, so I was also doing that. And the idea of staying in one place made my wife very happy."

That's how Ralph became the first musical director of the San Francisco Playboy Club when it opened in November 1965. He added, "Actually, I really would never have left Tony if my wife hadn't insisted."

Ralph's wife may have been happy, but Tony was desolate. As the recordings that the singer and the pianist made around the time show, the two had built up a remarkable rapport over the seven years they'd been on the road together. But Tony was not one to hold a grudge. At one point, when singer Herb Jeffries—another of Tony's friends and inspirations—was headlining at the Playboy Club with

Ralph, Tony made a point of dropping in and he sang three songs. A *Variety* reviewer noted that Tony "was just doing a favor for Ralph, but he's giving it the same effort as if he were getting his usual fee."

Ultimately, Ralph wasn't too crazy about the San Francisco gig, and it did little to mend his marriage; the couple soon divorced. As much as he liked the Playboy organization, nothing could compare with the thrill of playing for Tony night after night. Ralph soon realized that headliners such as Peggy Lee and Tony himself all had their own musical directors, and he was left playing for the "emerging talent." Said Ralph, "They were people on their way up, let us say, but after being with Tony... well, I couldn't believe it."

He ultimately left the clubs to go back on the road, this time with Robert Goulet. Not surprisingly, it was still less of a thrill, musically, than playing for Tony. Like the great Broadway leading man that he was, Goulet tended to do each number exactly the same way every night—as one does in musical theater—in contrast to Tony, who liked to change things up just to keep it all interesting. Ralph was dying to rejoin Tony, but the situation was awkward. "I couldn't just call Tony up and say, 'Hey, you know something, I'd like to come back to you!'" he said.

Tony continued working the Playboy circuit, headlining what the club advertised as its Festival of Stars in 1967, a unique event that united clubs across the country. There's a happy postscript involving Tony and Ralph; in 1980, Tony was again in the market for a piano player, and Ralph was available. They began working together again, and their relationship lasted another twenty years, a period that encompassed Tony's so-called "comeback" and his MTV triumph of 1994-1995. If you ask me, he's never been away.

# 11

# IT'S A PLAYBOY WORLD

After the turbulence of opening the New York Club had subsided and the club was running smoothly, Victor was again at sixes and sevens. He'd been functioning as a consultant for two and a half years, but he missed the security and challenges of being an official Playboy executive. After a brief negotiation with the organization, Victor was officially back in the Playboy family. He was a partner in the clubs, and once again had the title of Promotion Director. And, because he knew that Hef was exploring the idea of opening clubs overseas, he suggested that he might operate from London while scouting out the possibility of opening a club there.

London was the epicenter of the Swinging Sixties, and the jet-setters who fueled it were jetting there in droves. Clearly, the time was ripe for a Playboy Club—just as it had been in New York, a year and a half earlier. Victor arrived in London shortly after the Christmas holidays of 1963 and spent the first six months of the New Year tirelessly searching for the perfect property. He finally found it in a seven-story building on Park Lane, overlooking Hyde Park. A sixty-three-year lease was soon negotiated and signed. Nearly half a century later, he recalled that he could have purchased the place outright for about a million pounds at the time, but his colleagues at Playboy felt more comfortable renting. "It's easily worth forty million pounds today," he said wistfully. "The local developers were originally planning a block of flats, but when we took over the building, that idea went out the window. We did keep three floors for apartments, accessible via a separate lift on the other side of the building. My office was on that side as well, and so were the Bunny dorms."

Victor Lownes holding Bunny auditions in London. Rex USA garettes for customers. Image by BettmannCORBIS

Initially, the club was to be very much like those in the United States but, as plans took shape, a new concept began to form in Victor's mind. While scouting locations, Victor had seen a surprising number of casinos, card rooms, and other gambling venues which had sprung up as a result of the Betting and Gaming Act of 1960. The ostensible intention of the law had been to pave the way for church lotteries, bingo, and other amusements offering prizes. In effect, it opened the gates for any establishment to offer gambling, as long as it followed certain basic rules. Games of equal chance had to be offered and bettors had to have the right to take the bank if they wished.

Within the first few years after passage of the bill, some 1,500 casinos had opened in England, and Victor visited many of them. "I realized very quickly that the real money was not only in clubs but in gambling," he told us. "I said to Hefner, 'Let's start with a casino,' and he agreed."

In light of this decision, a new Bunny position was created, the specially trained Bunny Croupier.

Going into their new venture, Victor and Hef felt a bit as they had in 1959, prior to opening the first Playboy Club. Back then, concerned that they knew nothing about running a nightclub, they'd brought in Arnie Morton to guide them. This time, Victor entered into an agreement with Crockfords, a well regarded English gaming firm. It would rent the casino from Playboy and run it, in exchange for half the profits. But when Crockfords canceled the deal at the last minute, Playboy decided to manage the casino on its own, and brought on Mike Bassett as the organization's first gaming executive.

Eager to start promoting the new club, they began auditioning Bunnies. Tony Roma came over from New York with his new wife to assist Victor in the task. When the first six British Bunnies had been selected from among hundreds of applicants, they were sent to Chicago for Bunny training. Ever the publicist, Victor decided to whip up a frenzy around the new venture—using the girls as bait—that would top anything he'd ever done. The "Bunnies from Britain" flight to Chicago made newspaper headlines around the world. Their American Bunny sisters, waving banners of welcome, greeted the girls at O'Hare Airport and they were rarely out of the English press for the duration of their visit.

Keith Hefner explained to us that sending the British Bunnies to Chicago was a deviation from the norm; typically, veteran Bunnies would travel to the new location for training. The whole gambit was a publicity stunt, and it worked like a dream. A few months before the London Club was due to open, Keith—along with a battalion of "training Bunnies," including a Bunny Mother—as well as the British Bunnies who had just apprenticed in Chicago, all quietly made the trip over to London to finish passing on their skills and to make sure the British recruits were ready for action.

"Opening in London," said Keith, "was exciting for many reasons, but mainly because of the times. This was the era of the Beatles, Carnaby Street, and the King's Road—the time when, as the song goes, 'England swings like a pendulum do.' It was a mecca for all that was hip. There were lots of movies being made there and many of the stars came to our place to unwind. It was the place to be in '66 and we drew an international clientele."

It should be noted that entertainment on offer in the new club wasn't all mop-topped pop groups. Two of the most popular attractions were decidedly old-school: Victor's beloved Mabel Mercer, and the elegant song stylist Julie Wilson.

Victor's wife Marilyn—who, you'll recall, went on to become the Playmate of the Year in 1973—explained how she became a member of the hutch. "I was from Portsmouth, England, and I traveled to London with the specific purpose of being a Bunny. It wasn't as if I was living in London and thought, 'Oh, I'll work at the club.' I'd left home to be a Bunny, and was one, off and on, from 1971 to 1974."

On June 26, 1966, Hef stepped off the Big Bunny at Heathrow Airport escorted by thirty-two Bunnies who, at that point, could be considered genuine pop-culture icons. One hundred British cottontails joined them days later to welcome and assist all the globe-trotting partygoers who had gathered for the club's unveiling.

\* \* \*

The London Playboy Club opened officially on June 28, with a full complement of politicians, personalities, aristocrats, and celebrities from both sides of the ocean in attendance. These luminaries—many of whom partied well past four the next morning—included Rudolf Nureyev, Ursula Andress, James Garner, Jean-Paul Belmondo, Princess Lee Radziwill, the Marquis and Marchioness of Tavistock, the Earl of Suffolk, Laurence Harvey, Rex Harrison, Vanessa Redgrave, Lee Marvin, and Julie Christie.

Woody Allen chats with some London Bunnies. Photo by Ray StevensonREX USA

Trini Lopez—the singer, guitarist, and actor whose version of "If I Had a Hammer" became a number-one hit in thirty-eight countries—told us, "I was making the war movie *The Dirty Dozen* in London, and the whole cast was invited to the opening. Lee Marvin, Jim Brown, John Cassavetes, Charlie Bronson, Telly Savalas, and I all went, along with a few more guys I can't remember. It was some party! I remember that Woody Allen was up on stage at one point. I was dating Dolly Read at the time, who was one of the Bunnies and also a Play-mate. London was definitely swinging in 1966!"

Lopez hitching a ride on the Big Bunny and arriving in style! Courtesy of Trini Lopez

Trini didn't sing that night, but he went on to perform in many of the clubs over the years, as well as on *Playboy After Dark*. He was also one of a small coterie of lucky people who periodically got to hitch a ride home on the Big Bunny after visiting the Chicago Playboy Mansion. But perhaps his greatest honor was that his album, *Trini: Live at PJ's*, could be seen peeking seductively out from beneath Miss November 1966, Lisa Baker, as she luxuriated on a fur rug.

Applications for keys were so plentiful in London that member-ship had to be suspended at one point—and by the end of the first full year, net profits from the club were nearly $1 million. That's a whopping return on an initial investment of just about $1.5 million.

In keeping with Playboy's strict oversight of all departments, Bill Gerhauser was sent from Chicago headquarters to help Victor

Ursula Andress tries her luck at the London Playboy Casino.
Photo by Ray StevensonREX USA

with the financial and accounting aspects of the casino, thus freeing him from day-to-day business concerns. All went swimmingly until 1968, when a new gaming act was passed in England in an effort to clean up and control the industry more stringently. Whereas, under the previous law, only liquor licenses had been needed, from that point forward, gaming licenses were required as well, and foreign owners would not be approved for them. Additional directives of the new law stated that no alcohol could be served where gambling took place and that "no inducements to gamble" were permitted.

Playboy knew that in order to qualify for a license and comply with the new mandates they'd have to tweak things a little, so they quickly created a new British-based company called the Playboy Club of London. Victor and Bill already lived there at that point, so it wasn't a stretch. And, to be on the safe side, a so-called "modesty bib" was added to the Bunny Croupiers' uniforms, to obscure their "tempting" décolletage. Finally, since it might be argued that providing entertainment was an inducement to gamble, separate entrances were established, one leading to the casino and the other to the cabaret and restaurants. As soon as it was determined that Playboy had fulfilled all of the regulations, they got their license and the party continued unabated.

Sharon Tate and Roman Polanski enjoying a night out at the London Playboy Club.
Photo by Ray StevensonREX USA

* * *

Singer Lisa Carroll performed at most of the clubs on the Playboy circuit, but she has especially lovely memories of the London venue. "London was going to be my swan song," she told us. "I was going to stop performing after that, because I felt it was time to slow down and let some man catch up to me. When you're in entertainment, it's very difficult to maintain a relationship because you're always going from one city—or country—to another. Every time I met someone I liked and wanted to know better, I'd be off to another singing or acting engagement. But I guess I wasn't supposed to retire yet.

"I was offered a spot at the Playboy Club in London and I thought it would be nice to sing my way over on the *Queen Elizabeth*. It just seemed like an elegant way to get there. There was a well-known writer, Bobby Kroll, on board, going to France to do a TV special for Annie Cordy, and he said to me, 'You're very good, but your act needs freshening up.' I told him it didn't really matter because this was my last engagement, but he persisted. 'Why don't you let me rewrite it?' he said. I knew he'd be expensive because he'd written acts for famous movie stars like Linda Darnell, so I repeated that this was my farewell appearance and I didn't care whether it was outdated or not. I'd just do my best and hope they liked me.

"He called my cabin the next day and said he had an idea for my show and to meet him downstairs. Well, after four or five days on board, he'd rewritten my entire act. It was wonderful. It was a marvelous revision of what I'd been doing, a real face-lift. I got off in Spain and flew the rest of the way to England and he traveled on to France and I never saw him again—but what a trip."

Still determined that this would be her last singing engagement, Lisa wanted it to be special—and after the unique luxury of sailing over, she chose to spend her first night in London at the glamorous Dorchester Hotel before checking in to Playboy Central. While taking a casual stroll through the lobby, she ran into the celebrated American songwriter and lyricist Sammy Cahn. After an exchange of pleasantries, Sammy inquired as to which of his songs would be included in Lisa's Playboy performance.

"I hadn't included *any* of Sammy's songs and told him so," she said. "Well, that just wouldn't do, he told me, and overnight, he wrote special funny lyrics to his song 'Don't Talk, Just Sing' for me."

When he sent the lyrics to Lisa, the accompanying note asked that she please not thank him with a loud tie! People—and by this I mean men-people—always seemed to have Lisa's best interests at heart. Looking at her promotional photos from those days, we can see why!

"I loved singing at the Playboy Club," she said, "and as was the case with most of the artists, they put me up in the upstairs residences, where the Bunnies bunked. One morning, I was awakened by a noise. At first I thought maybe I was still dreaming because all of a sudden, my door flew open and Sammy Davis Jr. was standing in my room! He said, 'Oh, sorry, I thought this was Lola's room,' and left. He was dating Lola Falana at the time and she was also staying there.

"One night, Aaron Schroeder, a big music publisher, was in the audience. After the show, he approached me and said, 'I'm going to bring some people from CBS Records to hear you tomorrow.' I explained to him that I was leaving London after the gig was over and he said, 'Don't do anything rash.' The next night, he brought the head of London CBS. The guy offered me a four-year contract but only if I would promise to stay in London for the full four years—so I did! I swapped apartments with a British guy who wanted to move to New York.

"I became a regular on one of the most popular English TV shows of the time: *The Mike and Bernie Winters Show*. The hosts were very similar to Dean Martin and Jerry Lewis. I was the dumb blonde who made all kinds of *faux pas*, and whenever the guys couldn't find something vital, like a key or something, guess where it would show up? In my low-cut décolleté gown, of course. It

September 5, 1969 Hef and girlfriend Barbi Benton visit his London playboy Club.
Image by Hulton-Deutsch Collection CORBIS

was great fun, and I still had the opportunity to sing at the clubs. I played three separate engagements at the London Playboy Club during that time and just loved it. The Playboy Clubs were the best.

"Jack Benny's manager heard me sing at the club and hired me to go to South Africa to open for Jack, but they had to cancel because of the racial situation there. Almost all of the important artists were turning down and canceling jobs there, and there was even a petition circulated among performers stating that they would not work in South Africa.

"I eventually left the show because of a recurrence of an injury I'd sustained in an old car accident. I had to take time out to go back to the States for an operation. But my memories of London and Playboy are all great!"

* * *

One of comedian Rip Taylor's trademarks is his distinctive voice, which has helped him get numerous gigs doing voice acting for animated cartoons. We have fond childhood memories of him as the titular character in *Here Comes the Grump*. His signature rapid-fire delivery of gags, gags, and more gags, along with his use of zany props, costumes, and confetti, has made him a popular staple of variety and talk shows from Ed Sullivan to David Letterman, as well as on game shows including *Hollywood Squares* and *The Dating Game*. Based on his legendary gift of gab, it's difficult to imagine what Rip might have sounded like to audiences at the London Playboy Club—but he quickly filled us in on that.

As Rip told it, he "went native" even before the plane landed; as soon as he set foot on British soil, he almost unconsciously found himself talking with a British accent, "so thick that you could eat it." He was liberally peppering his speech with English-isms such as "teatime" and "cheerio"—phrases that no self-respecting yank would dream of uttering. Apparently, without even intending it, the Washington D.C. boy had turned into Terry Thomas! Fortunately, he had the mustache for it.

In addition to speaking the Queen's English, Rip couldn't resist the urge to dress the part. "I went nuts!" he told us. "I went to Moss Brothers costume shop and got the morning suit, pinstriped pants, the monocle, the bowler, the whole thing, and I*was*English!"

Rip remembered that his run at the club was a month long, and that he had never witnessed such a swinging scene in his life. And it wasn't just the Playboy Club that was hopping like a bunny. After Rip finished his last show and headed back to his hotel each night, he'd find the streets crowded with revelers. It was as if the English had finally gotten around to celebrating the Allied Victory in World War II, twenty years after the fact, he told us.

Rip recalled only one moment during his run when he felt conspicuously alien. In the middle of one of his late sets, a very rowdy, well-lubricated group of "ugly Americans" began heckling him. Rip realized that the only way he could shut them up was to literally shock them into submission. So, he started by addressing the crowd in his English accent, "Thank yew so much—anyone here from the jolly old colonies?" Of course, the yanks yelled loudly in response. At that point, he shifted back into an American accent, and shouted, "Big *fucking* deal," and then went British again, "Thank *yew* so much for coming!" At the time, it was still relatively rare for a mainstream comic to drop the "F-bomb"—especially in London. The Americans howled with laughter, nearly falling over in their seats, and they stopped heckling him.

Did Rip have any final memories of his London experience? "Yeah," he said, "it took me forever to lose that accent."

The "Singing Bunnies" Bunny Girl waitresses at the London Club, perform a song during the club's 'Showtime in The Playroom' spot, 1972. The ladies went on to record an album and are, Elaine

\* \* \*

Another veteran of the Playboy experience, Jon Hendricks, was living in London in the late 1960s, during the heyday of the London Club. Earlier, as a member of the vocal trio Lambert, Hendricks, and Ross, he'd participated in the 1959 Chicago Jazz Festival, and been a frequent guest on *Playboy's Penthouse*. Now, he was continuing to write songs and was working, mostly in Europe, as a solo artist, and living with his relatively new wife, Judith (they're still together after fifty years) and their daughter, Aria, in a house not far from Victor's. He frequently played the London Club and to this day, he remembers vividly what it was like to be surrounded by British Bunnies. But, he told us, the most beautiful woman he ever saw in the Club wasn't an employee at all, but the legendary Ava Gardner. He remembered that the word on the street was that she was staying in Europe, "because Frank [Sinatra] had told her not to come back to America!" Famously, the two ex-lovers could only deal with each other when there was a continent between them.

Jon was appearing at the London Club one day in 1968 when an old friend made his presence known: Sammy Davis Jr., in town for the London production of his hit Broadway show *Golden Boy*. "I had been to the dentist that day," said Jon, "and I'd gotten one of my top front teeth implanted but not very firmly. It was a plate. So Sammy decided to do a scatting thing, you know? He challenged me to a scatting exchange. And, of course, I accepted! He give me a *trip du challenge*! Now, in most jazz challenges or exchanges, the phrases sung by each participant get shorter and shorter; at one point they're exchanging eight-bar phrases, then fours, then twos, and so on. So, we got to fours, you know, and Sammy was doing magnificently hip things! He was just a knockout! And I was really trying my hardest, you know, to outdo that little rascal." Jon later admitted that he's not that much taller than Davis was.

"Ava was there that night—right at the front table—and there were pretty girls all over the place. So I was trying hard, but I was losing my plate! I was in the middle of a phrase and it flew out, right out of my mouth! I put my hand up so quickly that somehow I caught that thing, and I turned my back on the audience and put it back into my mouth. And, as you can imagine, Sammy was doubled over with laughter. He was laughing so hard that I finally said, 'Shut up motherfucker.' And Ava and the girls in front were all screaming! Oh, that was something else!"

After five years or so, London became too expensive for the Hendrickses. "To live there today you have to own an oil field or something," said Judith. "We never thought we'd return to the States, but we did, and we've been back here ever since."

Upon his return to the U.S., Jon founded a new vocal group, Jon Hendricks and Co., with which he has toured extensively. He continues to write lyrics and songs, and in 1993, he was named a Jazz Master by the National Endowment of the Arts. In 2014, Jon found himself back in London to record his latest and most ambitious project: a vocal adaptation of Miles Davis's classic album *Miles Ahead*, with lyrics for a full choir. He was ninety-three at the time of the recording.

\* \* \*

David Lawton—who comes from a town in Wales with so many unpronounceable syllables that even he has a hard time with it—was told early in his career that, "if you can sing and you can emcee, then you'll always work." He's found that to be true. For the last few decades, he's been a fixture on the Silversea cruise lines, serving as cruise director (another way of saying "entertainment director"), as well as singing emcee for many shows a day.

David started his career in the late 1960s, in what he describes as, "workingman's clubs," in Wales and England. "They were rough!" he told us. "You'd start to sing 'Strangers in the Night' and somebody would yell, 'Get your Bingo cards!' You would say, 'Hey! I'm trying

Anthony Newley gets carried away by the Bunnies at London Playboy Club 1972.
Image by Hulton-Deutsch Collection CORBIS

to do a show here' and they would say, 'Oh really? I hadn't noticed.'"

He eventually worked his way up to the Playboy Club in London, where he caught the attention of a magician who specialized in what David called a "pickpocket act." "He was very good," David said. "In fact, he had done a lot of undercover work during the war." The magician recommended him to Victor, who was impressed enough to send him to work the Playboy circuit in the States.

For roughly ten years, David worked primarily in the Chicago, Baltimore, Miami, and Jamaica Clubs. "Nothing about Playboy was cheap," he recalled, echoing what we had been hearing from a lot of entertainers. "Everything was sophisticated and classy—well done. Hefner was ahead of his time in the way he organized the Bunnies—there were very specific rules. Nothing was left to chance. We weren't supposed to date the girls but, of course, everybody did!

"They mostly used me to open for comedians. Playboy had some of the best comics out there—Bobby Shields, Dick Lord, Jackie Curtis.... It seemed like it would have made more sense to have a female singer open for a male comic—for the contrast—but their way seemed to work.

"The most important thing I had to learn was how to deal with hecklers. Jackie Curtis warned me, 'If you let them get away with it, then I'm fair game when I come on after you.'

"Early in the week, it would be slower, but come the weekend, big celebrities would come in, people like [Baltimore Colts player] Bubba Smith. The comedians were doing so many shows in so many rooms that they couldn't remember if they'd told a particular gag on one stage or another.

"The hardest thing was the long-distance travel. You'd close in Chicago on a Saturday and have to be ready to open on Monday evening in Miami. You had to spend all day Sunday traveling. I'd try to pick up some work along the way, to break up the distances."

David eventually obtained a green card and spent the largest part of his career in the United States. As the Playboy era began to wane, he gradually branched out and started working in other places, such as Lake Tahoe, where he opened for Don Rickles, Georgie Jessel, and Milton Berle. Later, he worked steadily at conventions for companies like Mary Kaye Cosmetics and Tupperware. "They always seemed to favor male singers for some reason," he said.

"Back in London, they said I had become 'Americanized,' but I really thought of myself as mid-Atlantic. Of course, being Welsh, I'd never really thought of myself as English to begin with. Then, after I got divorced, I decided to move back to the UK. I eventually started doing the cruise ships, where I still am.

"Overall, Playboy was an amazing learning experience. The pay wasn't spectacular but it was a really great stepping-stone for my career. It was a wild time!"

* * *

After London, the next major club opening was Montreal, almost exactly a year later. The main man in charge was Tony Roma, who had already enjoyed a long history with Playboy. He had been the general manager of the New York Club, then moved to London with the intentional of permanently settling there with his wife and their young son. But something in the British drinking water

Tony Roma surrounded by a Bunny contingent. BettmannCORBIS

made the boy sick, and as a result, they left the country within the year to run the even newer Montreal venue. Tony was both the manager and one of three partners in the establishment, making him one of a miniscule number of individuals who actually owned multiple Playboy franchises.

Montreal would be the only Playboy outfit ever opened in Canada, and the city was an unusual choice for such a venture, since the locals are fiercely independent and tend to be resentful of other Canadians—so you can imagine what they think of Americans. They weren't exactly enamored of the Playboy ethos—but when Hefner flew in from Chicago for the opening in July 1967, he was treated like a superstar. Reporters and photographers mobbed his path from the plane to the limo, and Hef inadvertently upstaged the singer Janis Ray, the venue's premiere act, who was supposed to be the star attraction.

The club itself was smaller than most of those below the border. Everyone remembered it as being more "intimate"; there were fewer Bunnies, too, but they were counted on to do more. They had to speak both French and English, and unlike elsewhere, were occasionally called upon to entertain as well; they were expected to be able to sing and dance, as well as execute the perfect "Bunny Dip."

With a capacity of 565, the main showroom was relatively large—more like a theater than a supper club. In fact, it may have been the single largest Playboy stage up to that time, thus anticipating the scale of the resorts that would open a few years later. A space that size could accommodate such major talent as Tony Bennett and Engelbert Humperdinck, who couldn't have played the smaller clubs; but of course, keeping it filled was more of a struggle. At one point, the three partners tried selling shares in the club, but it lasted only nine years.

Of all the Americans to work in Montreal, the ones who have the fondest memories of that club are the comedians Lonnie Shorr and Stewie Stone. Even though Lonnie was half a continent away from his native North Carolina, he said, the Canadian Club felt like a family. It was always packed on Saturday night, and there was a line to get in. At one point, as tensions were mounting, one Montrealer on the line was in a particularly surly mood; he interrupted Shorr, who was chatting innocently with the Door Bunny, by snarling at her, "What is he, your pimp?"

Stunned silence. Shorr saw red, and walked up to the guy—who was roughly six inches taller—and demanded he apologize. The two were screaming at each other when the night manager appeared and tried to console the guy, offering to buy him a drink. Of course, that made Lonnie even more furious. How dare he reward the bum for insulting one of the girls? "What are you buying him a drink for?' Lonnie demanded. "You should throw him out of here!"

Thankfully, at that moment Tony Roma appeared. Lonnie told him what was going down and Tony reacted as Lonnie had predicted. "He almost fired the night manager on the spot," Lonnie told us. "And he tossed Mr. Big Mouth out of the place, warning him not to come back until he learned some respect for women. Tony was strict but fair. You didn't mess with his employees, especially the girls."

This confirms Stewie Stone's memories of Tony Roma and the Montreal Playboy Club. There was one incident he can't forget, especially since it took place the first time he ever worked up there and met Tony. Stewie had come up from New York to open for Engelbert Humperdinck, and after the show, he heard Tony having it out with a disagreeable busboy. Stewie approached Tony and said, "Excuse me, Mr. Roma," at which point, the manager-owner said, "Wait a second," and then turned back to the busboy. "I told you to pick up that dish," he yelled and then—BAM—he flattened the guy! One punch and he was old cold. Tony then turned back to Stewie and calmly asked him what he wanted. It was all Stewie could do to mutter, "Oh… nothing," and back out of his way as quickly as he could. "He was a tough guy, that Tony," said Stewie.

After a decade or so of running three different Playboy Clubs, Tony withdrew from the corporation in 1970. His long-term plan was to open his own place so he launched Tony Roma's Place in North Miami. It was successful enough to attract the interest of financier Clint Murchison who, among other things, owned the

Dallas Cowboys football team. Together, they turned Tony Roma's into a franchise that, like the Playboy Clubs, soon spanned the world.

* * *

Hugh Hefner had maintained a close friendship with Ian Fleming since the early days of *Playboy,* when the weaver of international-spy stories had introduced James Bond to the magazine's readers in a serialized novel. Thanks to Hef, James Bond—with his passion for beautiful women, fast cars, and the perfect martini—was virtually synonymous with *Playboy* and had become a kind of role model for its readers. Via his adventures, the suave ladies' man and macho undercover agent had instructed millions of men on how to mix a cocktail, what music to select for a seduction, and what car to drive to make a quick getaway—all the basics.

While Ian was employed as the foreign manager of *The Sunday Times,* he would spend three months each winter on the island of Jamaica, and years later, that location would become central in several of his Bond tales. So it was only natural that Hef should turn to him for advice regarding the location of his next resort venture. Ian convinced Hef that Jamaica would be the ideal spot for the supreme Playboy getaway. Sadly, Ian died in August of 1964, just months before he would have been able to visit the club he'd envisioned.

Ocho Rios, as the Jamaica complex became known, was a lavishly appointed, seven-million-dollar resort stretching across ten acres of the north coast. It included 204 guest rooms, championship-quality tennis courts, an eighteen-hole golf course, a convention center, an Olympic-size pool complete with Bunny lifeguards in custom-tailored bikinis, and 800 feet of soft, white-sand beaches. Crocodile hunting was available in the Black Sea and limbo dancing on the poolside patio. The only question for keyholders was: Which was more attractive, the sun-drenched delights of the daylight outdoors, or the indulgences of the Bunnies, celebrity headliners, and local talent in the showrooms at night?

Pat Lacey, who had started as a Bunny in Los Angeles and would later become the Bunny Mother there, also worked in the Jamaica resort.

"At one point, the Jamaica Club was looking for stateside Bunnies to work there, and I was offered the opportunity to work out of the country. That resort was completely different from the U.S. Clubs in certain ways. For one thing, the showroom held about four hundred people—it was huge, with long banquet tables. It reminded me of a Las Vegas showroom, but longer! The bar was in the back of the room, and if you worked close to the stage, it was said you worked in 'Siberia,' because you had to go so far for cocktails. Plus, that was probably the first time I ever saw entertainers bomb, and by that I mean, not pull in a good crowd for the length of their engagement. But that was because the mindset of people staying at a resort for vacation was totally different from that of the guy taking a girl out on a Friday or Saturday night in the States. Vacationers were there for seven to ten days and the showroom was open every other night. So if you saw the show one night, you probably didn't want to see the same show later in the week—but it wouldn't have been profitable for Playboy to fly in new acts every few days."

\* \* \*

Singer and impressionist Duke Hazlett had already made a huge impression doing his unannounced imitation of Frank Sinatra at the 1959 Playboy Jazz Festival in Chicago, at the behest of Victor Lownes. After working Chicago and other American venues, he was thrilled when Victor hired him to bring his Sinatra act to London—it was his first trip abroad.

Duke remembered London vividly and, like Rip Taylor, described it in those days as the "city that never slept." "London in the '60s was peppered with small clubs, many of which doubled as casinos and such, but they were hard to get into because they literally weren't allowed to admit strangers off the street," Duke told us. "But all of them knew Vic. So either he'd come with me or I would drop his name to get in—anywhere in the city." Duke added that even though he was working multiple shows a night, into the wee small hours, he would still get up early in the morning for sightseeing. "There was so much that I had never seen before, so much history! Even just people-watching was great."

That engagement launched Duke on a round-the-world journey. "Doing Sinatra has brought me everywhere, even to Russia and Japan... everywhere! Everybody loves Sinatra and nobody portrays him better than I do. Wherever I went, they couldn't have treated Frank himself any better."

Duke has particularly warm memories—in both senses of the word—of the Ocho Rios Playboy Club in Jamaica. "It was amazingly beautiful—the resort, the showroom, the beach, all spectacular. But going to the other side of the island was also memorable, in a completely different way. The non-Playboy side was totally undeveloped, the roads were terrible, but the beach was gorgeous. You really felt like you were on a tropical island once you left the resort. But the Playboy side was completely modern, with every conceivable comfort."

\* \* \*

Kelly Monteith's first job as a solo comic was at the 183rd Street Art Theater in North Miami Beach. He described it to us as, "a strip club that also showed dirty movies. These same movies would be shown on prime-time television today, but back then, they were very risqué. There was a matinee and two or three showings a night and we'd do a show in between the movies. I was the comedian emcee and I'd go on stage after the movie and do five minutes, then I'd introduce the first girl, and after her I'd do another five minutes and introduce the second stripper. The best thing I can say about strip clubs is that you learned how to survive. It was a way most of us started out back then, but I knew I had to get out.

"I got to know Billy Rizzo who, at that time, was a booker for the Playboy Clubs, through other comedians. After paying my dues at the burlesque houses, I decided that I was ready to move on and called Billy, who arranged a weekend audition for me at the Chicago Club. I worked the Playroom—the smaller room with a bar—on a Friday and Saturday and Billy didn't come to see me until the last show on Saturday. I was really nervous because, up to that point, the audiences liked me and everything was great, but any comedian will tell you that you rarely hit a home run in all five consecutive shows. Somehow, it went well and Billy gave me some circuit work in the same room, starting at the Cincinnati Club about three months later.

"Playboy had a great circuit and they gave me the first steady income I ever had in show business. Jamaica was the most amazing job because you only had to work one show a week! Ocho Rios was just this little-bitty town. Jamaica back then was still very tropical and unspoiled—it was great. The people were nice, the club was wonderful… I mean you had the Bunnies, the pool, the beach, all the food and liquor anyone could want, and you could chill out for the entire week. How can you beat that? I always thought the Jamaicans were very sweet people.

"One of Jamaica's great products was *ganja*—the powerful marijuana that grew there. You would give one of the kids five bucks and he'd run into the jungle and come back with a *bale* of the stuff—it looked like a tumbleweed of pot. Of course, you'd have to clean it and weed out all the sand and twigs.

"Once when I was working at the New York Club, there was some kind of FBI investigation into the Mafia and they were calling the employees in for interviews. I never got called in, but I was nervous because I was sort of friendly with a guy who hung out at the bar a lot. He was an ex-boxer and I think he was a low-level enforcer—a strong-arm guy who retrieved money that was owed to *certain people.*

"I used to do a couple of jokes about the Mafia in my act, and the boxer guy told me once, 'Yeah, they're pretty funny but I don't think the guys downtown would appreciate those jokes too much.' I remember thinking, 'Whoa, maybe I better leave them out of the next show.' Nothing ever came of the investigation and I was sure glad I wasn't interviewed because I recall saying to myself, 'Jeez, if they ever call me in, I'm not going to squeal on *that* guy!'

"I worked the Los Angeles Club before I was really ready for it. I wasn't very good, to be honest with you. I worked with Arlene Golonka [best known for playing Millie Swanson on *The Andy Griffith Show*]. She had all her friends and family there on opening night and I followed her, but everyone just wanted Arlene back. To top it off I asked her if that was her real name. She got pissed off and said, sarcastically, 'No, I *changed* it!'

"Aside from that one time in L.A., I had great experiences at the clubs. The Bunnies were very nice girls. It was a good opportunity for them to make a lot of money—much better than if they worked as a secretary or clerk somewhere—and they were protected. No one was allowed to make rude remarks or touch them. Plus, there was a certain cachet about being a Bunny—a kind of status—and that costume made every one of them look amazing. We weren't supposed to ask them out, but we never paid attention to that. We had to be selective, though, because if you asked one on a date and she rejected you—well, you just blew your chances. The other girls would know immediately they you had hit on her and none of them wanted to be your second choice. I guess I picked well because my first wife was a Bunny from the Denver Club—Bunny Diane."

The clubs provided Kelly with the first steady income he ever had in show business and he told us it was, "a way to develop, in a lot of ways anonymously, since they didn't get much press because they were private clubs. It gave me the opportunity to evolve as a performer and a writer, and not to mention that it gave me a regular income to count on. I could actually buy clothes! "

Kelly got his break on *The Mike Douglas Show*. He was working at the New York Playboy Club when he got a letter suggesting that he take the train from New York to Philadelphia to audition for it. He aced the audition and landed his first television appearance. From there, he appeared on *The Jack Paar Show*, and was singled out in a review in *Time* magazine. Throughout this period, he continued to work at the Playboy Clubs, right up until he began appearing regularly on *The Tonight Show* and *Merv Griffin*. Kelly eventually landed his own show on CBS—*The Kelly Monteith Show*—and after an appearance on the English talk show *Des O'Connor*, he was offered his own series on BBC, which ran for six years.

While living in London, Kelly renewed his friendship with Victor, and he and his wife were invited to Victor's country home, Stocks, for the wedding of Victor and Marilyn.

December 1976 Rie Taga, a Japanese Bunny at the Tokyo Playboy Club serves drinks and lights

\* \* \*

The first Japanese Playboy Club opened in Tokyo on December 9, 1976. Others followed—in Osaka in 1978, Nagoya in 1979, and Sapporo in 1980. Interestingly, the franchise owners used primarily western-looking blondes in the advertising for the clubs—and the female singers they presented reflected this preference as well. But in addition to Japanese Bunnies, the clubs employed geisha to serve the keyholders. The truth is, the role of Bunny fell below that of geisha. Geisha did not have to follow the Bunny protocol of non-fraternization with customers, and could be seen cuddling with them while passing on drink orders to the Bunnies.

Because of the vast distance between Japan and the United States, the Playboy organization had difficulty maintaining their club policies. The franchisees were quite compliant when visited by Playboy executives—but once the coast was clear, all bets were off!

\* \* \*

Playboy's next beachhead was Nassau, the Bahamas, where they opened a casino on April 11, 1980. That one followed a unique business model: The Bahamian government owned the club and Playboy managed it. Val Lownes—yes, Victor's son—was the resident director.

Val had begun working in the family business a decade earlier, taking on various duties at the Playboy Plaza Hotel while studying at the University of Miami. At one point, Playboy offered a hotel-training program in which Val participated, working for various star department heads and picking up valuable skills from each. After a few years, he found himself troubleshooting at one club after another.

As Val remembered it, "I went wherever they needed someone—helping with labor disputes in one place, pitching in with catering in another. I floated among the clubs until going back to London, where my father was based, in 1975 or '76. There, I started dealing blackjack and working the roulette tables. I continued to pitch in where I was needed until the Bahamas became available. I remember my father giving a speech in which he asked for volunteers to go down to the Bahamas. He made it sound as if we would be pioneers—'Go west, young man'—only, in this case, it was more southwest!"

We ventured that we couldn't imagine Victor and Playboy having to do too much arm-twisting to get people to go work in a resort in Nassau.

"There were a lot of people with families that didn't want to relocate," Val replied, "But it was perfect for me. Sam DeStefano was my mentor in the entertainment arena. It would have been hard to put together a program for the showroom without Sam's help. His son Mike and I were friends, and Mike would usually come along with Sam. We'd play backgammon and he'd *always* beat me. He's a very bright guy.

"The Bahamian government was our partner and they wanted us to have Las Vegas—style revues with mainly local talent. We used a local lady to book the entertainment and it was really very good—so good, in fact, that we took some of the performers up to the Great Gorge Club for a week, and they were quite well received.

"A guy called King Pedro was a consistent hit. He did a fire act where he put a flaming Coke bottle on his head and then shimmied under a limbo stand. I never got bored watching him! Dionne Warwick came down for our opening night but, other than her, we didn't have a lot of stateside performers. Most of our customers came from the cruise ships and gambling junkets and they wanted to see island performers, so that's what we gave them.

"Gamblers from Chicago came down on overnight junkets. They had to show the organizers that they had a certain amount of cash—I believe it was $2,500—before they could get on the plane. We picked them up at the airport and immediately delivered them to the tables, where they got their chips and started gambling. They were expected to play green twenty-five dollar chips and, in exchange, we paid their airfare. Those who gambled a little more money got a room and dinner. At some point, most of them went downstairs to see the show, but they came back afterwards. Of course, less driven gamblers would come visit with their families and stay longer to enjoy all of the amenities of the island. That was more the norm."

Speaking of the local population—and understanding the government's fondness for seeing its people employed—we wondered if all the Bunnies were home-grown. Val explained, "There were two types of Bunnies—gaming staff and those that worked the back of the house, which included everything other than gambling—waitressing, promotion, all of that. The back of the house was all Bahamian staff, but the gambling side was all English. We brought them in from the English casinos. The Bahamian government didn't want the locals involved in the seedier side of the casinos, such as running gambling tables. In the beginning, they took a very moralistic attitude, but they knew they needed the revenue because Atlantic City was starting to take away some of their Paradise Island profits. When we first opened, and for a number of years after that, it was either Bahamians or English; I was the only one from the States."

Talking about Playboy and playboys conjured up one of Val's fondest memories. Every day, he told us, he'd look out from his office veranda over the pool and select a pretty girl. His assistant—quite accustomed to the task—would pick a striking orchid from the gardens underneath, put it in a vase or empty soda-pop can, and attach one of Val's business cards, on which he'd have written, 'Would you and your friend [or parents or whomever] please be my guests for the show tonight?' He'd have them seated at his reserved table and, of course, he would join them. He was young, living in paradise, and had a great job. Can you imagine a better life?

Although the foreign clubs followed the Playboy philosophy, they were responsible to local culture as well, and provided livelihoods for lots of local people—while spreading the Playboy brand around the world.

# 12

# PLAYBOY IN PARADISE

n the late sixties, an era when most hoteliers were shying away from new construction in favor of leasing existing properties, Playboy embarked on a typically groundbreaking plan—quite literally. Hef and the Playboy team hoped that a domestic resort would attract families in addition to their established clientele, and drive some essential new revenue.

An extensive search located the perfect 1,350-acre piece of real estate, just a half hour drive from the Chicago Club, on Lake Geneva in Wisconsin. When the Lake Geneva Playboy Club Hotel—as it was first called—opened in May of 1968, at an estimated cost of $18 million, it offered not one but two golf courses, horseback riding, ski slopes (Playboy was one of the first resorts in the country to install a chair lift), a stocked fifteen-acre lake for fishing, a wild-life refuge, and a freestanding convention center, in addition to the trademark nightclubs and dining facilities staffed by beautiful Bunnies. Guests could swim in either the indoor or outdoor pool, shoot skeet, and then relax in the luxurious health center—all before an evening of fine dining and spectacular entertainment in one of four showrooms.

The estate also boasted a runway large enough to accommodate a full-sized jetliner, and of course Hef's personal jet, the Big Bunny, had the best parking spot. The club's name was soon amended to the swankier Lake Geneva Playboy Resort.

As usual for Playboy, the sophisticated venue wasn't without its local detractors, who feared the encroachment of some sort of a den of iniquity—but once they saw the lovely, lush grounds and line-up of top-notch entertainment, they quickly threw their support behind the new resort, and government and local dignitaries joined Hef in cutting the ribbon at the opening.

\* \* \*

You'd expect a lavish resort like Lake Geneva to offer the pinnacle in entertainment, and that was certainly the case. But some rather raucous acts filled out the bill as well, creating at least one clash of "high" and "low." The comedian Gallagher, whose trademark act was hitting melons with a sledgehammer, opened there one New Year's Eve for Vic Damone, a singer so mindful of his suave image that he had his suits and shirts custom-made on London's Savile Row. What could possibly go wrong?

We had the good fortune to speak with Gallagher (bornLeo Anthony Gallagher Jr.) at the start of 2015, and he told me the story of that fateful night. "Vic was in the stage wings waiting to go on, and I swung my sledgehammer and hit the watermelon with the expected results. The melon guts flew and some of the mess landed all over his suit!

"The audience had to wait while Vic went back to his room to change, and the estate was so huge that it was quite a walk to his suite. He was fuming! I wanted his audience to have that midnight *smash* to remember and they sure did. Just the fact that you're asking me about it forty or so years later proves that. That's what I assume a comedian is supposed to do: shake things up, present the unexpected and violate the traditional. In the same fashion that the

Marx Brothers or Margaret Dumont did, you have to find some vain, self-important person to boot in the rump, and Vic Damone was a great foil for that."

Vic may have fumed at having to change his clothes after his watermelon bath, but he told us that he, too, really enjoyed playing the clubs. "The musicians were great," he said, "and Hugh Hefner was a super guy."

Jerry Pawlak, the resort maître d' told us, "Vic had it written in his contract that at each show, I had to seat at least two good-looking women ringside. He said he couldn't sing love songs to guys smoking cigars—he had to sing to beautiful women. I tried to fill his request each night but if I couldn't, I'd get some off-duty Bunnies to come in and sit there."

\* \* \*

The Four King Cousins can boast quite the show-business lineage: All are daughters of the famous King Sisters and part of the King Family. The dynasty began in Pleasant Grove, Utah, where large

The Four King Cousins, Tina Cole, Cathy Cole Green, Candy Conkling, Carolyn Thomas. Courtesy of The King Cousins

families were the norm; there were six King sisters altogether, who were in and out of the act at different times. The King Sisters were one of the major vocal groups of the swing era, and achieved a level of popularity comparable to that of the Boswell Sisters, their inspirations, and the Andrews Sisters, their colleagues.

The original King group sang with many of the most famous bands of the 1930s and 1940s, including Horace Heidt, Charlie Barnet, Artie Shaw, and Alvino Rey. And somehow, in between radio broadcasts, big-band tours, and making hit records, all of the sisters managed to marry prominent members of the Los Angeles music and movie community. Among them, they produced more than enough young singers for a new generation of harmonizers, eventually called the King Cousins. First introduced as the Five King Cousins on ABC's *Kraft Summer Music Hall* hosted by John Davidson (following a series starring the King Family), their names were Carolyn Thomas, Candy and Jamie Conkling, Cathy Cole, and Tina Cole. At the time, Tina was the best known of the bunch, having played Katie Douglas on the popular situation comedy *My Three Sons*. When Jamie resigned to finish her education at Brigham Young University, the ladies became the *Four* King Cousins. They were signed to a recording contract by Capitol Records and released their debut album, *Introducing the Four King Cousins*, in 1968. It was produced, arranged, and conducted by another cousin of theirs, Lex de Azevedo, and it showcased their signature four-part vocal harmonies. Their second album was produced by the Playboy/Trio Records label in 1976, two years after their initial appearance in a Playboy Club, and was released in Japan.

We had a great time talking with the King ladies, who tended to answer in unison. "We were part of a singing family," the girls all said at once. Tina Cole took over from here and told us, "The whole King family phenomenon was a surprise to us. We were just leading regular, normal lives—of course our mothers were still singing, but we were going to school and doing our thing—when we were handed this wonderful opportunity on a silver platter. None of us were expecting it or really aspiring toward this career we've had.

"We loved entertaining at the Playboy Clubs—mainly Lake Geneva and Great Gorge. We played Lake Geneva a few times. It was glorious. We went bicycling, picnicking, played all sorts of sports. It was a ball! We opened for John Byner and even went on a picnic with John and his family."

"All I knew about the Playboy Clubs going in," confessed Tina, "was that they were where the Bunnies were. At the time, I couldn't wait to go down to the Bunny hutch and get a Bunny suit! All the Bunnies that were there helped me get into it. The Bunny Mother was there too, and she was also into the spirit of things. When I put on the costume, she went over to the dryer and pulled a big wad of panty hose out—to give me cleavage, she explained. I had so much fun—I remember it vividly to this day!

"Our second album was produced by Playboy. We did the vocals here in the States and completed it on tour in Japan—that's when they added the orchestration, with all Japanese musicians. It actually was another one of those things that happened so quickly that it was over before we caught our breath. The album was completed in three days for about fifteen thousand dollars—which is really unheard of—and released in Japan to really good sales.

"Okay, back to Lake Geneva," said Tina. "Carlo Cirello was the room manager and he loved us—and we just adored him. He was always looking out for us. One day, he wanted to give us a break from the club, so he took us to an Italian restaurant in Milwaukee he was fond of. Well, we never asked, but we were sure that this one gentleman was what's called 'connected'—you know—with the *family*. Big Frank was the name everyone called him, and we think he was originally from Chicago. He sat in the corner booth with his back against the wall and his posse around him. Carlo must have told him we were coming because, when we walked in, Big Frank looked at us and said, 'Hey, these are the King Cousins! We'll be at the show tomorrow night!' And they were all there!

"It was a wonderful, fun, carefree time for us. We wore beautiful clothes for the shows, mostly gowns with slits up to the tops of our thighs, and jeweled tops. We had a couple of costumes we traded off and we did a lot of dancing in the act. We did a tribute to our mothers, the King Sisters, and at that point, we changed and added chubbies and ostrich feathers and headbands, and we had the King Sisters on tape, so we sang '40s tunes *with* them. We also had them talk to us about what to do and not do. It was really a very clever bit. And John Byner... he was so much fun to work with. What a gentleman!"

Mimi Hines told us, that the opening of Lake Geneva was almost stalled because, "They were still putting in plants and trees on opening day," Mimi said, "but overnight it blossomed into this wonderful landscape that looked as if it had been nurtured for years—when really the plants and trees had actually just been planted the night before. It was really cool. Everybody gussied up to come and see the show. The guys were in suits—and even a few tuxedos—and the ladies had on beautiful cocktail dresses. The Resort atmosphere was all old time glamour—plus the clubs were run so smoothly. At least that's how it appeared to us as entertainers.

"Phil and I loved the Wisconsin Club. We were married as well as partners, and during the day, we played golf, got a facial or massage in the afternoon, and then hit the deck for the show at eight. I miss Phil Ford and the fun of our act so much; I can't tell you. We always opened with a rousing song, then did a second kind of swing number, and from there, we'd go right into the 'Sayonara' sketch. Phil and I coined the phrase 'rots a ruck'; everyone loved it, so we always did a variation of that. After the show was over, we'd stay up late, giggle and laugh, and write down the ad libs that we had come up with that night."

Because of their brilliant shows, Mimi and Phil came to be called 'the spoilers,' and other entertainers weren't keen on following them.

Jerry Pawlak—who just filled us in on Vic Damone's contract

requirements—was perhaps the most legendary maître d' in the Playboy chain. As Victor Lownes put it, "Jerry was a grace under pressure kind of guy." In his eight years at the resort, he was a bartender, room captain, assistant maître d' in the Penthouse Room, and eventually he earned the coveted position of maître d' in the blue-velvet-draped VIP dining room. "It was quite an opportunity to get a job there and work your way up from the ground floor." Jerry recalled when we spoke with him." I started as a bartender, and it was my good fortune to have been working the night the maître d' of the VIP Room fired a captain. He looked around the room and asked the rest of us, 'Who wants to be captain?' I couldn't say yes fast enough. That was my first promotion. As I moved up the ladder I was eventually in charge of arranging the entertainment and reservations for all the big names. I took a lot of pride in pro-

viding the best experience possible to our clientele and visiting celebrities. If anything wasn't running smoothly I could usually fix it with just a look and not have to say a word to the staff. It was a lot of responsibility but I worked with Bob Hope, George Carlin, Ann-Margret, Peggy Lee, Buddy Rich and many other big names."

Jerry went on to talk about the first and only time George Carlin made an appearance before the conservative Wisconsin

Barbi Benton and Jerry Pawlak at the Lake Geneva Resort. Courtesy Jerry Pawlak

crowd in the Playboy resort. "He was almost thrown out of town—not just the Playboy Club! I really wasn't paying much attention to his show, but I was told he made a bunch of jokes about the Vietnam War that didn't sit well at all with the patrons. I turned around just in time to catch him flip off the audience and leave the stage. I had to comp the entire room—all 400 patrons—for their dinner and lack of a show! But I did get on stage and tell them that I guaranteed that George would never play a Playboy Club again. Hef agreed. He was all about free speech, but he was also a savvy businessman and knew that if he wanted to attract families to the facility, that kind of behavior couldn't be tolerated.

"You know," Jerry continued, "that was actually not the only time in my experience that we had a performer walk off stage. Another time, Buddy Rich didn't feel as if he was being appreciated and he put down his drumsticks and said good night. The only problem was that he had only said, 'Hello,' a few minutes prior. Joan Rivers also left the stage once, upset because a gentleman had his back to her. She said she'd return when he turned around. It's part of the job to deal with different temperamental personalities."

Apparently, Vic Damone's special requests weren't the only ones Jerry received. "Joan Rivers' contract stated that I couldn't have people who smoked cigars close to the stage. Not unreasonable, I guess, but how was I supposed to know if they smoke cigars or not? These were the days when everyone smoked!

"In that same vein, Frank Sinatra Jr. was here for a show—and I have to say he wasn't terribly friendly with anyone—and on his last day, his manager told me that Frank wasn't very happy because the staff wasn't being welcoming *to him*. Well… you have to be a diplomat in this job, so, before his last show, I gathered the Bunnies and told them that after the last song I wanted them to come on stage and give him a rousing ovation. Not only that but they were to take their Bunny tails off and toss them at him! I pictured it like a twist on people throwing flowers but the Bunnies saw it as lobbing eggs and really threw them at him! The Bunnies were never supposed to take off their tails so I thought this would really be something special—and it sure was. He actually put his hands up to ward them off! They were fluffy cottontails so they hardly hurt, but let's just say that it didn't make Frank feel any more welcomed.

"Shirley Jones and Gordon MacRae entertained at the club on various occasions. They were both in *Carousel* and *Oklahoma*, and a friend of mine who owned movie theaters in Chicago and had a house on Lake Geneva with a beautiful home theater asked me if Shirley Jones and her husband might like to come over to watch *Carousel*. I brought it up to Shirley and she said, 'We'd love to!' I drove her, Jack Cassidy and some other staff members over to my friend's house, and we had a great time! She sat right behind me, and the only sad part of the evening was when, about half way through the movie, she started to very softly cry very softly because a few of the stars had recently passed away. It's so interesting to view a movie with the star of it sitting right behind you."

We were on a roll, loving Jerry's journey back, so we encouraged him to tell us more. "Jack Jones was there once," he said, "with his *fabulously* gorgeous wife, Jill St. John. During dinner one night, I took it upon myself to wait on them, and Jack ordered a fine wine to accompany the meal. Well, Jill was even more beautiful up close and I couldn't take my eyes off her. At one point, I asked Mr. Jones if I should pour the wine and he nodded yes, but I guess I was distracted. As I started to pour, we both realized that I hadn't removed the cork. I had been so entranced by Jill that I was tilting the bottle but nothing came out! Jack made a joke out of it, saying that Playboy sure had their own procedures for everything—that other places removed the cork before attempting to decant it!

"It was very special when the big boss, Mr. Hefner, came in. The entire club wanted to shine for him, and VIP Room Chef Jean Banchet offered to make him anything he wanted. Prior to coming to Lake Geneva, Chef Banchet had worked in a restaurant in Chi-

Ray Anthony and Jerry Pawlak. Courtesy Jerry Pawlak

cago called La France—it was voted the tenth best French restaurant in the world—he was the best and we had to have him. That's the Playboy way. All Hef requested was fried chicken and mashed potatoes!"

Jerry explained that Lake Geneva was a kind of testing ground where performers could premier a big show before moving it to bigger venues in Las Vegas or elsewhere. It was like an "out-of-town tryout" and some of them just didn't work out.

"Sally Struthers had a show that she was going to use to open for Alan King. Alan came to see it the last night and hated it. We were all dining together in the VIP room and he not only criticized the show in front of all of us, but he complained about her choice of outfit—a tuxedo suit. I don't think she ever did another major show anywhere.

"Ann-Margret was the first singer at any of the clubs or resorts to use a wireless mic. As she came off the stage someone had to be there to grab the mic from her, and the first few nights her husband Roger Smith took care of that. But he had to head back to California before her run was up, so on the night before he left, he looked around and appointed me with that duty. 'Let Jerry do it,' he said, and of course I was happy to. Well, she always came *charging* off because she was so ramped up from the show, and I'd have to actually grab her —almost like a halfback. It wasn't a bad job at all! When I'd get home I could still smell her perfume on my suit jacket, just from holding her for that short time. Wow, Ann-Marget!"

A near disaster was averted one night when musical director Sam DeStefano had to deal with an emergency outside the club. Jerry told us, "Sam always played the piano as either the comic or singer finished their act. The room manager said, 'Someone has to play the piano,' and he looked at me in my tuxedo, and said 'Let's have Jerry play him off.' I'm all for helping out but I don't play the piano. *I know nothing about the piano*! Well, the band came up with a plan. The bass player said, 'I'll play two keys and all you do is go *bum-bum-bum-bum*'—and he showed me what I should do. But when

Sally Struthers giving a great show on stage.
Michael Mauney The Life Images Collection Getty Images

the comic saw me sitting on the piano bench he said to the audience, 'Look who's behind the piano, the maître d' Jerry! Jerry, why don't you play us something?' I motioned him over and explained what was going on, and right then the bass player started his notes and I played my *bum-bum-bum-bum* and we played him off.

The funny part was that I had to go back to the door to wish my clientele good-night, and you'd be surprised how many people told me, 'Jerry, you play a great piano!' I only played two keys!

"You probably wouldn't guess that Ed McMahon's entire show was about W.C. Fields—OK maybe a little Johnny Carson. He even wore a big top hat. His opening act was three singers—triplets! After each show we always had a little party. Just a small get together. Nothing ever happened, but you can imagine me, I'm saying, *triplets*. It was a good act.

"Trini Lopez was always a huge hit. He had the whole audience on their feet dancing and singing along with him. And boy, did he give them a show. He dressed up in a white gaucho outfit covered with rhinestones." When Trini told me about the same show, he said, "I resurrected Liberace's gym suit with humongous sequins. I felt I should show up in lots of bling." Jerry really enjoyed Trini's company but was surprised when, on a visit to New York's Stage Deli, he heard someone call his name and turned to find it was Trini. "I never would have thought that superstar Trini Lopez would recognize me at the Stage Deli!" he said with typical humility.

"The entertainers were the biggest in the business," Jerry recalled in wrapping up our chat. "Peggy Lee, Tony Bennett, Liza Minnelli, Dyan Cannon, the list goes on and on. It was the best job ever. I just found an old menu from 1968 and added up all the items we offered. The entire menu—I'm talking about appetizers, soups, entrees and desserts—everything added up to $89. I could hardly wait to get to work each day. Now, I can tell you—I would have worked for free—it was that good!"

\* \* \*

With one resort up and running, Playboy went even further out on a limb and found the perfect, sprawling property for another. In 1971, the Great Gorge Playboy Resort in MacAfee, New Jersey, opened with Ann-Margret headlining. Like the one at Lake Geneva, this resort was built upon a sprawling estate and featured every conceivable recreational option, this time with an emphasis on winter sports; it was a particular draw for skiers. An added appeal was its close proximity to the metropolitan cities of New York, New Jersey, and Connecticut. Playboy executives envisioned city-dwellers bringing their families to the country for weekend get-aways and vacations.

Since the London Casino had turned out to be a raging success, the Playboy team was elated when, in 1972, New Jersey officials began to hold talks about legalizing gambling in the state. They were certain that Great Gorge would provide them a perfect foothold in the nascent U.S. gaming arena.

A regular at Great Gorge, Shecky Greene is one of the few elite comedians who were compensated in six figures to headline in Las Vegas during the '60s and '70s. I found Shecky to be a sweetheart—and extremely generous with his time and colorful stories—but from what he told me, he was a different guy in the old days. Show business had been just a means to an end for him, he told me, and that end was gambling and drinking. His favorite vice was betting on the horses, and it wasn't unusual for him to make $150,000 in a week and give his bookie $130,000 of it.

"Great Gorge was supposed to be a big deal for Playboy—a really big deal," he told us, "and they paid me a lot of money to play there, which I feel a little bad about, because they weren't making any money at that time. But they were setting the stage for the legalization of gambling and I always drew the gambling crowd. Unfortunately, there were nights when we had probably seventy Bunnies and no customers. It was sad, because it was a gorgeous place, but people just didn't take to it. If New Jersey had legalized gambling throughout the state, that club would have done amazing business. But—they didn't."

* * *

Outside of Las Vegas, gambling wasn't something that government officials were willing to agree to sanction very hastily. It wasn't until 1976 that gambling came to New Jersey, and even then, it was only permitted in Atlantic City. That didn't help the Great Gorge Resort, which cost a staggering $30 million or more to build.

The Playboy organization forged ahead in its attempt to replicate the success of London by opening a club in Atlantic City. In order to finance the proposed $135 million venture, they formed a partnership with the Elsinore Corporation. In 1981, the group was issued a temporary gaming license, and the club opened on April

Shecky Greene surrounded by a bevy of beautiful Bunnies and still he tells us, "Not one, no not one, would go out with me. So I dated the doorman." We find that hard to believe! Courtesy of

14. The timing, alas, wasn't propitious. As the ribbon was being cut in Atlantic City, the organization found itself at the center of an investigation of its business practices at

the London casinos—but that is a story for another chapter.

* * *

Larry Storch traveled a remarkable path before arriving at the Playboy Clubs. He grew up during the Depression, in a brownstone on Manhattan's 77th Street, where his mother took in boarders to help make ends meet.

"My first job," he said, "was at a striptease joint in Albany. I went on between two striptease dancers who would come out wearing outfits no bigger than a Band-Aid. My salary was twenty-five dollars a week, which was a lot of money in those days, and I could send home fifteen of it."

With World War II raging in Europe, Larry joined the Navy. It was onboard the USS Proteus in 1942 that he met Tony Curtis. The two became fast buddies and remained lifelong friends. "When I got out of the service, I was hitchhiking around in my uniform.

I wanted to see the country, and I figured that with my thumb in the air, wearing a sailor suit, I couldn't miss! 'Where do you want to go, sailor?' a guy in a car would say, and I'd reply, 'I'm just going west, sir. I want to see the country.' One guy [let] me off in Palm Springs and said, 'Sailor, you won't have any trouble getting a pick-up from here.' I decided to stay there for a little while, and I was sitting in a bar, and the guy next to me turned out to be Phil Harris—'Hiya Jackson' from *The Jack Benny Show*. 'Whaddya do?' he asked me.

"Well, I started doing impressions of Cary Grant and all those guys for him, and he said, 'Listen, I'm taking you back to Hollywood.' He pushed me into a car, and we drove right to Hollywood, right up to Ciro's, a nightclub on the strip. I was still in my uniform, and sitting by the stage was Lucille Ball, and on stage was Desi Arnaz rehearsing his band. Phil Harris said to Lucy, 'Don't ask questions.'

"To me he said, 'Do some of your voices.' I did the English things and the Frenchmen, I did the Germans and the Russians, and finally Lucy said to me, 'Desi opens tomorrow night. I want you out of your sailor suit—buy a dark black suit—you're in the show with him.'

"All this happened so fast. I mean, it was too much! I opened up for Desi for two weeks. My salary was one hundred fifty dollars a week—a lot of money. It was amazing!"

As many know, Cary Grant never actually uttered the line famously attributed to him—"Judy, Judy, Judy"—in any film. Perhaps you'll guess where it came from. Cary himself attributed it to one of Larry's appearances at Ciro's, when, in the middle of a Cary Grant impersonation, Judy Garland walked in, inspiring Larry to utter the now immortal words.

"There were only a few nightclubs in Los Angeles," Larry went on, "and Ciro's was it. After I played there, I had an agent from William Morris, Benny Holtzman, who booked me into the Copacabana in New York. 'How close to a thousand can you come?' I heard him saying. Mind you, it wasn't so long before that that I'd been making twenty-one dollars a month. Benny got off the phone and said, 'You got seven fifty! You got seven-hundred-fifty a week.' I'm thinking, *I must be dreaming.* That was the beginning of it.

"I performed everywhere, including all of the Playboy Clubs. It was at a Playboy Club that I first told a story that was the least bit—*whoops!* The story was about two ladies of the evening and it got a big laugh, and I remember thinking, *whoops* is the way to go. Not dirty, but with a little bang.

"Once, I opened at the Great Gorge Club in New Jersey, and the next morning, I got a call from the manager who said, 'Larry, if you look out your door, you'll see two police officers.' I said, 'The jokes were that bad?' He said, 'No, we have a woman who works here as a telephone operator and she's also a psychic. She had a dream where she saw you being shot by a bald man wearing a green suit.' 'But she's only a telephone operator,' I said. Then the chief of police was also on the line saying, 'Yes, but her record of being psychic and calling future shots is alarmingly accurate.'

"So the cops followed me around for the next two weeks—two in uniform and two in plain clothes. They even came to my shows. 'Don't worry, and don't ask questions,' they told me.

"I hadn't told anyone about the psychic or the cops, so the bass player couldn't figure out why I was doing a lot of jokes from behind his bass fiddle. As soon as I finished the gig and left the grounds, it was, 'That's it kid, you're on your own.' My patrol detail disappeared.

"My wife traveled with me most of the time, but especially when I had a Playboy gig. I'm not complaining, but every evening before I went down to do my show, she wanted to make love. Finally, one night, I asked her, 'Why do you always want to make love before I go to work?' She said, 'Because that way, all those half-naked Bunnies will look like John Wayne to you.' I told that story to my buddies one night, and the manager overheard it and said, 'You have to tell that story from the stage'—so I did.

"I loved playing the Playboy Clubs, and every once in a while, a friend of mine, another comedian, would be in the audience, and I'd bring him up. Shecky Greene came up once and tore the place apart. They loved him."

Larry worked steadily in nightclubs, in movies, and in theaters, but it was on television that he fulfilled one of his wildest dreams. "Jackie Gleason was an idol," he told me, "and why not? He was a giant. I had done an impersonation of him in one of my shows, and one day, I received a call asking me to go see him at the Sheridan Hotel where he was staying. He came out of the bedroom in a bathrobe at twelve noon—just like Hugh Hefner—and said to me, 'Larry, I've got to take a ten-week vacation from the TV show. I'm giving the gig, the show, to you. Remember, we run live. Hundreds of people will be watching'—really it was millions—'so just don't say *fuck* and you'll be fine. Can you remember that?' He was my idol.

"At one point, I was in a Broadway play called *Who's That Lady?* playing a Russian spy. Tony Curtis called me and said, 'I hear you're on Broadway doing a show, but I'm making a movie, so pack your bags and get on a plane. We start in a week.' He put me in *Some Like It Hot*, *Forty Pounds of Trouble*, *The Persuaders*, and others."

Today, Larry lives just blocks from the turn-of-the-century brownstone in which he was raised and was inspired by his mother's multicultural tenants. Smart money management has provided him with a double penthouse on Central Park West, where he can point out his childhood home from his luxurious wrap-around balcony.

"It's all from telling jokes! I can't believe how fortunate I am," he told me. "Now, I get my kicks from going down to the park and blowing my saxophone. There is one last story I have to tell you. One day recently, I was playing my saxophone in the park. I had my eyes closed, searching for the notes, you know, and feeling my sax pull, when a little boy came up and put a dollar into my horn. His mother was standing with him and said,

'I told him we had to help you out.' I said, 'Thanks lady, but I really don't need it.' Jesus, I thought to myself, if another Depression ever comes around, I'll take my saxophone over to West End Avenue and play on the corner."

Why West End Avenue?

"So I can keep an eye on my penthouse."

\* \* \*

Teen idol Bobby Rydell first began performing to sellout crowds of screaming high school girls while still a teenager himself. By the early 1960s, he had accumulated five gold records, including one for his bestselling single "Wild One," and one for his ever-popular "Volare." A few bars from that one are the ringtone on his phone. When I reminded Bobby that he was the youngest person ever to sing at the famous Copacabana nightclub in New York, he replied, simply, "I believe I was." After a little more prodding, he expanded on the experience.

"I was nineteen the first time I was booked at the Copa, and it was prom season so the place was packed with kids. That meant the chorus girls couldn't come out to do their Carmen Miranda-style dance routines—there just wasn't enough floor space. I remember looking forward to seeing the Copa girls dance, and they told me, 'No, no, Bobby. No Copa girls tonight. You go on right away.'"

After playing the Copa, Bobby went on the road, as well as performing in movies and on numerous television shows. In 1963, he played Hugo Peabody in the movie *Bye, Bye Birdie* with Ann-Margret and Dick Van Dyke. He also had a recurring role on *The Red Skelton Show,* as Clem Kadiddlehopper's cousin Zeke, and was a regular on *Milton Berle.*

"All of a sudden," he told us, "the Playboy circuit came up. The first club I played was New York, and that was a marvelous job with great musicians. Jack Lemmon and Tom Jones were in the audience the same night, and that was a real hoot for me. In general, the Playboy circuit was a ball to work. The people were wonderful and there was no BS. As performers, we had to have everything in place and worked out. We had to know what we were doing. The clubs were all the same, yet each one had a little slightly different flavor. For example, the Chicago Club was a little smaller than the others because it had been the first one to open—but it was a hit with me because it was almost like a jazz room, intimate and a very cool place to work.

"Lake Geneva was great to play because of all the activities and the larger showrooms. Carlo Cirello, the room manager, was a funny guy. If you met him, you'd never forget him—but you might have a difficult time *hearing* him he was so soft-spoken. Let's say I said to him, 'Carlo, what time is the second show?' [Mumble, mumble] 'What, Carlo?' I'd say. 'Talk to me! What are you saying?' Sometimes, I wondered if he was putting us all on!

"One time, Buddy Greco was working Lake Geneva and he called Carlo from his hotel room and said, 'I'm not coming down for the second show unless the piano is tuned.' Carlo said, 'Do me a favor. Stay in your room. There's no one here.' Ha! Carlo was funny. I mean, very funny. I played golf with him at the great courses right on the property.

"The club in Dallas was my favorite one, because the band was made up of all these guys from North Texas State. They had what was called a lab band, with Galen Jeter as the lead trumpet player. It was such a ball to play with them every night, because those musicians were absolutely ridiculous. They were so good that once, when I was in Dallas doing a gig somewhere else, I went over to the Playboy Club to see them, hoping for a chance to sit in with Jeter. After the hugging and kissing, I said, 'Galen, do you mind if I sit in and play one of the charts?' He said, 'We'd love you to join us.' So I sat in with the big band and played a jazz track.

"Dallas was pretty hip, thanks to those guys. They knew how to work me over, but in a sweet, funny way. One of them would say, 'You know, Bob, when Frankie Avalon was here, he bought us all five cases of Jack Daniels.' I don't know if they were lying or not, but I'd buy gin or whatever they wanted. It was a great time!"

An interesting sidebar to Bobby's Texas stories concerned the rivalry between the famous Dallas Cowboys Cheerleaders and the Playboy Bunnies. It evolved into a publicity war, with each group trying to outdo the other at just about everything, including softball, charity fundraising, and general peacock strutting.

Bobby teamed up with Frankie Avalon and Fabian in 1985 on a show they called *The Golden Boys*. The public response was phenomenal, and there were sold-out crowds most everywhere they performed. Bobby told me that one night, over dinner, Frankie asked him how long he thought they might be able to keep the show on the road, to which Bobby replied, "I don't know, Frank, a year maybe? Two tops. Then it's over."

Bobby couldn't have been more wrong. Thirty years later, *The Golden Boys* is still playing in the largest venues in the country—to full houses.

* * *

Lorna Luft played both the Lake Geneva and Great Gorge Resorts, and refused to pick a favorite. "I *loved* working there," she told us. "I had a great time, and they were both beautiful clubs with great sound systems, great lighting—truly a marvelous night club feel—and they had a great behind the scenes crew. It was amazing and, because it was Playboy, they couldn't have been more professional. When you were booked to play there, you knew you were going to have fun. The resorts offered so many activities, and it amazed me because you wouldn't have thought Playboy would be so acclimated to *daytime* fun.

"My show included two boy dancers, and was your typical cabaret show where I sang pop songs of the seventies. The Ace Trucking Company opened for me and it was a lot of fun seeing Fred Willard later, in every single movie I turned on! It was a great time and we all enjoyed ourselves—the Bunnies, Ace Trucking, my crew—everyone.

"I loved going to the clubs as much as working there, but you needed a key to get in. If someone invited me and I had other plans, I'd cancel them. It was special to be invited to the Playboy Club—an event. I've been to the Mansion and whenever I was in Hugh Hefner's company, he was nothing but charming and lovely to me. And he'd always say, 'Thank you so much for working at the clubs, the resorts.' He's just always been a class act, a great host, and incredibly generous.

"If they start opening new Playboy Clubs again, I would be more than happy to go back and work them. You know why? Because it was the kind of place where you thought, 'When's my next booking back here?'"

\* \* \*

Fred Willard entertained at the Playboy Clubs many times and with different partners. "One of the first times was at the Phoenix Club and I was part of a comedy duo—Greco and Willard. Then we moved on to Boston, Cincinnati, New Orleans. New Orleans was a tough job because you worked a *lot* of shows. If there were enough customers you might work six shows a night! We'd start with our A show upstairs, then the manager would lead us downstairs for the B show and then back up for another A show. It got to be a little confusing. The Boston Club was one of my favorites—only two shows a night—and great atmosphere.

"The one unique thing about the clubs was that the room manager would always submit a written report on each entertainer. It would go to headquarters in Chicago as well as your agent. You didn't get graded in a regular club! People came for the Bunnies and because it was a key club. They also expected a certain level of entertainment. It wasn't like playing at coffee houses, where the guys would go on stage after a folk singing duo, in the Village with the hippies. You really had to have your act down well."

In between career revolutions, Fred spent a year at Chicago's Second City before being asked to join a newly forming comedy group. "We became popular pretty quickly," Fred told us. "Before we even had a name for the group we were recruited to appear on *The Tonight Show* and *The [Ed] Sullivan Show*. We did some sketches and some improvisational routines, and one of them involved a man-on-the-street interview. In the skit, one of our characters says he works for the Ace Trucking Company in New Jersey, and we thought this was the funniest thing because every place had companies with the name Ace—Ace Typewriter, Ace Plumbing etc.

So we called ourselves the Ace Trucking Company!"

By the time Fred hit the resorts, he was one of five comics performing together as the Ace Trucking Company. "Lake Geneva was kind of the gem of the whole Playboy Club rotation. You got to stay right on the property, which was a beautiful resort, and when you weren't swimming or whatever, you'd spend time with the other performers. I remember hanging with Lorna—who was terrific—and also Jesse Jackson. My wife had a long conversation with him while he held our daughter, who was just a toddler at the time, on his lap.

"It was such a well-run organization. I don't know if they have any place like that today. Those days are pretty much over if you want to go out and have an evening with dinner and a show. I hope they come back!"

You'll learn more about come back plans later on, but we doubt Fred would have time to appear at any new club. He put improv on the back burner as he segued very successfully into movie and TV roles.

* * *

Everyone we questioned loved working at the Resorts. There's no question about that. Well, who wouldn't? They were architecturally beautiful, with state-of-the-art play toys, dining, and entertainment. But as far as being profitable to the organization, they weren't, and even Playboy couldn't carry the losses forever.

# 13

# A WOMAN ON TOP

O f all the thousands of beautiful sights ever witnessed in the pages of *Playboy* magazine, one of the most astonishing was a special pictorial in October 1970—not one of the regular centerfolds, but a special guest star. She was a singer-actress who already had an impressive résumé of television, nightclub, and recording work under her belt—not that a belt (or any other garment) was visible. She looked amazingly feminine, yet incredibly empowered; there was something soft and sweet yet, at the same time, feisty and independent about her—this was one sexpot who was able to take care of herself. The visual image of her was so overwhelming that the comic book auteur Jack Kirby was inspired to create a Wonder Woman-like female superhero ("Big Barda" of the *New Gods* series) using her as a template. It was an auspicious beginning for a long and productive relationship between Playboy Enterprises and the marvelous entertainer Lainie Kazan.

Few entertainers have had to endure the up-and-down extremes—both professional and personal—that Lainie Kazan (nee Lainie Levine) has experienced over her half-century career in show business.

Lainie Kazan. Photofest

After graduating from Erasmus Hall High School in Brooklyn—
two grades ahead of Barbra Streisand, although they never met
while there—Lainie joined the well-regarded Carol Haney dance
troupe, *Up!* When Carol began work on a new Broadway play, she

suggested that Lainie audition for the show. The play was *Funny Girl*, and Lainie lost the lead role to her former schoolmate, Barbra Streisand. *Down!*

At the time, Lainie was singing at a Manhattan nightclub on Second Avenue called the Living Room. One night, Carol, brought a few of her colleagues to see the show—Garson Kanin and Ray Stark among them. After hearing Lainie sing, Ray persuaded her to audition for the part of Vera the showgirl. Having already lost out on the lead, Lainie was not keen to chase after a minor role, but she auditioned anyway.

Meanwhile, Lainie's run at the Living Room (an important club where Jack Jones and Marilyn Maye also played in the mid-1960s) continued, and she also was offered work in several clubs in Canada. One night, Irvin Arthur, who was already working with the Playboy Clubs chain, came in and told her that he was impressed and would find something for her. In the meantime, she went north to sing in Toronto, and then Winnipeg.

Ontario and Manitoba are not known as particularly warm parts of the world, and Lainie's first taste of road life left her cold and lonely—and far from home. But, unexpectedly, two phone calls reached her within a few days of each other that completely changed everything. Phone call number one: the producers of *Funny Girl* called to offer her the part she wanted. The second was Irvin Arthur; he lined up three months' straight work for her on the Playboy circuit. She took option number one. She had had it with nightclubs, at least for the time being. "I was done with the road for awhile," she said, "I wanted a crack at Broadway."

Lainie may not have won the role of Fanny Brice, but she negotiated hard with Ray Stark. In addition to playing Vera, she would be Streisand's understudy for an additional fifty dollars a week. And—perhaps even better—she'd also snagged a movie contract with Stark's Seven Arts Production Company.

One night in 1964, Ms. Streisand was sick with the flu, and

Lainie was tapped to step into the role of Fanny. Lainie's mother contacted all of their friends and relatives, as well as the press. But, alas…. Barbra, clearly shaken at the thought of ceding the limelight (and perhaps of inviting comparisons), rallied at the last minute and went on. Luckily for Lainie, the star's recovery was short-lived, and Barbra was forced to surrender her part to her for two performances the following day. One matinee and one evening show were enough for Lainie to show her stuff. The audiences and the press loved her; her star had been launched.

In spite of her budding success on the Great White Way, it wasn't long before she left Broadway and *Funny Girl* to return to the nightclubs—but now she could command headlining gigs at such top-notch venues as the legendary Persian Room in New York's Plaza Hotel.

What could possibly go wrong for Lainie at this point? Apparently, fate had a few more twists in store. In 1970, Lainie's career was sidetracked for several years by a life-threatening injury. Later in the '70s, she experienced two setbacks on Broadway. The first was when she was fired from *Seesaw*, and another when a proposed revival *The Women*—where she was to share billing with Alexis Smith and Myrna Loy—never got off the ground.

She had an important appearance on *The Ed Sullivan Show* in December 1968 (Lainie was already singing her classic medley of "The Trolley Song" and "Gotta Have Me Go with You"), and around that time she also had a very successful run at the Playboy Resort in Lake Geneva. Yet none of her proposed roles on Broadway or in Hollywood seemed to be materializing. Her marriage was on the rocks, and she needed money, to, among other things, support her young daughter. She had to take whatever work she could get, and it turned out to be from the road-weary world of nightclubs that she thought she had escaped years earlier. She spent several years working primarily in dumpy, midwestern joints that she referred to as, without much exaggeration, "the toilets of the USA."

Was this a happy time? Far from it: "It was the low point in my life," she says. She was traveling from city to city, and from paycheck to paycheck, most of which bounced. For practical reasons, she could only carry one performance costume with her—one working "gown"—and tried to change the look, just for her own sake, by switching around the jewelry. She mostly played in the Midwest—Milwaukee and the less fashionable areas of Chicago. These were all dives run by the lower echelon rings of organized crime, the last gasp of the mafia's involvement in the field of live entertainment and gin-joints where the booze was usually watered down. She remembers a club known as the Centerstage in Milwaukee, a ghastly haunt where her room had a refrigerator that had been painted orange, and a floor that was as crooked as the owners. "The sign only had two lights lit on the tiny billboard, and they didn't pay me. We did three shows a night, and had to wear our coats because the guy would turn off the heat after the second show. I remember screaming, 'I can't stay here another second!'"

It seemed like a long way from the Lake Geneva Playboy, where she enjoyed working so much in 1969. But then, she realized it may have been a long way metaphorically, but only a "hop, skip, and a jump" geographically. Lake Geneva wasn't far from Milwaukee, "So I called my old friend, Sam DeStefano, then the Lake Geneva Entertainment Director." All she wanted, Lainie told Sam, was to lie down in a comfortable bed. He responded with predictable generosity and hospitality, and told her to bring her daughter, her boyfriend, and her whole band—which she did. Compared to the dives she'd been staying at, the resort was like, "a slice of Heaven. Plus, Sam gave me *carte blanche* to the whole resort."

This was about 1976, and the entertainment she discovered at Lake Geneva, however, was far from heavenly. Lainie was distressed to see that the Lake Geneva Resort was floundering just like she was. The Playboy Resorts were never a notable success, but this was downright embarrassing: "The place was so empty you could shoot buffalo in the balcony," she said. "A second rate rock band called The New Zealand Trading Company was playing to a miniscule and unenthusiastic audience, and a group called The Shaggy Gorillas Minus One Buffalo Fish—*I am not kidding*—[was] in one of the other rooms."

Never one to keep her opinions to herself, she had dinner with Sam and gave him her reaction—mainly, why should Playboy, an organization always associated with the best in jazz, be booking these bottom-feeding rock bands? By now she had enough experience with different kinds of clubs and different kinds of bands to have a well-informed take on the situation. She vented to Sam, "You know this is criminal. This gorgeous place…I would do this and change that …and on and on." Sam was impressed enough to inform the main office back in Chicago what she was saying. Soon, word came back from Chicago—from Hef himself no less—that they were interested in hearing what she had to say.

By this point, Lainie's fortunes were so low that she didn't have a car—or suitable clothes for a business meeting. "The Playboy folks were wonderful," said Lainie, "and rented me a red-white-and-blue 'Freedom Van,' with flags on it, to drive to the meeting in Chicago. I had only jeans and tee shirts, so that's how I dressed." She drove from Lake Geneva to Chicago (daughter and boyfriend still in tow) where she met with Hefner. This was mainly a formality, because he then passed her along to Victor Lownes. "I was afraid of Victor at first. He was larger than life to me, so incredibly intelligent, and his brain processed everything so fast." Victor put all of his cards on the table. The corporation was distressed with the way business was going at the Los Angeles Club; the area around it had gotten somewhat seedy, and the venue itself was losing money, not attracting the kind of A-list clientele it had in the old days. He then uttered a sentence that would change everybody's lives: "Why don't you take it over for a while," he said, "and see if you can turn things around. We need someone who has a real knowledge of the nightclub world." Lainie and her boyfriend looked at each other and just nodded in agreement, as if to say, "Why not?" She was thirty-five years old and had never worked on the business end of a club before, but that fresh approach was precisely what Hef and Vic wanted. Still, the over-riding thought was, "I was stunned. My own club! How totally fabulous!"

* * *

Lainie quickly relocated to L.A., renting an apartment on Wilshire and Beverly Glen Boulevards. Never without her entourage, she brought her boyfriend, daughter, nanny, and a girlfriend who also functioned as her assistant—and they all set up housekeeping in the two-bedroom apartment. "We squished in," said Lainie, "and when I answered the phone, I'd say, 'Hello, this is Lainie's room'—just to identify myself from one of the other people living there. Lainie's Room stuck in my head, and when I suggested it to Victor as the name of the club, he said, 'Terrific.'"

For the first time, a Playboy room had, in effect, a subtitle, "Lainie's Room," within the Los Angeles Playboy Club. She immediately set about changing many honor policies that had been set in stone since the L.A. Club opened a dozen years earlier. To make it more like her own room, she removed the existing paintings from the wall, and instead mounted posters and photos of herself— Lainie's Room was truly Lainie's Room. Fortunately, she stored the original paintings—which were by the most famous of all Playboy artists, the celebrated LeRoy Neiman—in the basement, and then moved them back to the Playboy office later.

Victor became Lainie's mentor. She describes him then, in the mid-1970s, as much like the Victor Lownes we know today, "Suave, dapper, brilliant. I checked everything with Victor. I learned about attending to details from him. Nothing was unimportant, from the color of the tablecloths to making sure the hanging pictures were dusted." And he treated Lainie with Playboy's characteristic generosity. In addition to her regular salary, Lainie also was given fifty percent of the all the profits (exclusive of food and beverage sales). Who played Lainie's Room? Virtually everyone—"You name a major jazz singer, and I had them!" The list includes singers Sarah Vaughan, Esther Phillips, Freda Payne, Anita O'Day, Lana Cantrell, Lorna Luft, Roslyn Kind, Carmen McRae, Morgana King, Mel Tormé, Frankie Randall, and Marilyn Maye; piano headliners Buddy Greco, Bill Evans, and Earl 'Fatha' Hines; comics Shelley Berman, Steve Rossi and Marty Allen; entertainers Tom Sullivan, Liz Torres, Maxine Weldon. Playboy also backed Lainie in an extensive campaign of print and media ads, with her face over slogans like, "Lainie's Back!" and, "Come to my room—Lainie's Room."

Sam DeStefano was also a major contributor; she describes him as a "silent partner," and he gave her nuts-and-bolts advice as to how to run a club and get certain things done. "I'd always go over my entertainment list with him because he handled all the entertainment for all the clubs." Lainie reports that it was all especially satisfying, since jazz seemed to be fighting a losing battle against rock and disco, and the rejuvenated L.A. Playboy Club was now leading the charge for the good guys. She was also proud to hire close friends whom she admired: Marilyn, Lana, Lorna, Roslyn. "They weren't just my close friends," she says, "they were the absolute top talent that was out there."

\* \* \*

Lainie may have been the first woman in a position of authority within the Playboy organization, but she ruled with an iron hand. She had no shortage of very definite ideas as to how she wanted things done, and not much patience when they weren't done to her satisfaction. Maybe that's why the Bunnies at the Los Angeles Club didn't embrace her. To hear Lainie tell it, they hated her. One of the changes she made that probably didn't sit well with the cotton-tail set was that nothing could be served during performances. Surely, that cut into their tips.

"I was the first person to do that in the club," Lainie said. "I felt the artists deserved that respect. They didn't need to be distracted because someone wanted more French fries during their show. I think the Bunnies resented me. They resented a woman giving them orders, because it had never happened at Playboy before. I caught more than one of them passing through the spotlight giving me the finger. The girls were used to being the big attraction, and I took some of the focus off them and put it on the artists."

Lainie demanded excellence from everyone, and that included herself. "The most exciting thing was the control I had," she continued, "the control of being the first woman ever to run a Playboy Club and make it the very best that I possibly could.

"I wanted my room to be a place where good work could be seen. I was just there to provide the best space possible for the singer or artist—and I called them 'artists.' I was horrified when people referred to me as an 'act.' People's careers developed in places like that. I was able to offer work for ten weeks a year because I had two clubs. They could play five weeks in Lainie's Room East [the outpost Lainie later opened in New York City] and five weeks in Lainie's Room West.

"I also prohibited smoking. I actually had that in my contract! That was a real hard one for many people to adjust to, but again, I felt it was important for everyone. I made the room conducive to the singing. When I first got there, they had speakers hanging from the ceiling. I installed a great sound system and better lighting. I had a designated spotlight operator; prior to me, they didn't even have a spotlight!

"I revamped the menu and decorated the room to my specifications. I also renovated the dressing rooms so the performers would have a nice place to relax. I put tablecloths and flowers on the tables—it was very elegant.

"It was a hard road, because I would get home at three, sometimes four o'clock in the morning and then get up and be back at the club taking reservations by eleven a.m."

I speculated that Lainie had really enjoyed everything about that job, even though she'd given up any free time she might have had for it. She quickly agreed, saying, "I didn't *give up* anything. I'm a workaholic, and I loved it."

As surprising as it sounds, Lainie even got Hefner to suspend the members-only policy for Lainie's Room. She explained, "I realized right away that none of my friends could come in because they weren't members. Nowadays, the price of a Playboy key doesn't seem like a lot of money, but then, we were all struggling artists. I wanted everyone to be able to enjoy the place.

"The L.A. Room was very eclectic. It was a jazz club, but I knew a lot of people in other areas of the business, and they would come in to be with friends. It was like a clubhouse. We were all just good friends. The musicians in there were aces—the best. David Benoit played piano and conducted. Milcho Leviev was famous, famous, famous, and he was my keyboard player. On drums, I had a guy named Doug Senibaldi, though eventually, Nate Neblett, who played with Marvin Gaye, took over. Another really well-known musician, Jimmy Stewart, played guitar. John B. Williams, who was later on *The Arsenio Hall Show*, was my bass player. He ended up marrying Jessie Rich, one of my background singers, after meeting her on my bandstand, and they've been married thirty-five years. My other background singer, Carolyn Dennis, married Bob Dylan, and they had a baby. That was my basic band and we were quite a little family."

\* \* \*

John B. Williams had just left *The Tonight Show*, after playing with the band for seven years, when he received a call asking if he could fill in for Henry Franklin, Lainie's bass player. "Henry got ill," John B. told us, "and right as I was finishing up with a bass student I was teaching, I got the call asking if I could come down to Lainie's Room at the Playboy Club to sub for him.

"I got dressed quickly, grabbed my bass, and rushed down to the club—and that's how I first met Lainie. I rehearsed with her and she loved the way I played. I filled in that evening, and after that, she asked me if I would come back, because Henry still hadn't recovered from his illness. When he finally got well, he had another commitment and couldn't continue to work the club, so she asked me if I would do the job. It was a really nice, intimate, beautiful club, and I said yes, and that's how I started."

And that was the night John B. first turned Jessie Rich's head. We were lucky enough to have them both to talk to, so we asked her if it had been love at first sight. "It was for me," she responded, "and I did the chasing. I was ready for him!"

"She started singing and making eye contact," John chimed in, "and a few times, I took her home. Maybe a month after that first meeting, we started dating and hanging out. We actually had a bit of an argument with Lainie, because whenever we went out of town—once in a while we traveled to another club—Lainie would have everyone double up in the rooms. Lainie *always* had everything mapped out and organized to the last detail and she didn't like to be thrown off her plan. She had it figured that the band members would share rooms and the singers would share rooms. Well, on a trip to Lake Geneva, Jessie and I wanted to bunk together instead of being separated. We didn't see why it should matter, but Lainie had it all figured and didn't want to change. We held our breath and kind of said, 'No, we're not going to do that. Jessie and I are going to double up!' It worked out—and very nicely! We've been together ever since."

Once John B. slowed down enough to let Jessie catch him, they were married—just about a year after they'd met on Lainie's bandstand. "To this day, I thank Lainie for that," said Jessie. "Way back when, she said to me, 'You really like him?' I said, 'Yeah!' She said, 'Well, he can sure play nice, and he smiles all the time he's on stage.'

"I remember the day that John B. shaved his head. It wasn't a popular style then—I think he started the trend. His hair was thinning, so I said, 'Well, shave your head!' He did, and he's been like that ever since. Later, when he became a regular on *The Arsenio Hall Show*, it was easy for me to pick him out on TV. But on this particular day, the first day that he shaved—Lainie didn't notice until she was on stage. She turned to look at him and screamed! He looked like the man in the moon. She just went 'Aaaah!' The audience must have thought she spotted a mouse!

"Bob Dylan was a standard in the room. He was like a piece of furniture. He would come in at least twice a week. He was dating Lainie at the time." Later, he would meet and marry Carolyn Dennis, another of Lainie's singers.

"He'd come in incognito, with a hat pulled down over his head, and he'd sit back in Lainie's booth, which she held for herself or her guests. That way, her special guests could sit where Lainie would come out and make her entrance. Bob would be there twice a week seeing Lainie. Nobody recognized him because he always looked like a little bum. He'd sit back and watch the show and when Lainie came off the stage, they'd sit and eat and talk. He'd be there after hours, too, because she was his girlfriend! She had been in *Playboy* magazine and was stunning. She had a lot of admirers."

Perhaps tiring of the gossip and 'girl talk,' John changed the subject back to the music. "We did a live recording called *The Chanteuse Is Loose* at the club. The band was really top-notch."

But there was no keeping Jessie quiet for long. At the mention of the band, she chimed back in, "The band was always into doing weird stuff. Jimmy Stewart was a guitar player and he sat next to Lainie on the stage. He would always shock her without even trying. It was just the way he looked at you. Theo Saunders, who was the first piano player at that club, would come out with a pyramid on his head—yeah, he'd have a steel pyramid and he'd wear it on the top of his head for energy or something. I personally think he did it just to get a reaction from Lainie."

Jessie continued singing with Lainie from the time the club opened until Lainie left, but John B.'s tenure was shorter.

"I got into an argument with Lainie," he explained. "She loved to conduct the band. There are just some singers who love to turn around and conduct the band and have that control—Lainie was one of them. Everyone in the band was griping about it and somehow, I was elected to bring it up to Lainie. I told her, 'That doesn't look good on stage. Don't do it.' I should have predicted the results, which were not good. She got mad and threw her drink at me! Now, looking back, this is the funny part. Her assistant Felix was there, and leaped to her defense. I was not happy about having a drink thrown at me and I let her know that, but Felix jumped between the two of us and we had a little wrestling match. It wasn't a fight—no blows—we just kind of wrestled around the dressing room. You had to see it to see the humor—two grown men just dancing around.

"I should have known better, because something similar happened to me when I was with Doc Severinsen. That time, the band was mad over money and I was telling them, 'Stop complaining to each other. Complain to the source! Complain to Doc.' They said, 'Yeah, that's a good idea. Let's have a meeting and all go talk to him.' We were performing at the Persian Room in the Plaza Hotel and decided to meet at Doc Severinsen's dressing room and voice our differences. Well, the appointed time came, and I was the only one there—with Doc. He just kind of looked at me and said, 'Now, let that be a lesson to you.' I guess I didn't learn my lesson very well. It was the same thing with Lainie! I was the only one who showed up, so on behalf of the band, I started letting her know our grievances, and she got mad.

"After I left the Playboy Club, I went on the road with Michael Franks and then Nancy Wilson. I worked with Nancy for twenty-five years—thirty, all told. She'd never let me quit. When I was offered

*The Arsenio Hall Show* in 1989, she said, 'Don't quit. Just take a leave of absence.' Five years later, when the show went off the air, I got a call from her, asking, 'When are you coming back to work?'"

Nowadays, John B. is getting ready to release his latest album—recorded in Austria—called *The African Queen: A Tribute to Horace Silver.* "I recorded with a wonderful assembly of Austrian musicians and Jessie singing," he told us. "I had the privilege of working with Horace from 1967 to 1969, and that's where I got my start as a professional musician. I'm hoping that this recording calls attention to his huge and important body of work. The songs that Jessie sings are three of Horace's hits that Ron McMaster put lyrics to. Jessie also graces the cover.

"When I started doing *The Arsenio Hall Show*, I endorsed a German bass company called Warwick. They make the finest basses in the world—the Rolls Royce of basses. Last year, they started a 'bass camp,' where they have great bass players from the US and Europe come to their factory in Markneukirchen Germany and teach master classes. I'm honored to be included and to be able to share my love of music with these young musicians."

Returning to the Playboy years, John B. said, "Lainie fired me—but, you know, today we laugh about it, because we're the best of friends. She's a great lady and I have the utmost respect for her as a singer, an artist, an actress, and a friend!"

\* \* \*

Freda Payne loved jazz, and told us she remembered when, "you could go to Birdland—or a similar NYC haunt—and see the Count Basie Orchestra *with* Count Basie or the Village Gate, and listen to Nina Simone, or any of the other wonderful small clubs with Miles Davis or Dizzy Gillespie. I even got to schmooze with Sarah Vaughan, and was privileged to have had Duke Ellington play for me. I got to tour with the great Lionel Hampton and his

Freda Payne. Photofest

band, as well as tour South East Asia with a cat by the name of Bob Crosby—Bing's brother—Bob Crosby and the Bobcats. I got to rub noses with these guys and do a lot of interesting things. The '60s and '70s were *interesting times.*"

Freda classified herself as a cabaret singer when she was starting out, and said that although she has always had a special place in her heart for jazz, she tried to pattern herself professionally after Lena Horne and Diahann Carroll. "I was working in supper clubs and singing popular songs such as 'Son of a Preacher Man' and 'Moon River,'" she said, "the hit songs from that time."

Freda played the L.A. Playboy Club "many times," in her words, "both before and after Lainie ran the Room. But Lainie and I had more of a relationship than just the Playboy Club. We were in the same yoga class with Bikram Choudhury for years. This was when he practiced *warm* yoga. He had a couple of little space heaters in the room and it wasn't that bad. He started to get progressively hotter until you had the temperatures we have today, which I can't endure.

"I have great memories of Lainie's," Freda continued. "One Saturday night, I was playing there and the room was packed. I was excited because I heard that Berry Gordy, the head of Motown Records, was going to come and catch my act. I peeked out and saw him sitting in the audience and couldn't be happier. Then, the maître d' came back—all excited—and said, 'Ms. Payne, Magic Johnson is in the house! He came to see you.' I had no idea who he was and replied, 'Magic Johnson, is he a magician? Does he do a magic act?'

"The poor guy was shocked that I didn't know who he was and said, 'No, he's the new star of the Lakers!' The truth is that at that point I could have cared less about Magic Johnson. I was more excited about Berry. After the show, I introduced Berry and Magic, and got to talk to Magic and he said, 'I have to tell you Ms. Payne, when I got drafted to play with the Lakers in L.A., I told myself there were two women I wanted to meet, you and [the actress] Jayne Kennedy.' Ha! Yeah, it was fun [and] we became friendly, although we never dated, but to this day when I see him, I bring it up.

"Lainie's Room was the local place to work in town. It was cool. It was nice. And it was [an] intimate room."

\* \* \*

Milcho Leviev was thirty-two when he arrived in the United States, but he had already amassed a lifetime of experiences, both musical and political. Born in Plovdiv, Bulgaria, he was the product of many intersecting cultures and became as well versed in jazz as he was in classical music. He played with a quartet called Jazz Focus, based in Bulgaria's capitol city, Sofia, and his résumé also included conducting and composing for film, television, and theater. His expertise encompassed Bulgarian traditional music as well as American and Western European styles. By the time he left Bulgaria, he'd already served as musical director for the prestigious Bulgarian Drama Theater.

In 1970, Milcho defected from East to West Germany and, from there, he made his way to Los Angeles. The innovative trumpeter, composer, and bandleader Don Ellis immediately sought him out and he spent most of the 1970s shuttling between Ellis's various bands and that of the jazz-fusion drummer Billy Cobham.

"I was a piano arranger for Don for five or six years, and I have to say that he was a legend. He was very avant-garde, and I learned a great deal from working with him.

"In the early '70s, I was touring with his twenty-two piece orchestra. When we reached New York, Don got an additional engagement to play with a small group—Don and myself, and the rhythm section at the Playboy Club.

"Now, the Don Ellis Orchestra was notorious for playing in unusual rhythms—5/4, 7/8, 9/16, and so on—called 'irregular rhythms.' Don liked to compose musical portraits of the orchestra members, and for me, he wrote a funky, slow, blues number in 11/8 called 'Blues in Elf.' It was musical poetry. Don thought I looked like an elf with my long hair, and also, *elf* in German means *eleven*.

"In this piece, instead of four beats divided in four groups of triplets, the last group had two instead of three notes. The feeling was like walking three steps cool and limping on the fourth!"

One time, Milcho reports, the group's use of this particular irregular rhythm backfired. "Don said to us, 'Lets start with a slow blues so people can dance relaxed.' He counted four even beats—we started playing—but after a couple of bars, the dancers were limping! Unconsciously, we were playing in 11/8 instead of 12/8! When we straightened out the rhythm, the people straightened up and danced normally. I think only the musicians knew what had happened.

"It was the well-known bassist John B. Williams, who played with a veritable Who's-Who in the music business, who told me that Lainie Kazan was looking for someone to play piano and be the musical director at her Playboy Room. When the show was touring, I had to conduct, since we sometimes used big bands and strings and such. This required a second pianist, so we brought in David Benoit. Lainie then decided to keep him in the smaller band also. The music sounded bigger and richer and, at the same time, David had the opportunity to learn some things from me so that he'd be ready to take my place when I decided to concentrate on my own music.

"Our home gig was at Lainie's Room in L.A. The band consisted of me and David on keyboards, Charlie Black [from the Don Ellis Orchestra] on woodwinds, the great John B. on bass, and Nate Neblett, a highly in-demand and seasoned studio musician, on drums. I would say we had one of the most prestigious gigs in town—well paid, with good food and celebrities in the house! In fact, Hugh Hefner himself stopped by quite often.

"After we'd played the club for a year or so, Lainie decided to document the show, and that's how the album *The Chanteuse Is Loose* happened. We recorded it live at the club.

"The music we played was a rich combination of pop, jazz, and classical. At the time, I was a bit of a jazz snob. Leonard Feather, who was preparing his *Encyclopedia of Jazz* and sending questionnaires to musicians, was surprised that I didn't list my gig with Lainie. When he asked me why, I answered that we weren't really playing jazz. 'Nonsense,' he said. He told me that, after a performance of one of Duke Ellington's *Sacred Concerts*—which also featured classical singers and musicians in addition to the legendary Ellington Orchestra—a critic asked Duke Ellington, 'Was *that* jazz?' Duke answered, 'Young man, there are only two kinds of music: good music and the other kind.' I learned my lesson!

"Anyway, I liked Lainie immediately. She's tough, but you have to stand up for yourself if you're in show business, and especially if you're a woman. She has a great ear, is a wonderful singer, loves jazz, and has some great jazz intonations. That's why she hired all those great jazz musicians."

Milcho served as house pianist and musical director at Lainie's Room until he eventually left to tour extensively with iconic bebop saxophonist Art Pepper. That was quite possibly the most celebrated gig of his career—even more so than his Grammy-winning arrangement of Dave Brubeck's "Blue Rondo à la Turk," which he did for Al Jarreau on the 1982 album *Breaking Away*.

Milcho's arrangement of Charlie Parker's "Confirmation," which appears on Manhattan Transfer's 1981 album *Mecca for Moderns*, was also nominated for a Grammy, but he considers his highest accolade to be the praise he received from a good friend of that vocal quartet, Jon Hendricks. The legendary jazz singer and songwriter said, "Milcho combines black blues and his own heritage in such a way that I tend to think that, once upon a time, his Slavic roots and my African roots were actually in the same place."

In 1980, Milcho was permitted to perform in his home country for the first time in ten years, and eventually, he moved back to Europe. He and his wife now live in the neighboring country of Greece. "I'm still touring, prophesying, and teaching. Bulgaria is a free country now and my roots are there. As they say, 'Life is a circle.' You go back to where you started."

* * *

Lainie's Room became so successful—and she became so ubiquitous as a spokesperson and performer—that in 1978, Victor Lownes asked her to replicate the room at the Playboy Club in New York. She didn't have to think about it very long before agreeing. "I had quite a nice advertising budget in New York, too," she told us, "and I used it wisely. I took ads on planes, in *Backstage*, and even in *The New York Times*."

It's difficult to imagine how she fit it in, but it was around this time that Lainie began working on her acting by studying with Lee Strasberg at the Actor's Studio in New York. As she described it, "Kids from the Actors Studio started coming over to the club late on Monday nights and putting on little plays or readings. Bob Dylan, Joni Mitchell, Shelley Winters, Flip Wilson, and many others were involved, or just hung out after hours. Bob would come in wearing his hoodie, sit in the back, and watch what was going on. Once we closed the club, we'd have jam sessions or he'd compose songs. These impromptu gatherings weren't paid or even scheduled or publicized. It was wonderful. We would sing and have a great time. Word just got around that maybe someone interesting might show up and doodle on Monday night. They'd come in after hours, hang out, and sing a song or two."

Once Lainie's Room East was open, she spent a lot of time in the air. By 1978, she was not only running the two clubs but singing in them as well, for approximately twenty-six weeks a year.

"The two clubs were really very different," she told us. "The one in Los Angeles was a hangout; it was *the* place to go—the clubhouse. The New York place was more exciting—the show was the thing. I had great managers at both places; both were old friends. Carol Soskin, who managed L.A., was my best friend in the world, and Cynthia Friedland managed the club in New York. It seemed as if she was calling me every five minutes, because something was always going on and she needed to know what to do."

Once Lainie had breathed new life into the two clubs, the Playboy organization started showing interest in them again. When she'd first taken over in Los Angeles, Lainie had had control over all aspects of the business. Later, though, she found herself having to argue for and justify her decisions. "They called me the Singing Tycoon," she said, breaking into a laugh, "because, in addition to running the clubs, I'd have to fly to Chicago for quarterly board meetings where I was the only woman. Many times, I'd have to dash from there to one coast or the other to sing.

"All of a sudden, the corporate types decided, 'Oh, this is interesting, what's happening at Lainie's Room? This is a good thing for us and we should start taking some of the control back and rein in Lainie.' I almost lost it over their meddling, so that's when I started going to corporate meetings with my little briefcase. I wanted to be taken seriously and to make sure nothing was decided without me—but it was always a battle. I learned how to be very political, and that in itself was a great lesson because I'd always been so direct. I didn't have time for games."

Lainie sang at the opening of both the L.A. and New York Lainie's Rooms. She hadn't planned to perform at the New York opening, but as she put it, "Whenever there was a problem with the artists, I had to fill in, and with two places, it was a little crazy. I had booked Morgana King to open in New York. I was in L.A. the day before opening night and I got a call from her: 'Babe, listen, it's Mo. I don't feel like singing tomorrow.' I said, 'What do you mean you *don't feel like singing tomorrow*?' She just flat-out said, 'If you want someone to sing, you'll have to do it yourself.' She didn't feel like it! So I had to get on a plane and open the New York Room.

"Another time, I had accepted a rare booking outside of Playboy, to sing at the Fairmont in San Francisco, and Barbara McNair was all booked to sing in New York. Well, I was relaxing in the sauna or the steam bath, I forget which, when the attendant came rushing in to say I had an emergency call. This was before we carried cell phones with us everywhere, of course—so they brought in a phone and hooked me up. It was the New York manager, just hysterical, saying, 'You're not going to believe this, but Barbara McNair's husband was just shot dead at the airport. You've got to catch the first plane and get here immediately and do the show!'

"People would die to work in my rooms… I fed them, the working conditions were superior, and I tailored the contracts to their weird individual requirements. Lana Cantrell had a clause saying she'd get five beers before each show because all her musicians drank beer. They could have had beer anyway, but she wanted it in the contract. Esther Phillips wanted two vodka stingers before each show. When she sang, it was like a revival meeting—she was wonderful."

Lainie was one of the few club managers who gave her artists time count-downs, just like they do in the theater: "Half-hour until you're on… fifteen minutes… five minutes until show time." No one we spoke to had ever heard of anyone extending this courtesy in a nightclub setting before.

"Anita O'Day once walked off the stage after only her third song because someone was talking," Lainie told us. "She just walked down the stage steps and started toward the elevator; I was running after her screaming, 'Anita! Anita! Come back!' What could I do but get up on stage and finish the show myself? That happened all the time. I actually initiated a 'Billy Eckstine' clause in everyone's contract, stating that they had to stay on stage for forty minutes in order to get paid. It got its name because once, someone was doing something in the audience that Billy didn't like and he walked off just a few minutes into his show.

"Carmen McRae was very rough and tough—very difficult, but a great singer. She'd come into the club with her sensible shoes, her little black shirtwaist dress, and her purse, and when it was time for her to go on, she'd walk directly onto the stage—without saying anything to either the audience or me—put her purse down, kick off her shoes, and say, 'Uh-one, two, three, four,' and she'd start to sing. Never a 'hello' or 'good-bye' to the audience, never a song introduction, and when she was done, she'd put her shoes back on and walk right out the door.

"One night, Carmen was singing and her drummer's drums were getting wet because (we later found out) the air-conditioner was leaking. You could actually hear the water softly splattering on the drums. She came off stage irate. She said to me, 'Who's responsible for this? Fix this goddamn leak!' So we did—right on the spot. My boyfriend and a few other people redirected the water from the air-conditioner to a kitchen sink. I called her the next day and said, 'Ms. McRae we fixed the leak.' She shot back, 'Take your goddamn club and shove it!' I was horrified. I didn't know what to say, so I just said, 'Thanks.' Now, I want you to know that she was one of my all-time favorite singers, but I never went back to see her ever again."

Not all of the artists were difficult, of course. According to Lainie, most of them were wonderful, talented, hard-working professionals. "Shelley Berman was great," she told us. "He'd come up on stage before I introduced him and goof around, saying, 'Am I on yet?' I'd say, 'No, not yet, Shelley,' and he'd grab the microphone and go, 'Ladies and gentlemen, Shelley Berman, Shelley Berrrrrman!!'"

\* \* \*

Shelley was probably the most celebrated comedian to appear in Lainie's Room. In 1977, he was filmed live there for an HBO special that was recently released on DVD. It was a rather unique period in cultural history; the Playboy Clubs were at

Shelley Berman appears fascinated by New York Bunny Vi Hebel's lighter. Courtesy Shelley Berman

their zenith, but there was a new player in the entertainment game, what would eventually be called premium cable TV. When Shelley's show was filmed, it was so early in that particular game that the comedian didn't even say "HBO"; he referred to the company as "Home Box Office," as if it were an exotic new thing that his audience might not be familiar with—and many of them probably weren't!

In hindsight, some thirty-five years later, it's clear that the rise of HBO and other cable channels was double-edged for the entertainment industry. While it certainly paved the way for comedians to garner huge audiences and become superstars, it usurped the role of live venues such as the Playboy circuit, which had previously been the only places to see big-name comedians do full-length shows.

Shelley's case is textbook. In the 1960s, he appeared on every TV variety program and talk show from *The Hollywood Palace* to *The Jack Parr Show*—but only for a few minutes at a time. In fact, he was so ubiquitous on TV that he guest-starred alongside Ethel Merman on *The Perry Como Show* in 1960, and then again four years later on *The Judy Garland Show*; one wonders if the two ever considered co-hosting their own program, which they might have called *The Merman-Berman Hour*! Shelley's brief, hysterically funny bits only served to whet viewers' appetites for more. If they wanted to see him holding forth at length, they had to go out and see him live—probably at a Playboy Club.

But, once he appeared at length on HBO, the itch to see him in person was very likely satisfied. So, while cable TV created a boom in comedy in the 1980s, it was at the expense of the live venues that had nurtured the very talent it presented. In a sense, when HBO filmed Shelley at the Playboy Club, it was the beginning of the decline of Playboy.

To give Shelley his due (and cheer yourself up a little), check out the HBO special. It remains a classic, right from the trademark opening "telephone routine" for which he'd become so well known that all he had to do to incite gales of laughter was hold his hand to his ear. In fact, that's how Shelley will probably always be remembered—hand to ear.

The comedian turned ninety in February of 2015, but he remains as vital and funny as ever.

* * *

Before he was a five-time Grammy nominee, David Benoit—then only twenty-two years old and just beginning his career—was asked to fill in for Lainie's pianist, Russell Turner, who'd dropped out suddenly. David told us, "I had never had any experience accompanying singers, but Lainie needed someone to sub for her while they looked for a permanent replacement. I was just a green kid from the suburbs and this was a whole new world for me. Funny story—my father drove me to meet Lainie and, when she saw him, she thought *he* was the replacement."

As Lainie tells it, she was getting ready to go on the road with the Duke Ellington Orchestra when her pianist disappeared. "He was brilliant, but a very disturbed young man. One day, he just didn't show up for rehearsal. So I asked Jimmy Stewart—my guitarist, not the actor—for help in getting someone for the job. I was panicked, because we were leaving the next day, but he said, 'Don't worry, there'll be someone at the airport.'

"The next day, I went to the airport and there was a good-looking guy in his fifties with a kid about seventeen. I went over to him and said, 'Oh, thank you so much for coming on such short notice. I really appreciate this.' He stopped me and said, 'Oh, no, I'm not your pianist—it's my *son*.' And he introduced me to this pimply-faced kid! That was my introduction to David Benoit and I thank God for it! His first job was playing with me and the Duke Ellington Orchestra!"

David continued, "Starting out, I had to sight-read Lainie's music but I did a good job. After my first night, I guess she liked the way I sounded so she hired me permanently and, eventually, I became her musical director. I learned so much from her. There were nights when everything went well but then there were nights when she was just *screaming* at me. The neat thing about her is that she never gave up on me. She saw my talent and she never—you know—fired me! She was actually very encouraging, telling me over and over, 'You can do it.' I just love her. She was tough but she taught me a lot. I think of her as a teacher.

"We had dual pianos. Milcho Leviev played a grand piano and I played an electric Fender with some synthesizers. We switched off. We needed a two-keyboard kind of group, what with Lainie doing more contemporary music and less cabaret.

"I remember Hugh Hefner coming in with women, gorgeous women—just like you see in the movies. He was always very nice. Later on, I had a chance to meet him a couple of times at the Playboy Mansion because he used to host a lot of jazz events there. I guest-conducted the Henry Mancini Orchestra a few times there and found Hef to be a *really* nice guy and a great lover of jazz.

"Yeah, the Playboy Club—Lainie's Room—was quite an experience for me. I loved meeting all those people and being thrown into a whole other world! It was really an education."

"David learned a lot playing for me," Lainie said, "He loved going out to dinner, and he'd always order Pouilly Fuisse. So when he'd play too much on the piano I'd say, 'Lighten up on the Pouilly Fuisse!'"

"It's weird, the little things that stick in your mind. I remember that Lainie served all the drinks in wine glasses—even beer. I thought that looked so elegant. Another thing that really impressed me was, once, after a gig, I was getting my notes—Lainie always made notes for everyone—and I heard someone knocking on the door. I went to answer it and asked, 'Who's there?' A voice said, 'It's Bob Dylan.' I was like, 'No, no, c'mon. Who are you, really?' Again, he said, 'Bob Dylan.' I opened the door, and sure enough, there he was, standing right in front of me.

"Lainie's Room in New York involved a whole other set of stories. One time, a mobster had us all go to Brooklyn between sets to perform at a charity function. The scene was like something right out of *The Godfather*. All the musicians knew we *had* to do this. There wasn't any discussion about how much we got paid or anything else."

Lainie elaborated. "It was a charity event for the Saint Andrews Orphanage, in the bowels of Brooklyn. They came to get us in what seemed like getaway cars and drove at least a hundred miles an hour the *wrong way* over the Brooklyn Bridge! When we got to the place, there were only men, sitting at big round tables with a bottle of Scotch in the middle of each one. We did three shows on Friday and Saturday, and they got us back just in the nick of time, but it was hilarious. Something out of a movie!"

David said, "Lainie had to stand by this tiny little piano, and it was *horrible*. I started to complain about it, because it was almost child-size, but Lainie said, 'Don't go there.' You know? We just had to deal with it. So we did the event and got ferried back to the club for our third set. I think I was twenty-four at the time. When I think back to those days and how I was fresh from my nice little suburban life, I wonder, 'Did that really happen?'"

Lainie told us that she had a lot of friends who helped her out during those years. "They protected me and were wonderful. So I did a favor for them. I never dreamed of asking to be paid."

"One of my favorite times," said David, "was when we decided to book Bill Evans, the great jazz pianist. He was one of my all-time favorite musicians. I was so excited to see him and couldn't understand why we didn't have more people in the audience. When I asked Lainie about it later, she said they were waiting for a singer to come on but no singer ever came. Bill was the act. It was really upsetting to me because, here we had this genius pianist at the end of his life and the audience wanted a singer. We couldn't get people to come. They didn't know who he was! Some people actually asked for a refund. After hearing Bill Evans! Lainie loved him as much as I did and we thought it was a great coup to get him for the club. It was a tragedy.

"A lot of established New York musicians would play with Lainie and the band, so I got to meet a lot of greats, including Jack Logan, the jazz guitar player. After our last show, we'd go to another bar and stay out until very early in the morning, talking and comparing notes and sometimes playing. These experiences are incredible training for young musicians. It's like getting thrown into the deep end of the pool.

"One place we played was the Lake Geneva Club, which was *beautiful* and very exciting for me, because they had the Sam DeStefano full big band. I never studied music formally, just learned the old-fashioned way, by going out there and playing. I learned as I went."

David also entertained at the Playboy Jazz Festivals. "Hefner loved jazz," he told us. "The whole jazz festival seemed to come from a very sincere place. He would always be hanging out and listening to music. He was gracious and nice—a really nice man.

"Thinking back on it, the whole experience with Lainie was a big deal—a really big deal. I remember the first night I played the L.A. Club and how nervous I was. Later, I invited my parents to come, and they were so excited to be there. I credit everything that happened to me to Lainie, because she was my ticket into this whole world that I hadn't known anything about—Playboy Bunnies, Hugh Hefner, the mob—stuff you see in movies, but this was real!

"The thing about Lainie is that she was demanding. She wanted the best from everyone, and maybe that's why everyone still keeps in touch with her and loves her. She helped so many people get their careers started over the years—she's like this wonderful *grande dame* of entertainment."

Today, David keeps a full schedule of touring. At the time of our interview, he was getting ready to leave for Asia, including the Philippines, where he was slated to play a relief concert to help victims of the 2013 tsunami disaster. When he's home, he has a wonderful morning radio show on KKJZ in Los Angeles.

\* \* \*

The incomparable Ella Fitzgerald once said that Marilyn Maye was, "the greatest white female singer in the world"—and many people agree. Marilyn appeared a record seventy-six times on *The Tonight Show*, received a Grammy nomination as Best New Artist in 1966, and has had one of the longest show-business careers of any kind. Now eighty-seven years young, Marilyn took time from her still-busy schedule to talk to us about her days at the Playboy Clubs.

Marilyn Maye. Photofest

"That was a long time ago," she began. "Lainie's Room was great. She always had a well-known singer and I don't know if that helped draw people in or not, but it was good business.

"I remember playing both of her rooms—in L.A. and New York. In California, you'd get Asian tour groups in the audience—that really are not known for being very demonstrative—and I was getting a little insecure, because they just sat there as I was singing my heart out. No applause or smiles or anything! I thought they hated me but at the end of the show, they'd mob me and rave and rave about how good it was. That was just their way.

"In those days, waitresses and waiters weren't as considerate of the entertainer as they are nowadays. They weren't supposed to serve during performances in Lainie's Room but... sometimes they did. For whatever reason, I was able to forge an understanding with the Bunnies. Maybe they sympathized with me. I'd ask them, 'Please try not to serve if I'm doing a ballad. If I'm singing an up-tempo tune, then you're home free.' And they worked with that. If a customer wanted a drink and I was singing a 'happy' song, I wanted him to have it, because the happier they were, the better for me.

"Lainie and I became good friends during that time because she was there every night. She'd sit in her corner booth and watch the show, and then we would dissect what I did. We've been good friends through all these years. I loved playing both of her rooms. It was great fun because I knew a lot of people in L.A., and they'd come to hear me sing and then we'd all go out afterwards."

Lainie told us that Marilyn was a good singer at the time they worked together but that through the ensuing years she developed into a world-class talent. "Between the two clubs, I gave Marilyn ten weeks every year," she said. "Marilyn's daughter Kristi occasionally traveled with her mother, and on one of her visits, we met and became friends, and I actually hired her as my assistant. She was great and worked for me for about a year."

One extra perk of playing the Los Angeles Playboy Club was that

Hollywood celebrities were known to stop by, including the incomparable Steve Allen. To this day, Marilyn cites Steve as the single most important figure in her career. Allen not only put her on national television for the first time, but his support led to her extremely fruitful relationship with RCA Records in the 1960s. Another TV star who tended to come in whenever Marilyn was in residence was known less for his love of good music than for his trademark lollipop, the detective-show star—and role model for clean-headed gentlemen of multiple generations—Telly Savalas. "He was a big fan," Marilyn confirmed. "He'd come to hear me often."

Marilyn's history with the Playboy Clubs goes back well before Lainie's Room, however. She'd worked in the Playboy Club back in her native Kansas City in its early days. "The fabulous thing about playing Kansas City was that it had two rooms, the showroom and the lounge. My daughter Kristi is also a singer, and around the holidays, they'd book her to sing in the lounge with a trio while I performed in the main room. She was nineteen or twenty and it was a great way for us to be together for Christmas.

"In those days, I was doing a 'trouble' medley—I sang every trouble song in the world. Nowadays, I do a medley of 'happy' songs, but back then, it was 'Trouble in River City' from *The Music Man*, 'You've Got Your Troubles and I've Got Mine,' and a bunch of others. My middle name is 'Medley,' you know," she added with a wink.

On any given night, Marilyn is still knocking them dead somewhere, and she has captivated a new legion of devoted fans in major cities as well as at resort hotspots from Provincetown to Palm Beach. Already the recipient of a raft of performance awards, on October 14, 2012, she received a Lifetime Achievement Award from the Chicago Cabaret Professionals Association.

Telly Savalas sucking his signature lollipop. Photo by James FortuneRexREX USA

\* \* \*

Lana Cantrell was impressed with Lainie's attention to detail. "It was different there, in that Lainie wanted to make sure the singers had what they needed to give a good show. She made sure we had monitors, which we didn't always have at other clubs. It's important to be able to hear yourself so you know if you're singing softly or really loud. Probably only another singer would understand that—Lainie clearly did. She also had fabulous lighting and sound systems for us.

"She was a really good boss and ran the room well," Lana went on. "There was always a cup of hot tea waiting for you. These are things that business people don't think about.

"Through the years, Lainie and I followed each other around Vegas—because of our names! Lana Cantrell, Lainie Kazan—a lot of times, bookers would mix us up and say, 'Oh, I thought you were the other one.' They were expecting voluptuous Lainie and got scrawny me! She was great!"

\* \* \*

Trini Lopez visited Lainie's Room in L.A. often—as a patron, not a performer. "I never played the clubs," he told us. "They were too small for me, but I did play the resorts many, many times. I did go to see a whole bunch of artists—including my brother Jesse—at Lainie's and the other clubs. Jesse is a musician and a singer who plays great tenor sax and guitar and a real funky blues harmonica, plus, he sings. He really enjoyed entertaining at Lainie's—it was one of the nicest of the Playboy chain."

Lainie confessed that she and Trini were actually dating for a while, so, clearly, listening to Jesse wasn't the only attraction!

\* \* \*

While attending Hofstra University on Long Island, Lainie became friends with fellow classmate Francis Ford Coppola. They stayed in touch through the years as best they could, while pursuing their separate business and personal lives. It wasn't until 1980, when Lainie was singing at the San Francisco Fairmont, that Coppola caught her show. After they greeted each other and caught up a little, he said, "God, you're funny!"

"I had no idea I was funny," Lainie told us. "Well... in college,

Francis and I had done plays together and I guess I was funny then. 'You're hysterical,' he told me that night in San Francisco. 'Listen, I have a script. Why don't you come up to Napa, and I'll show it to you?' So I went up, loved it, he loved me in the part, and he put me in his movie, *One from the Heart*.

"Suddenly, I was at the center of the action—the eye of the storm—and I couldn't run two clubs and do movies. So I licensed my name to Playboy for two years and focused on acting. Sadly, without me to oversee things, Playboy ran the clubs into the ground. Both rooms closed for good a year later."

Lainie really took off as an actress in 1983, with her hilarious turn in *My Favorite Year* starring Peter O'Toole; at forty-two, she played the mother of Mark Linn-Baker (who was then twenty-eight). She followed that with memorable parts in *Harry and the Hendersons* (1987), *Married to the Mob* (1988), *Beaches* (1989), and—perhaps most notably—*My Big Fat Greek Wedding* (2002). On television, she has shown up in *Desperate Housewives*, *Ugly Betty*, *Touched by an Angel*, *Will and Grace*, and *The Nanny*, and was nominated for an Emmy for a guest spot on *St. Elsewhere*.

"I don't have any regrets," she says, "I didn't have a game plan going into the Playboy venture, other than that I would make a success out of the clubs, and I did. It was a hot club! I wanted to make these artists shine to the fullest in the best environment I could supply. I tried—and I believe I succeeded in—showing them off to their best advantage, giving them as much work as I could, and paying them as much as I could wheedle out of Playboy. I wanted the two Lainie's Rooms to be places where everyone wanted to work. And you know what? They were."

Part Three

# THE BEAT GOES ON

14

# JUST A BOWL OF JAZZ

n 1959, Playboy produced its first jazz festival in celebration of its
fifth anniversary; twenty years later, the organization returned to
the idea of a big, weekend-long festival as a means of celebrating
its twenty-fifth. The two events bracketed the golden era of
Playboy, during which it operated some forty clubs all over the world.
By 1979, however, the clubs were beginning to wind down. Many
were still open, but it was becoming increasingly clear that the focus
of the music world (jazz and otherwise) was moving away from small
clubs and on to ever-larger-scale arena shows and music festivals.

By 1979, Hef had been deliberating over whether or not to get
back into the festival business for a few years. He'd decided that if he
did so, he'd want to partner with George Wein, the man who almost
singlehandedly invented the outdoor music festival. So, when Hef
and Victor sat down to brainstorm about a fittingly grand way to
celebrate the magazine's twenty-fifth birthday, they quickly agreed
that—with George's help—it was time to host another jazz festival.

George Wein had been twenty-eight when he produced the first
Newport Jazz Festival in July 1954; equally ambitious events followed, including the Newport Folk Festival and the New Orleans

Comic Bill Cosby, left, shares a moment with singer Mel Torme, and Hugh Hefner, backstage at the 1986 Playboy Jazz Festival. AP PhotoMichael Tweed

Jazz & Heritage Festival. As he recalled in 2012, "By the time I was brought in to talk to Playboy, Dick Rosenzweig was doing a lot of the day-to-day management because Victor Lownes was running things in London."

Dick had come to Playboy in 1958 as assistant to Victor, who was then Vice President of Advertising. Dick rose through the ranks, moving to Los Angeles in 1977 to take the reins of all West Coast operations and eventually becoming the senior executive vice president. Today, he is responsible for advising Hef on the company's initiatives in publishing, marketing, licensing, and television and video entertainment. He has also assumed the title of chairman of Alta Loma Entertainment—Playboy's film and TV subsidiary. Until 2014, he was president of the Playboy Jazz Festival. Together with George Wein, they have been the executive producers of the festival since 1979.

As George told it, "Through the years, Dick had called me several times for different things but nothing came of it. So, when he called to talk about the twenty-fifth anniversary festivities, I said, 'Don't waste my time. You've called me before. Are you asking me to make a bid or do you want me to do a festival for you?' Right away, he said, 'No, we want you to do the festival.' That's when we came up with the Hollywood Bowl concept, which has pretty much been in place ever since."

George admitted that he was especially receptive to working with Hefner, who was a friend, and that he always felt an affinity for the Playboy organization because, as he put it, "we started at the same time. *Playboy* magazine's first year was 1954, and the first year of the Newport Jazz Festival was also 1954. I wasn't involved in the first Playboy festival in 1959, but I definitely heard about it. It received wonderful reviews and a ton of publicity."

The 1979 event at the Hollywood Bowl was produced by George, in conjunction with Darlene Chan, who, in ensuing years, gradually took over the job completely. Most of the PJFs of the last thirty-five years have been her babies. "Darlene's been with me for almost forty years and the Playboy Jazz Festival has been an incredible success," George said. As Hef put it, "In the beginning nobody thought that jazz could work to that extent in the Hollywood Bowl. But the combination of George Wein and Playboy has been unbeatable! The community embraced it and here we are, thirty-five years later."

The decisions as to musicians and shows have been entirely up to George and Darlene; George knows Hefner's taste, but he also knows that Hef respects the two of them and allows them to do their jobs the best way that they see fit. There had always been a place in the lineup for Hef's dear friend and favorite jazz singer, the late Mel Tormé, and Bill Cosby—who has always been exceptionally close to both Hef and George—served as the emcee for thirty years.

There's always been a wide variety of different kinds of jazz, from smooth jazz to straight ahead jazz, hot jazz to cool jazz, singers to big bands, and every conceivable instrument.

From the very beginning, the Playboy Jazz Festival (PJF) in the Hollywood Bowl was a record-breaker. Early on, it broke certain rather unusual records: the highest number of t-shirts sold since the Beatles 1964 concert (1979), the highest number of programs sold (1980), the largest press turnout for a non-rock concert (1981). It was also during the 1981 festival that 10,000 individuals participated in what the record books recognized as "the largest jazz jam session ever." In 1981, the festival sold out a week before the event. In 1982, the most expensive seats, the boxes, were sold out five months before the event.

Count Basie was a key figure in the first five years of the Playboy Jazz Festival at the Hollywood Bowl; in 1981, Helen Humes, the great jazz singer long associated with Basie, gave her final public performance as part of Basie's set at the PJF. In 1983, Joe Williams, Basie's most celebrated vocalist (who was part of the band at the Chicago Festival in 1959), was honored with a star on the Hollywood Walk of Fame, an event which the Festival celebrated. When Basie himself died in April 1984, that year's PJF, a few months later, was dedicated to his memory. Two years afterwards, the festival honored Benny Goodman, who had performed at both the 1979 and 1980 festivals and died a few weeks before the 1986 event.

This isn't to imply that all the highlights of the Playboy Jazz Festival have been farewells. It's safe to say that nobody *actually* started their career at the PJF—you can't really begin a career at the Hollywood Bowl! But the PJF has seen plenty of imposing debuts over its first thirty-five years; appearing there doesn't mean the start of a career, but it often means the entry of an artist into the major leagues. As Gregory Porter, who made his PJF debut in 2013, put it, "There are certain festivals that amount to stamps on your passport of success! Newport is one of them, as is the Playboy Jazz Festival."

\* \* \*

When Darlene Chan was asked to name her personal highlights from thirty-five years of experiencing the festival, her mind immediately went to two vocal-centric concerts in the mid-1980s.

The first featured Weather Report, led by Wayne Shorter and Joe Zawinul, and Manhattan Transfer. "This was in 1982," she said, "and a highlight for sure. Manhattan Transfer was a surprise, and the audience went bonkers." Indeed, it could be said that the combination of Weather Report and the Manhattan Transfer represented to the jazz world of the 1980s what the Count Basie/Lambert, Hendricks, and Ross combination had been twenty-three years earlier.

Hendricks himself played a key role in the other PJF that lingers prominently in Darlene's memory. Titled, "Sing, Sing, Sing," it starred Hendricks leading a vocal quartet that included three rising giants: Dianne Reeves, Bobby McFerrin, and Janis Siegel of the Manhattan Transfer. "This was another huge crowd favorite," says Darlene. Reeves made her solo debut in 1989, and continues to make regular appearances at the PJF to this day.

Ray Charles at the Playboy Jazz Festival 1988. AP Photolra Mark Goslin

Other established stars fresh from Newport and other major jazz events around the world made their way to the Playboy festivals, including Ray Charles in 1984, complete with his big band and the vivacious Raelettes. That same year, Mel Tormé, one of Hefner's personal pals, teamed with another old friend, trumpeter Shorty Rogers. In 1993, he joined forces with another trumpeter and friend of Hef, Ray Anthony, for a set that was recorded and later released by Concord Jazz. Miles Davis, who had been a rising star at the 1959 festival, was easily the biggest and most controversial name in all of jazz by 1985. It was Davis, more than anyone, who helped turn the PJF into a sellout event, breaking records for attendance and gross sales at the Hollywood Bowl that year. Considering that the Bowl had been in operation since 1922, that was quite an accomplishment.

* * *

Everyone who was there remembers the 1982 festival—in part because the two nights were extensively recorded and filmed. That was the year that longtime jazz supporter Bruce Lundvall accepted a position at Elektra Records, and produced the album *In Performance at the Playboy Jazz Festival.* The two-LP set features parts of six different sets, including performances by Dexter Gordon (with Woody Shaw and Kirk Lightsey), the smooth-jazz trio Pieces of a Dream, tenor saxophone star Grover Washington Jr., and the Weather Report/Manhattan Transfer set that Darlene so loved. There were also two all-star ensembles: The JazzTet, the long-running partnership between trumpeter Art Farmer and saxophonist Benny Golson, was joined on this occasion by the outstanding singer Nancy Wilson and her rhythm section, with Michael Woolf (the famous jazz pianist and father of the famous "Naked Brothers"); and the well-named "Great Quartet," with trumpeter Freddie Hubbard, pianist McCoy Tyner, bassist Ron Carter, and drummer Elvin Jones.

In addition to Art Farmer and Freddie Hubbard, the other

superstar trumpeter at PJF 1982 was Maynard Ferguson, whose set was captured on video. His band had enjoyed a huge hit single just a few years earlier with "Gonna Fly Now," the theme from the film *Rocky*, and Ferguson and his very young band were still performing in a jazz-funk-pop vein. Later, Ferguson would return to his bebop roots, but in 1982, his playing was aggressively pop.

The 1982 festival was also significant in that it marked the first of thirty-one years that Bill Cosby served as the host. Cosby has told the story many times about how he started in showbiz working as a bartender and aspiring jazz drummer in a club in his native Philadelphia. As he tells it, his dreams of becoming a professional musician were dashed by saxophonist Sonny Stitt, who convinced the young Cosby that he was better off going into some other line of work. In addition to being a cultural icon in his own right, Cosby has always been a great spokesman for jazz, as well as a lifelong buddy of both Hefner and George Wein.

Another legendary entertainer who remains close to Hef and George is Tony Bennett, who made his PJF debut in 1996, shortly after his album *MTV Unplugged* had just won the Grammy for Album of the Year. With his appearance at the Bowl, Bennett had headlined in virtually every Playboy outlet, including both *Playboy's Penthouse* and *Playboy After Dark*, the local clubs, and the big resorts.

Likewise, vocalist Al Jarreau, whose music combines jazz, R&B, soul, standards, funk, and pop, is a veteran of the clubs who graduated to the festivals. As he put it, "I got my wheels going as a jazz singer about the time the Playboy Jazz Festival moved to Los Angeles in 1979. Playboy was a big part of my background." By the time he first appeared at the Bowl, in 1993 (the same year that marked the PJF debuts of Buddy Guy, Patti Austin, Dr. John, Joe Zawinul and the Zawinul Syndicate, and the McCoy Tyner Big Band), he had already won his fifth Grammy Award. Al continued to appear at the Bowl every five years through 2008, and noted, "It's always a big deal for me to be able to play for a sellout audience of

17,000 fans in Los Angeles, at one of the marquee events for music in this sector of the universe."

Al made a specialty of the music of Dave Brubeck almost from the beginning of his career. "Take Five," composed by the pianist's longtime partner Paul Desmond, is featured on Al's 1977 live album *Look to the Rainbow*, and in 1981, he recorded Brubeck's own "Blue Rondo à la Turk" on the album *Breakin' Away.* Considering that both of these performances won Grammys, it's not surprising that Jarreau and Brubeck felt a mutual affinity before they had even worked together. Their most celebrated collaboration was a joint concert at the Playboy Jazz Festival in 2003.

When we interviewed Al in 2012, shortly after Brubeck's death, his friend was very much on his mind. "We just sadly said good-bye to a friend and amazing artist," he began. "It was just a few years ago [2003] that Dave and I played 'Take Five' together at the Playboy Festival. It was a fantastic experience that people are still mentioning—the coming together of Dave Brubeck and Al Jarreau. I did 'Take Five' as often as he did. It's been one of my signature pieces going back to 1965, before I was even recording…. It was a special moment in my career."

\* \* \*

Dee Dee Bridgewater has been headlining at the festival for almost twenty years. She had spent considerable time in Europe in the 1970s and 1980s, a period in which the irrepressible vocalist and experimenter was singing a lot of R&B, musical theater, and world music, as well as jazz. In the early 1990s, Dee Dee shifted her focus back to "mainstream" jazz and began working in the United States again. She started recording consistently and playing major American festivals including Kool-JVC (George Wein's ongoing New York event) and Playboy. Her first appearance at PJF was in 1998, the year that her tribute album to Ella Fitzgerald, *Dear Ella,* won a Grammy. In 2008, her Afrocentric *Red Earth: Malian Journey* CD was released, and her festival appearance, which incorporated authentic Malian singers, musicians, and instruments, was the hit of the weekend. In 2014, she celebrated the collaboration between Ella Fitzgerald and Count Basie, sharing the honors with soul diva Patti Austin and Las Vegas headliner Clint Holmes.

But the Playboy Festival that meant the most to Dee Dee was in 2005. That was the year that the biggest jazz festival on the west coast honored the memory of a legendary band from back east—the orchestra of Thad Jones and Mel Lewis. Dee Dee had first come to the attention of the music world in the early 1970s as the vocalist with the orchestra led jointly by trumpeter-composer Jones and drummer Lewis, which played Monday nights for many years at the New York's Village Vanguard (and continues to do so even without its founders). She recalled, "I started with Thad and Mel when I was twenty. Thad was my mentor. Everything that I still do today is because of what he taught me. Thad showed me how to program a set list, how to work with the arrangements—that all came from Thad and Mel's band. If you get up on stage without a plan, you say to yourself, 'Oh let's just call some tunes,' then you're going to end up going to the same cliché endings and beginnings. You can experiment more when you have a 'roadmap,' as I call it. You can make your detours but everybody knows when they're coming back, so there are no bumps in the road. And I like it *tight*. Thad's band was tight. Thad would take a chart and rearrange something while it was being played, pull out a section or repeat one, if that's what was working. That was my music school, those four years. So *everything*, I know about music, I learned from listening to that band."

The singer was working under her original name, Dee Dee Garrett, when she married one of the band's trumpeters, Cecil Bridgewater. She toured Europe and the Soviet Union for the first time with that band. So, in 2005, she welcomed the opportunity to pay tribute to Thad (who had died in 1986 at age sixty-three) and Mel. Trumpeter Jon Faddis, who, though best known as Dizzy Gillespie's protégée, also played in the Thad-Mel Orchestra, shared the stage with her. The two led an all-star ensemble but, as everyone agreed, the highlight came when Dee Dee made an entrance carrying a baby—who turned out to be Thad's granddaughter—while singing his best known song, "A Child Is Born."

George Wein has been a long-term supporter of all those artists—Jones, Lewis, Bridgewater, Faddis, and so many others—and even though he no longer oversees the logistics of the festival, he still participates in its programming. In fact, you might still run into him at a club in New York, where he continues to scout new musicians for Newport, New Orleans Jazz and Heritage, and Playboy. Doubtless that's where he first heard Gregory Porter.

Gregory was forty-one when he made his Playboy debut in 2013, so he had been singing around New York for quite awhile before he became famous, but his rise to the top, when it happened, happened very quickly. As recently as 2010, Gregory was singing in small clubs, but just a year or two later, he was headlining at the Hollywood Bowl and his major-label debut album, *Liquid Spirit*, won a Grammy.

Gregory views the difference between a 100-seat house and the multitudes that populate the Bowl with a particular philosophy: "You have to maintain the intimacy," he says. "In a way, it's an exercise in theatre. You take all the different houses—sometimes you're up on stage looking *down* at the audience, sometimes, like in the Bowl, you're looking out looking *up* at them. But you still have to open up—you can't let that make any difference. Even in a place like the Hollywood Bowl, the voice doesn't necessarily have to be larger, the physical presence doesn't have to be larger, but you have to just be *aware*, you know? You have to keep an awareness of your surroundings. The magic comes is when you can take a place like the Bowl, which is a savage beast, and bring it down to people size, to keep it intimate enough so you could sing a ballad. If you can do that, that's cool."

Wynton Marsalis and his Quintet perform during the 26th annual Playboy Jazz Festival, Saturday, June 19, 2004. AP PhotoDamian Dovarganes

\* \* \*

In 2014, the Playboy Jazz Festival was acquired by the Hollywood Bowl itself from Playboy Enterprises. For the first time, the 36th annual event was officially produced by the Bowl organization—with Darlene Chan still at the helm and George Wein on call. And, rather than downsizing the event, as has happened to some similar institutions, Playboy is currently making plans to branch out and produce other jazz events in conjunction with the extravaganza at the Bowl. Some may even take place outside of the Greater Los Angeles area.

As George said when we interviewed him in 2012, "It still sells out. It used to sell out clean. Now it sells out early for the first night and eventually for the second night. We don't have the same names in the business that we used to have."

One aspect of the Playboy Jazz Festival has been integral since 1959 in Chicago, when Victor Lownes came up with it: the famous "turnabout" stage. For fifty-six years, that innovation has kept the huge operation flowing smoothly. As George Lopez, the comedian who took over from Bill Cosby as emcee in 2014, observed, "They spin that stage whether you're done or not!"

Each artist deals with the revolving stage in his or her own way. "The funny thing is, when I did the Playboy festival, I somehow forgot the stage spins," said Gregory Porter. "I got on the stage and I was about to discuss the set list and, all of a sudden, the stage starts moving! I was like, 'Oh, yeah, that's right! I have to do this!' So I grab a hold of the piano or whatever was there and go along for the ride. I have to say it was *gorgeous*, the experience of opening up to the audience like that! It was really cool—not even in a silly way."

Most artists get the big surprise at the end of their sets rather than the beginning, or—in some cases—slightly *before* the end. Dee Dee Bridgewater, who tends to pay more attention to the crowd than the clock, reports, "It was very exciting, but I didn't quite finish before they started pulling us off!"

\* \* \*

One of the single most joyous documents of the whole thirty-five-plus year Playboy experience is a video of the remarkable Latin percussionist Willie Bobo leading a band at the 1982 Playboy Jazz Festival. Bobo (1934-1984) played with many leaders, including Tito Puente, George Shearing, and Cal Tjader. He was widely admired in the Hispanic music community but, unlike Puente or Tjader, never had his own hit singles, the kind that would make him more widely known to a general audience. Drummers, in particular, adored him, as Cosby clearly did. The surviving video begins with Cosby informally interviewing Bobo, who talks about having worked at the Los Angeles Playboy Club ("with the Bunnies") the night before. The video features special guest Grover Washington Jr., best known as a smooth-style tenor and soprano sax player, here playing full-bodied Latin jazz on the alto sax. Tragically, Willie died of cancer a few months after the next year's festival, in September 1983; he was only forty-nine. Cosby produced and hosted a special tribute to the percussionist featuring his son, Eric Bobo, in 1984.

But it is the 1982 Willie Bobo that makes the deepest impression. Viewing the video, the biggest surprise is the percussion section, which includes no fewer than four drummers: the Manhattan-born Puerto-Rican leader himself on timbales (a la Tito Puente); his young son Eric playing on a smaller timbales and cymbal kit; a conga player (conguero); and—here's the shocker—Cosby himself, banging away (and keeping very good time, at that) on a cowbell and other miscellaneous percussion implements. Hefner can be seen sitting out front with the requisite stunning blonde, at a table with a champagne bucket and several glasses of the good stuff. He has clearly just realized exactly who that fourth percussionist is and he's delighted. It's a moment that helps define the very nature of jazz—you'd never see a famous comedian spontaneously sitting in with a string quartet for a bit of Mozart, to the undisguised joy of his friend, employer, and fellow aficionado. Considering what Hef was drinking, who he was with, and what he was hearing, how could he not be in heaven? It's an amazing moment, frozen for all time.

## 15

# PARADISE LOST

The opening of the resorts was to be the last bold move in the Playboy playbook—at least so far. The three buddies who'd impulsively decided to get into the nightclub business in the late '50s couldn't possibly have envisioned the empire they'd build, the lives they'd change, and the careers they'd launch—but nothing lasts forever.

It wasn't that the Playboy Clubs "jumped the shark," in the parlance of a later generation, but that the world changed around them. In 1960, it was worth waiting in line for an hour to see a sexy waitress in a Bunny costume; by 1975, those same outfits seemed pretty tame compared to what you could see in any club in any large city—or even on Main Street. By 1970, pop music and even jazz were going the route of mega-venues and festivals, of which Woodstock was merely the most famous. George Wein was staging jam sessions in Radio City Music Hall, Sinatra and Elvis were both playing Madison Square Garden, and top jazz stars such as Miles Davis and Ella Fitzgerald wouldn't play anything smaller than a huge concert hall. Almost overnight, it seemed that there was little room on the scene for the kind of intimate venue Playboy had

A relaxed and confident Hugh Hefner as he faces the New Jersey Casino Control Commission hearings in Lawrenceville, New Jersey on January 12, 1982

made popular. Between 1979 and 1991, the clubs became less and less profitable to the corporation, even as the annual Playboy Jazz Festival at the Hollywood Bowl grew into a bigger and bigger deal.

By the 1970s, some of the clubs, and especially the resorts, had begun hemorrhaging money, and something had to be done to stanch the flow. As each new club or resort opened, hundreds of thousands of dollars were funneled from Playboy's general coffers to cover the costs of construction, furnishings, and general operations.

There were also challenges at the magazine itself. By the early 1970s, circulation had reached an all-time peak of an astonishing seven million readers per month—virtually the highest of any magazine in all of publishing history. But, having attained such a pinnacle, there was no place to go but down, and the flow of money to the ailing clubs didn't help matters.

Other men's magazines showed up on the scene, looking to steal a piece of Hefner's action; the greatest rival was Bob Guccione's *Penthouse*. The outlook throughout the organization was growing dire. A new strategy was called for.

Playboy brass, or at least some of them, clearly had faith in the idea that you had to spend money to make money. Rather than coming up with ways to cut back, they argued for expanding the resort business—the "family-oriented" aspect of the Playboy empire. The senior executives who favored this plan reasoned that, by creating luxurious destinations offering horseback riding, tennis, swimming, archery, and even skiing in the colder climates, they would broaden their customer base. Playboy would become synonymous with top-notch family fun and they'd be back on top. The pro-expansion faction prevailed and—in typical Playboy fashion—no expense was spared in outfitting each new location.

As the saying goes, hindsight is twenty-twenty. It's clear now that Playboy probably should have followed the lead of other, more cost-conscious hotel chains of the time and leased existing spaces. Instead, they bought up properties and set about remaking them in the luxe Playboy image. Budgets had never been a concern to the organization—why start cutting corners now? Only one reason: because its life depended on it.

In Miami in 1970, Playboy purchased the Hilton Hotel, spent $1.5 million renovating it, and dubbed it the Miami Playboy Plaza. It never caught on as they had hoped. It was only sixty percent occupied, on average, even during high season. After losing millions on it every year, Playboy sold the property in 1974.

The first Playboy Resort, Ocho Rios in Jamaica, had been profitable from its opening in 1965. Riding high on this triumph, the organization had spared no expense in developing the 1,350-acre Lake Geneva Resort. It hobbled along for years, contributing only modest profits to the corporate balance sheet, and was finally shuttered in 1981.

The luxurious Great Gorge Resort, conceived as the jewel in the crown of Playboy's Hotel and Resort Division, was the most family-friendly of all the properties. The corporation poured more than *$33 million* into that one. Suffering from competition with resorts in the nearby Pocono Mountains and Catskills, Great Gorge never came close to breaking even. During the first four years of operation, it lost over $5 million. It's no consolation to Hefner that none of the subsequent corporate owners have been able to make a go of it either. Since Playboy de-acquisitioned the property, it has been a Four Seasons Hotel and more, infamously, the Legends Resort and Country Club. Neither could be called a success.

When the losses could no longer be denied, a variety of "fixes" were implemented. For decades, Playboy had pursued a policy of hiring great—but not superstar—entertainment for its clubs. In an effort to attract more customers to the resorts, the company decided to bring in A-list headliners who might lure large crowds. The strategy succeeded in packing the showrooms, but the much-needed bump in profits never materialized. After all, big name performers such as Diahann Carroll, Peggy Lee, Vic Damone, Sonny and Cher, Mitzi Gaynor, and Steve and Eydie don't work cheap.

At certain points in the history of the clubs, they blurred the distinction between an "act" and a "show." In other words, they would bring in a show that had been running elsewhere and use one of the clubrooms roughly as the equivalent of a Broadway Theater. This was the case with the improvisational troupe that starred Lily Tomlin and played the New York Club as a show onto itself, as well as the Ace Trucking Company, the comedy revue that starred Fred Willard.

In 1973, Irvin Arthur helped produce a show called *Minsky's Follies* in the Miami Club. This was burlesque such as the old-timers might remember; the combination of slightly risqué baggy pants comics telling dumb blonde and mother-in-law jokes and statuesque cuties stripping down to pasties and G-strings. The *Follies* was an unprecedented smash in Miami, where it kept being extended until it ran an amazing eighty weeks. Irvin's first thought was to bring it to the other clubs, but a grander idea dawned on him. Why not bring it to a bigger theater, as what might have been the first and only Playboy theatrical production to tour outside of the clubs.

Newspaper ad for the long running Minsky's Follies.

Alas, the venue they chose was just too darn big—the Hollywood Palladium. This was a huge cavern and a former ballroom. From the back of the house one needed binoculars to tell whether the girls on stage were naked or wearing beer barrels. Needless to say, it was an expensive disaster and set Playboy's live entertainment division back even further. It also proved to be a public relations catastrophe for the corporation and Hef personally. It seemed like there was a huge flock of journalists and editors who, rather than being happy for Hefner, had been sitting around wringing their hands and waiting for one of his ventures to fail. Irvin told us, "If the newspapers had panned me or the show alone, things might not have ended as they did, but they castrated Hefner personally." In London, Victor was distressed to receive a call from his old friend and employer telling him to deal with this financial and PR nightmare. Victor had to deliver the message to Irvin telling him, "'Irvin, the party's over.' But we gave him some time to figure out his next move and he received a characteristically generous severance package." In the late 1970s, Playboy published several special collections of pictorials of Bunnies, then currently working in clubs around the world. This was a clear sign that the live entertainment division was floundering while the magazine continued to flourish—there was more money to be made in selling naked pictures of Bunnies than having them actually do what they were hired to do—serve drinks and work in a nightclub.

In another ill-advised effort to keep up with the times (and lure more women), the New York Club experimented with adding male "Rabbits" as servers. The result wasn't quite what they had in mind. For the short time the policy was in place, the club attracted a primarily gay clientele rather than the bachelorette party crowd they'd envisioned.

* * *

Clearly, bolder moves were called for. In 1975, Hef brought Victor back to Chicago headquarters and tasked him with doing whatever it took to turn things around throughout the organization. Victor soon earned the nickname "Jaws."

"By that time, the hotels alone had lost over fourteen million dollars," Victor told us. "Severe measures would be necessary if we were going to keep the Playboy organization viable."

The writing was on the wall—some properties would have to be closed—but Hef was extremely anxious about the message that would send to the public. After all, he'd spent his life building up the Playboy brand, and was hesitant to do anything that might tarnish its image. With that in mind, Victor exempted the flagship clubs—Los Angeles, New York, and Chicago—from the initial wave of closures.

Closing ill-performing clubs was not Victor's only strategy for stabilizing the organization's finances. The number of staff, at both the corporate offices and the Mansion, was dramatically slashed. Salaries, including Hef's own, were radically cut, some by as much as twenty-five percent. Playboy charge cards, used by keyholders at the clubs and hotels, were abolished to stem the tide of uncollectible debt. And, in what might have been the most painful move of all—at least for Hef—the *Big Bunny* was to be unloaded, a move he had roundly rejected on previous occasions.

The black DC9-30 with the Bunny logo on its tail sat empty at the Los Angeles airport most of the time, yet continued to devour well over $1 million a year in parking fees, salaries, and service charges. She was quickly sold for $4 million—close to the asking price—and for the first time in many years, Playboy executives, including the big boss himself, were forced to fly commercial. To add insult to injury, most were required to ride Coach.

Victor recounted that many of the clubs, including those in Los Angeles, Detroit, Atlanta, Kansas City, St. Louis, Montreal, Cincinnati, Phoenix, and even Chicago and New York were in need of costly renovations or, in many cases possible relocation due to deterioration of the surrounding neighborhoods from chic to shabby. By the mid 1970s, the domestic clubs and the hotel and resort division—pretty much all the clubs but the English ones—were costing Playboy a collective $8 million in losses a year. Victor thought that removing the Playboy name from the resorts might attract more families, but that didn't make any difference at all.

According to Victor, the cutbacks, closures, and belt-tightening succeeded in shaving almost $3 million off the annual overhead, but it was too little, too late. The clubs were still burning through corporate funds at a fast clip. The brutal fact was that Playboy could no longer afford to carry them for vanity's sake.

Putting aside the issue of their obligation to dues-paying key-holders, Victor started shuttering the nonproducing clubs in 1975. The first to go were those in Kansas City, Atlanta, Montreal, Boston, and Detroit. By that time, business had dwindled so profoundly that little notice was taken when their doors were locked for the last time.

Perhaps Playboy's mounting problems should have been addressed years earlier, but the revenue coming in from the London Club and Casino had been so massive that Hef and his cohorts could afford to live in a state of denial, at least for awhile. The oil-rich Arab gamblers who frequented the London venue on Park Lane made it the most profitable casino in the world at the time. In 1980, the club contributed a massive $32 million in profit to the corporate bottom-line—a godsend since the other divisions realized a net loss of $31 million!

The delicate balance was short-lived. The very next year would mark the beginning of the London casino wars, which would end in Playboy's crippling defeat.

* * *

Playboy had opened the London Club in 1966, and from the start, officials of the UK gambling goliath, Ladbrokes, were plotting its demise. They seized their opportunity in 1981, squealing to the Gaming Commission about "major breaches" on the part of Playboy. The police investigation that followed turned up at least seven violations of the 1968 Gaming Act, including the fact that the club allowed its members to gamble on credit. With the organization in free fall, Victor was summoned from London to Chicago. The Chicago Playboy executives convinced Hefner that their situation would improve without Victor and he was unceremoniously fired on April 15, 1981.

On October 5, the court ruled that Playboy was not "fit and proper" to be allowed to run casinos in England. Devastated, the organization had little choice but to minimize its losses rather than fight the ruling; in November, Playboy announced that it had sold all of its British casino holdings to Trident Television.

In fiscal year 1982, Playboy showed a loss of $51 million. Without gambling profits to shore up the balance sheet, the empire was crumbling fast. In 1982, in the hope that infusing new leadership and a youthful viewpoint into the organization would create new energy—and profits—Hef's daughter Christie was appointed President of Playboy Enterprises at the age of twenty-nine. Hef continued to be

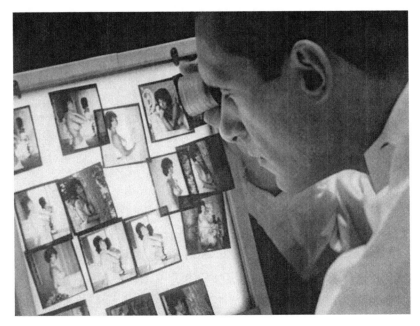

Hef in Chicago 1983 scrutinizing photos for Playboy Magazine. BettmannCorbis

the driving force and to have final approval on most issues.

It hardly seemed as if things could get worse—and yet they did. At that point, Hef and his team had one more ace up their sleeve. They pinned all of their future hopes on the opening of the first Playboy casino stateside—in Atlantic City. But bad news travels fast, even across an ocean. Upon hearing the outcome of the investigation in London, the understandably skittish New Jersey Gaming Commission created one roadblock after another for Playboy. The worst of it was the dictum that, if they wanted their gaming license, Hefner and his current management team would have to step down. Needless to say, that was a deal breaker—and the license was denied.

With that, it was "game over" for the Playboy Clubs. The remaining ones were shuttered over the next few years, including the Chicago flagship on February 29, 1986. The last U.S. Playboy

Club, in Lansing Michigan, closed in 1988.

Devil-may-care management may have been a contributing factor to the clubs' downfall but, more than anything else, they were the victim of changing times. As the '70s gave way to the '80s, people were finding new ways to walk on the wild side. The veiled sexual fantasy offered up by scantily clad Bunnies in an exclusive key club no longer had the power to make everyday Joes feel like powerful and desirable VIPs. But perhaps the greatest loss of all, when the last club announced "last call," was the demise of the many showrooms, large and small, that had been the training ground and mainstay of a whole generation of top-notch entertainers. As each one of them has told us—it was the end of an era.

The Playboy Clubs were at the center of an iconic period of our cultural history and they helped define it as a carefree, liberated time when boundaries were pushed—and sometimes broken. Over nearly three decades, the impact of the clubs on musical taste and entertainment standards is undeniable. They provided a home, a school, and a livelihood for a multitude of musicians, singers, comics, and restaurant personnel—all the while helping to topple the color barrier in entertainment. You could say that they trained a generation of audiences from around the world to appreciate good music, good food, and good company.

When the last Playboy Club closed in 1988, some 2.5 million keyholders had passed through their doors. By then, Studio 54 had come in with a bang (in 1977) and gone out with a whimper (in 1981)—but, once the disco era arrived, nightclubs were consigned to history. The new nightlife involved less fantasy and more reality. Men were no longer content to ogle the girls from a distance while listening to live performers in polite silence. They wanted to get up on the dance floor and do the hustle, up close and personal, to the elaborately recorded sounds of Donna Summer, the Bee Gees, Gloria Gaynor, and the rest.

But... when one door closes, other doors open.

## 16

# PLAYBOY REBOOTED

A fter a thirty-year hiatus, doors to new Playboy Clubs
are opening. This time around, the organization's
business plan is to license the Playboy name to managing partners. There have been a few fits and starts,
for sure—most notably in Las Vegas, Cancun, and Macau—but
hopes are high for a robust physical presence in the near future.

A brand-new club in Las Vegas opened in 2006, amid much
fanfare, on the top floor of the Palms Casino. But don't go online
to book your reservation—after six up-and-down years, it closed in
2012. Playboy Macau, located in the penthouse of the Sands Hotel
there, enjoyed an even shorter run, opening in 2010 for two years.

The club in Cancun, which opened in 2010, was going strong
until political changes within the country created problems. In
2014, the Interior Ministry decided to crack down on gaming and
abruptly shuttered the club.

If you're looking for good news, check out London—where
history seems to be repeating itself in the form of a very successful
new operation situated right across the street from the original.
London Playboy "2.0" is run by Caesars Entertainment Corporation,

the parent of Caesars Palace, Bally's, and other top-drawer casinos worldwide—a recipe for success if ever there was one.

When we visited the club to check it out for ourselves, its director, Phil Shephard, pointed out, "It's diminutive in size and configuration compared to the original club—a much cozier club than the one that was across the street. In terms of numbers, we have about eighty-five Bunnies, as opposed to the two-hundred they had in the '70s. But we pride ourselves on emulating the same level of sophistication, the same level of elegance, the same level of service that the Playboy Club has always been famous for. Looking at the videos from the '60s and '70s, it's clear that their training program and attention to detail were second to none. They even had a correct procedure for how the Bunnies were to place their cufflinks—they had to face each other!"

Like its predecessor, the new London Club is located in the swanky Mayfair district—this time at 14 Old Park Lane. The original was at 45. Its doors are open every day of the year but Christmas. We were immediately struck by the way the designers

London Gaming Bunnies working roulette tables. Courtesy Playboy Caesars Entertainment

have succeeded in blending classic British glamour with contemporary nightlife flair, while capturing the free spirit of Playboy—or *the* playboy. I asked Phil what was the main attraction these days, the Bunnies or the casino?

Without missing a beat, he confirmed what we suspected: "The primary attraction is gaming. We're expanding our membership base, and we have a nice, eclectic mix of people who come in. Some come to sample Salvatore Calabrese's delights at his beautiful bar. If you're into vintage cognacs, it's a fantastic experience. The ambience is lovely, the service second to none, and the Bunny services are really quite exceptional. This is a place to immerse yourself and enjoy.

"Baroque is our live-music venue, which is still morphing. It started out as a nightclub within the club, but we found that attracted a much younger crowd that was almost diametrically the opposite of our customer base and we started to lose business in our key area, which is obviously the casino. So for awhile, it evolved into more of a cabaret club."

Cabaret in England, I very recently learned, is slightly different from what it is in New York—more of a "circus" or sideshow. Salvatore's son was a consultant for Baroque, which began to mix in a variety of cabaret acts with its music offerings.

"We brought in a lot of different stuff," Phil continued, "glass walkers, contortionists, acrobats, you name it. Four or five acts would come on and work the floor, in and amongst the customers. That also wasn't a total success, and now we're experimenting at using the space as a dinner salon with a singer and live music during the meal and then a DJ for the rest of the evening. We're excited to have the English singer and recording artist, Matt Goss coming up there. He's currently a regular at Caesars Palace in Las Vegas, but he's taking a holiday from that to come here to perform a show for sixty of our exclusive VIPs over dinner. It'll be 'an intimate evening with Matt Goss.' Our VIPs are very pleased when we can offer a Caesars headline act here at Playboy.

Only in London! Tea time at the Playboy Club. Courtesy PlayboyCaesars Entertainment

"The Bunnies will always be a huge draw for Playboy customers, and we've taken part of the original training manual and added our own approach, resulting in what we think is a wonderful training program for everyone. One of the key changes we made was that instead of having a Bunny Mother, we operate with 'Head Bunnies.' We have four of them: two valet Head Bunnies, and two gaming Head Bunnies. This way, we have real-time correction—so if the Head Bunny is working the floor and she sees a girl who isn't suitably dressed or her hair in the wrong place, or she isn't delivering appropriate service, the Head Bunny can make an immediate correction. This replaces the old routine of reporting that kind of behavior to the Bunny Mother; it works better for us. Aside from that, the training program is still based very much on what was done in the 1960s. We still teach the 'Bunny Dip.' The particular styles the girls must adhere to are the same—nail varnish has to be neutral, eyes should be smoky, that kind of thing. Bunnies aren't allowed to have their hair up—which would give them two sets of ears... and so on."

I had to admit that I'd never heard about that last rule, but when you think about it, it does make sense. Who has two sets of ears?

"We also feel we've improved on selecting Bunnies," Phil went on. "We have a 'Bunny casting,' rather than just conducting interviews. If we have an opening for, say, five Bunnies, we'll invite thirty ladies for the day. We start off by showing movies—newsreels of Playboy Clubs and what they used to be like. Then we show some of the recent events we've had at the club—Kate Moss's birthday party, or some of the larger events we plan for Halloween and Midsummer.

"Once all their paperwork is completed, we take the group on a tour and then we settle in again and they are encouraged to introduce themselves and say why they would like to be a Bunny. They have to tell two truths and a lie about themselves, and the rest of the group has to guess which the lie is. We try to make it as informal and fun as possible at the beginning, to break the ice. The we hit what I call the audition, where we break the ladies up into groups of four or five and give them a challenge, such as, 'Go write a song,' or 'Compose a singing telegram.' And off they go, with a Bunny chaperone looking after them. After fifteen or twenty minutes, they come back and show off what they've done in front of the others. This gives us some insight into their characters, how they get along with people, and whose personalities shine through."

I couldn't help but comment on the psychology at work during the process.

Phil explained, "Absolutely, there has to be, because the Bunny ethos is more than just presenting yourself as a good looking lady in a costume. You have to be able to project the right personality. There's something quite specific in being a Bunny—plenty of very beautiful girls don't make the grade. We want women who are aware of what it means to be a Bunny and really want to do it. A lot of our girls have Ph.Ds. Some have their own businesses. They're very smart ladies, not just waitresses.

"So, once we've done the auditions, we have to make the cuts—

and we disappoint some people. We have to say, 'Sorry, you did very well but now is your time to go home,' and we give them a little goody bag with an invitation to the next party, some makeup, and some memorabilia of Playboy, and they go off, while the others stay.

"We then divide up the finalists and shoot their photos dressed in something akin to a Bunny costume—not the real thing, because no one other than a Bunny is allowed to wear the outfit. And then the training begins! Salvatore is the maestro, so he actually puts them through a lot of their paces, and he's quite a hard taskmaster. He's been known to put little obstacles in the way while the trainees are walking around with their trays.

"After some training, we make another cut and have our final count of new Bunnies—though they still aren't actual Bunnies, but Bunny trainees. They have to go through a minimum of two months' training before they earn their ears, and if they can't make the grade, chances are they'll never wear the uniform. So, the entire process has been made into something quite meaningful. If they get through those two months, they've earned their ears!"

As with the younger clubs, fine dining is an integral part of the experience. Executive Chef ElmarBasziszta is tasked with overseeing the cuisine in The Dining Room, The Players Bar,

The Playboy Club London New Years Eve 2013.
Courtesy PlayboyCaesars Entertainment

Salvatore's Bar, and Baroque, as well as private dining and events. It's his responsibility to ensure that the menus across Playboy London expose members and guests alike to not only his passion for French cuisine but also offer dishes that have been inspired by his extensive travels.

Originally from Austria, Elmar has worked in leading hotels including Kempinski in Moscow, the Burj Al Arab in Dubai, the Shangri-La in Istanbul, and many others, after serving his internship (yep, even chefs have to intern) with Alain Ducasse at Louis XV in Monte Carlo.

"We have a loyal customer base here," Said Phil, "and a lot of history, because, when 45 Park Lane closed all those years ago, a significant number of its patrons moved to the Rendezvous Casino. I was actually working there in 1983, right at the time Playboy closed and the Rendezvous opened. Now, many of those same people are back at the new Playboy Club. We even had Victor Lownes, who is considered Mr. Playboy London, here for the opening in 2011—with his lovely wife Marilyn, of course. He made the original Playboy the most successful casino club in the world!"

After our wonderful and extremely informative visit with Phil, he passed us to a lovely Bunny Host—Bunny Eleni—for a tour. Eleni wasn't dressed as a Bunny at that moment because of a couple of issues with her costume. Luckily, a qualified seamstress is always on duty.

\* \* \*

Just when I thought it couldn't get any better, I had the honor of spending some time with Mr. Salvatore Calabrese—the Maestro himself—and learning about his legendary watering hole, Salvatore's at Playboy.

The word I hear most often associated with the clubs is "experience." Everyone from management to staff makes it his or her personal mission to insure that every guest has the most enjoyable

Playboy *experience* possible. In that context, Salvatore's bar is the ultimate experience! One sip of the iconic Salvatore's Legacy provides over 730 years of history in four luxe ingredients: 1788 Clos de Griffier Vieux Cognac, Dubb Orange Curacao from the late 1860s, 1770 Kummel

The famous maestro, Salvatore Calabrese, in his bar Salvatore's in the London Playboy Club. Courtesy Salvatore Calabrese

Liqueur, and a 1915 Angostura Bitter. The cost of this signature cocktail is dear at 5,500 British pounds, but you won't find it at your corner tavern—or anywhere else in the world, for that matter. If you think about it, these sips of history date to the time of the French Revolution, the American Constitution, President Washington's reign, the discovery of Australia, the Unification of Italy and many other things we've only read about in our high school history classes. To me that's mind blowing!

Salvatore designed a sexy, unique, and elegant honeycomb to display his assemblage of mature cognacs and other fine vintage liqueurs, along with authentic bar accessories and glassware. Many of his potions are so rare that they constitute a Liquid Museum. This intimate, sexy bar also boasts of the largest variety of vintage champagne in Europe. The brilliance of Salvatore's stylish lounge is that, if you aren't in the mood to sip cognac from the era of King Louis XVIII, you can order a simple, classic cocktail for £14.50 and feel just as pampered.

Salvatore has opened and runs establishments worldwide, rubbing elbows and making friends with untold celebrities along the way. He told us that Stevie Wonder is a friend, and whenever he's in London he stops by to relax with his own special cocktail, the *Wonder.* "It's something I created for Stevie," Salvatore says, "a Champagne cocktail. He carries the recipe with him so whenever he fancies it, he can ask for it. When he's here in town I make it for him personally. He once came to my bar and I could tell he was enjoying the piano player. When the guy took a break I asked Stevie if he wanted to play. He said he did, so I led him over and he played for over a half hour—at my bar! It was magical for everyone who was there at that moment to listen to Stevie Wonder perform live. Then he went back to his table and carried on with his night. As he stood up to leave, I went over to say goodbye to him and he started clapping. I turned around and said, 'Stevie, what's that for?' And he said, 'It's from one artist to another!' That was very moving for me. He's a wonderful man."

When I inquired how—at twenty-one years old—Salvatore had become the youngest maître d' on Italy's Amalfi Coast, he said, "I was a bit of a wild boy, even at age eleven, so my dad found me a job in a hotel bar to keep me busy through the summer and so I could make a little money. It was at that bar that I found my mentor, Signor Raffaello. He was a Humphrey-Bogart-in-*Casablanca* sort of person. He knew exactly how to charm the women's socks off, spoke several languages, and was Mr. Hospitality. I *definitely* wanted to be him! He taught me so much about making people feel special.

"But I had other dreams, too. I loved the sea and desperately wanted to be the captain of a ship. I studied with that goal in mind, but I had an accident before I was old enough to take the test and became almost blind in my left eye. I couldn't pass the physical. I was crushed, but it turned me toward the second love of my life and that was working in bars and restaurants.

"At twenty-one, I had twenty-eight people who worked for me. It was quite a challenge but I did pretty well. I've always been a leader. Eventually, I became an expert on organizing the dining areas of bars and hotels. If anyone had a problem with how to make the best use of a space, I was the one they came to. I was clever that way. Eventually, I moved from Italy to London, where I met my English wife and found a job in this small, charming little bar called Duke's

Hotel. The Duke's Bar is famous for the martini, and I developed a way of creating the *perfect* martini.

"It was at Duke's that I developed the concept of selling liquid history. The idea caught on, and wealthy people and celebrities came in. I started to develop a following among the Who's-Who—Paul McCartney, Elton John, and the like. They all wanted to 'taste history' and I made that bar extraordinarily famous. I even managed to serve Her Majesty and some American Presidents. Princess Margaret was a regular customer."

Of course I had to ask what royalty drank.

"Princess Margaret? Whiskey. She's a whiskey lady. And Her Majesty likes a good martini and dubonnet. So I had that pleasure, and was there for twelve years. From there, I move to larger rooms: Lanesborough and then my own place at Fifty St. James. When we closed Fifty St. James, I started a wonderful relationship with Caesars. After a few years, they contacted me to say there was a project they were entering into with Playboy and asked me to participate.

"Now, you have to understand that in the late seventies and the eighties, I used to take the bus from home to London, and I'd pass by the old club at 45 Park Lane. Playboy was an iconic name and an iconic place. People like the Rat Pack, Sean Connery, Muhammad Ali, royalty—everyone used to go to the Playboy Club. Beautiful women in exotic Bunny costumes—there is nothing tacky about it. It's an art. And those girls are not *just* girls. They have to have some intelligence and skill and know how to charm.

"So, Caesars came to me and asked about putting my name on a bar at the club. That was in 2011, and it's been magnificent. As you can see, it's a beautiful bar; I designed it. And I am proud to be able to offer one of the finest selections of vintage spirits in the world, some going back as far as 1770. I broke the Guinness record for the most expensive cocktail in the world, and I'm very choosy about who I sell it to. For me, it's not the fact that it's the most expensive that matters, but that was the only designation the Guinness Book people would give. I take pride in making the *oldest* cocktail in the world. The four ingredients represent 730 years of history and that's massive! For me, it's about making it unique.

"I consider my bar a theater where I get to create the atmosphere and manage what my customer will experience and enjoy. The drinks are the final touch. Caesars and Playboy are bringing back the fun and mystique of a great club—it doesn't matter who our customers are. If we can make them feel good and make them happy, that's what it's all about.

It doesn't get any better-- Salvatore and the Rat Pack. Salvatore in Salvatore's at the London Playboy Club. Courtesy Salvatore Calabrese.

"We've only been opened since 2011 but there have been so many memorable events and so much pure fun here. We celebrated Playboy's Sixtieth Anniversary with a party attended by absolutely everyone—from those who had been to the original London Club to those who weren't even born then. Tom Jones and Donatella Versace were here… Kate Moss, so many others. Kate was also on the cover of the Anniversary Issue of the magazine. At the end of the evening, Kate, whom I've known for quite a few years, came to me to say goodbye. Now, I have a separate entrance that celebrities can use, so I told her driver to go down to the car park and started to walk Kate and her security team down the back stairs. She'd been wearing very high heels and this was the first chance she had to take them off. I didn't want her to have to walk barefoot, but she kept saying, 'No, no, no, I'm OK.' I was walking next to her and couldn't stand it anymore, so I picked her up! She was quite shocked—and so were her bodyguards—but I said, 'I can't stand to see a beautiful woman walking without shoes.' 'Ahh, I love Italian men!' she said, and we laughed.

"We also have lots of Bunny reunions, and we get to see all the lovely women who were the stars of the club in the sixties and seventies. You can tell there's still a real bond among them all."

Salvatore recently resigned his position as President of the United Kingdom's Bartenders Guild to concentrate on his global organization, but he is still available to consult when they need him. He's written ten cocktail books, which have sold over a million copies collectively, and I'm hoping that he may soon start on his memoirs—though there are many chapters still to come. What fun reading they would make!

In the second decade of the twenty-first century, Playboy Enterprises is a much more streamlined and well-directed company than it was in its free-wheeling heyday. It is also a more solidly profitable one. Plans for the future include more than two hundred reconceived clubs in entertainment hot spots around the globe and, with partners such as Caesars, how can they be anything but fabulous? More than one entertainer has echoed Lorna Lufts sentiment, "If they start opening clubs with cabarets again, I'm first in line. I'd be more than happy to work at the Playboy Clubs again." Nobody knows exactly what will unfold, but you can be sure that Hef's global brand will continue to evolve as long as there are pretty girls and men who love them.

CPSIA information can be obtained at www.ICGtesting.com
Printed in the USA
BVOW02s2016190515

400987BV00003B/6/P